AFTER HITLER

Jürgen Neven-du Mont is chief television reporter for North German Radio. He has been a journalist, a producer of the Munich Youth Theatre, political correspondent of the *Süddeutsche Zeitung*, chief reporter for the *Münchner Illustrierte* and chief correspondent for the *Berliner Illustrierte*. He has worked on the news programmes of Bavarian Radio and has been chief television reporter for Hesse Radio.

Mr Neven-du Mont sees in television the synthesis of his former interests. He produces political programmes, largely on Germany and on Eastern Europe.

JÜRGEN NEVEN-DU MONT

After Hitler

REPORT FROM A WEST GERMAN CITY

Translated by
RALPH MANHEIM

PENGUIN BOOKS

Penguin Books Ltd, Harmondsworth, Middlesex, England
Penguin Books Australia Ltd, Ringwood, Victoria, Australia

—

Zum Beispiel 42 Deutsche first published in Germany
by Nymphenburger Verlagshandlung 1968
This translation published in Great Britain by Allen Lane The Penguin Press 197·
Published in Pelican Books 1974

—

Copyright © Nymphenburger Verlagshandlung, 1968
This translation copyright © Pantheon Books, 1970

—

Made and printed in Great Britain by
Cox & Wyman Ltd,
London, Reading and Fakenham
Set in Linotype Pilgrim

CONTENTS

INTRODUCTION
WHY I CHOSE HEIDELBERG

This book is a self-portrait of people in a West German town. Though all the persons who speak in the book live in the same city, their common West German character far outweighs any regional traits.

The English or American reader may have rather a romantic notion of Heidelberg: the old houses with their high slanting roofs, the old-time comfort of the wine shops, the Neckar shining silvery in the sunlight, the Philosophers' Walk twining its way up the hillside, the old university, world-famous for its scholars and its duels, the out-of-door concerts of works by Bach, Mozart and Beethoven in the courtyard of the ruined castle. All very nice, friendly and *gemütlich*, quite free from associations with the Kaiser or Hitler, with Marx or Krupp.

From this point of view Heidelberg might seem to be an anomaly among German cities. Actually I selected it because it is quite typical of present-day German cities. I know what I mean, but I cannot explain, in the context of this city and its inhabitants, what it is that I mean by 'typically German'. I do not think that there is a precise definition of 'typically German' any more than there is a definition of 'typically British' or 'typically American'. Nations and people are too complex for such simplifications.

The specific reasons for my choice were as follows:

1. I wanted a medium-sized city. The population of Heidelberg is 125,000.

2. I wanted a city with a certain amount of industry. Heidelberg's industry has developed very considerably since the war and today there are 102 factories. Furthermore many residents of Heidelberg work in the more important industrial centres of Mannheim and Ludwigshafen, which are only a few miles away.

3. I wanted a university town because I needed professors and students, who play leading roles in shaping the country's present and future intellectual life.

4. I wanted a city with a cultural life which was average for Germany: Heidelberg has one large theatre and two small ones; concerts are held daily all year round; there is a local radio station and a people's university.

5. I wanted a city that was neither overwhelmingly Catholic nor overwhelmingly Protestant because the two religions are evenly balanced in the Federal Republic. 36.1 per cent of the population of Heidelberg is Catholic and 48.4 per cent Protestant.

6. I wanted a city governed neither by a Social Democratic nor by a Christian Democratic majority. The CDU (Christian Democratic Union) was long the government party in the Federal Republic, but the Social Democrats polled almost as many votes. In the last few years the country has been governed by a Great Coalition of these two leading parties. The political picture in the Heidelberg Town Council is as follows: Christian Democrats: twelve seats; Social Democrats: twelve seats; FDP (Free Democrats): four seats; NPD (National Democrats, neo-Nazis): one seat. A good deal will be said of these last in our book.

7. I wanted a city that reflected the changes of the last forty years. The reader of this book will see how very much this city and its population have changed in the period since Hitler.

Although, thanks to its many American, English and French friends, Heidelberg was not bombed during the war, its inhabitants heard the explosions in Mannheim and Ludwigshafen, and the sky over Heidelberg itself was often red. Fugitives from the nearby towns took refuge in Heidelberg, and later on numerous refugees from the new Polish territories beyond the Oder and Neisse and from Communist East Germany settled there. Thus almost every region of Germany is represented in the population.

I spoke with 121 inhabitants of Heidelberg. Forty-two of these interviews were selected for publication, not because they seemed more striking or colourful than the rest, but because they struck me as most representative of Heidelberg and the Federal Republic. By and large I took the same approach as my

American colleague Studs Terkel when he began to write *Division Street, America*. I was not interested in prominent or outstanding persons. Plenty has been written about them. I just wanted 'people'.

What then was my principle of selection? I built a little pyramid representing the various social strata, occupational groups and generations – a pyramid because of course there are more proletarians than professors, more employees than employers, more young people than old. My pyramid corresponded roughly to the overall social structure of the German cities.

I spoke from three to five hours with each of these persons, and with some I had several conversations. I saw them chiefly in their homes because people tend to be most themselves in their familiar surroundings, but some of our talks took place in wineshops or while walking or driving about. I made use of shorthand notes and tape recordings as aids to my memory.

How did I find these people? I have a few friends in Heidelberg and these know other Heidelbergers: artisans who paint their windows, sell them their meat and their milk, the waitresses who serve them their wine, the friends and professors of their student sons, the workers in a friend's factory, and so forth.

Of course there were people whom none of my friends knew or admitted they knew and whom I nevertheless needed, such as former members of the Waffen-SS, prostitutes and policemen. These I had to find by my own resources. I spent three months in Heidelberg, talking with people whenever opportunity offered and when possible expanding these contacts into regular conversations.

Of course I was specially interested in certain points, but I did not use a questionnaire or any formal interviewing technique. I put in a word now and then to keep the conversation going, but mostly I listened. That is all. I have recorded what my interlocutors said. Many passages are published verbatim. Elsewhere I have deleted certain repetitions and irrelevant transitional remarks, and in general condensed. But I have nowhere tampered with the content or style. I feel certain that what little editing I have done has merely brought the texts closer to reality, to what the speaker meant to say. These forty-two Germans are in every sense the authors of this book.

What struck me most about them is this: among the Germans I found little of the civic spirit and social initiative that are common in the Anglo-Saxon world. The answer is almost always: Why should I? That's not my business. That's the affair of the government. Almost always 'others' are expected to do everything. The idea of personal initiative in the social and political sphere strikes most Germans as utopian. They solve technical and intellectual problems, they do their jobs efficiently, but when it comes to human problems they are failures. The Germans know how to work, but not how to live.

It is often said that the Germans are unwilling to come to grips with their National Socialist past. I believe this to be a gross exaggeration. In conversations with my fellow Germans I have been struck time and again by the trauma with which the National Socialist period has left them, by their feeling that they are still living in Hitler's shadow. It is true that many of those who were in varying degree guilty still try to repress their feelings of guilt and that many of the innocent are still caught up in complexes induced, even if they reject the thesis of collective guilt, by a sense of collective shame. Nevertheless the vast majority need no prodding to talk about the National Socialist period and show a willingness to bring it out into the open.

In this dilemma, the young people in particular are looking for a new national consciousness free from the old nationalism; they aspire to a united Europe, which most of them believe should include Eastern Europe, and look upon themselves as German Europeans.

Perhaps the reader will find among the forty-two Germans in this book certain Germans whom they know or think they know. Perhaps too they will discover that the Germans of our post-Hitler times are different from what their preconceived notions had led them to believe. Perhaps this presentation of forty-two Germans from a West German city will provide a new picture of Germany.

JÜRGEN NEVEN-DU MONT

UNDINE GARTMANN

42, married, bookkeeper

They came around the corner very cautiously with fixed
bayonets.

You might think my first name Undine came from the opera or
from Giraudoux's play. Not at all, I was named after the cruiser
Undine. My father was a marine aboard the *Undine* in the First
World War. He was in Turkey, in the Dardanelles, and so on.
My father talked a lot about the First World War. It all sounded
very romantic. The Second World War must have been a lot
worse. I didn't see much of it. But I still remember the end of
the War clearly. We were living on Hauptstrasse at that time
and I saw the Americans coming into town. They came around
the corner very cautiously with fixed bayonets and looked to
see if the street was clear or not. They looked scared. But we
were scared a lot worse, we thought they might do something
to us. After they'd occupied the city, they put up big posters
all over, saying that anyone in possession of arms should report
them. But after three or four days they saw there was nothing
to worry about. We were all so glad the War was over. Our
strongest impression was that the American soldiers looked so
neat and clean, especially compared to us. We hadn't had any
soap in a long time and no decent food. At first the Americans
were very reserved but they were very well-disciplined too. I
can't say that they were friendly but there was never any real
misconduct. Most of us had hardly been able to wait for the
War to be over. Of course we were good Germans if you want
to put it that way, we'd have liked our side to win, but we were
really happy and thankful that all the killing was finally over.
It was all news to me and I was very much surprised to hear
about all the things the Nazis had done, we really had no idea,
really.

Maybe we were too innocent in those days.

As far as I was concerned the Nazi period was okay up to the War. I can still remember. The only unpleasant thing that happened to me was one time when we were having an air-raid drill the people in our building were too slow. Some block leader or whatever he was gave us hell. He said we hadn't gone down to the cellar fast enough, that it was a lousy performance. He said we were a lot of goldbricks and it mustn't happen again. But that was the only time I was kind of disgusted. I never heard a word about the concentration camps, strange as it may sound. Definitely not. Now and then you heard somebody say: 'You ought to be in Dachau!' But it was about the same as saying: 'Here comes the black Maria' or 'you'll end up at the police station or in an insane asylum.' Well, yes – come to think of it – I did see the persecution of the Jews. That's right. I was still in school. There was that night . . . what did they call it again? That's right: *Kristallnacht.* We went to school in the morning and it looked terrible on Hauptstrasse. The windows of certain stores had been smashed. I mostly remember the furniture store. And I remember that my mother bought a lot of material from a Jewish dry-goods store because the owners – they were Jews – had to leave and they sold their stock very cheap. Long after the War my mother still had some of that material. Then when the Jews began running around with their yellow stars, yes, that was bad. It was awful. And for instance when they put signs on park benches saying: 'No Jews allowed'. That was bad. You didn't feel like sitting on that bench yourself. And outside a lot of stores there were signs saying: 'No Jews wanted'. Same as they say today: 'No dogs allowed in the butcher's shop'. I know my mother felt very sad about it because we had a lot of Jewish friends, nice people. It was very sad to see them taken away. But we thought: they're being sent to the East, they're being resettled.

And there was nothing we could do about it . . .

No, I can't remember my father ever saying anything about the treatment of the Jews. But it was different with my mother. I can remember when we children played 'store', we used to write 'No Jews wanted' on our little doll's store. But then my mother came in and took the sign away and said: 'You don't joke about things like that.' After the War, when we heard about all those concentration camps, we thought a lot of the stories must be anti-German propaganda, but we also realized that such stories can't be made up out of the whole cloth, and of course we were horrified too, and we didn't know how we could make amends for such things. How could we explain to our friends that we really had nothing to do with it? It was obvious to us that no one would believe us when we said we really hadn't known and had never wanted anything like that. How were we going to prove it? And now the same kind of lunatics are back again. When I think of the NPD that's flourishing right now. Recently an NPD meeting was announced. I'd heard they were like the Nazis and were drawing big crowds, so I wanted to see for myself what they were up to. So I turned up punctually at eight o'clock. But I didn't get into the meeting because the hall was already jammed and about 200 students were standing outside. I was surprised that so many young people wanted to go, because after all they'd been hearing for years how our parents had drifted into that mess. Well, I'm afraid they're ready to drift too. Just think: if even fifty per cent of them fall for it. Maybe it's curiosity at first. But that's the way it started the other time. On the other hand, there's nothing to be surprised at, because these young people really have no ideals any more.

Every youngster is looking for ideals and if he hasn't found them yet, he thinks maybe the NPD has something to offer.

Nowadays, the young people aren't offered any real ideals. Look at the television: folk dances from Yemen, folk songs from Israel. You won't find such things anywhere in Germany. German folk dances or German folk-songs just haven't the right to exist. And the young people simply have no sense of belonging to a group. Of course there are Scouts and various youth organizations, but they don't get enough publicity. Very different things pour in on the young people. All the stuff you see in the illustrated magazines, all the sex and rubbish that's thrown at them. The one thing you don't find is anything worthwhile. Of course the young people can go out in the evening to a gymnastics club or a bar. But it would do them more good if they went to the Scouts or some other sensible youth organization. They're not publicized enough. The government doesn't care, it doesn't do anything for the young people. When we were little, we played in the woods, we had treasure hunts or cross-country races. We were in the Hitler Youth or the League of German Girls.

We went rowing and then there was a parade with a brass band. That was fun and it was worthwhile, and that's what's lacking today.

Nowadays the young people feel the need of a certain discipline. They don't just want to lounge around all the time, and that's why they're so unhappy. They want to belong to something. You see, they don't seem to find much of an ideal in democracy. I definitely get that impression. Our democracy doesn't offer them enough that's worth striving for, it doesn't set an example. The politicians we have today are always humming and hawing. People haven't the courage of their convictions and there's not enough morality. People talk a great deal about morality today, but there isn't any. When I was young, people didn't talk so much about morality. It was taken for granted. We were decent and well-behaved. In the League of German Girls the ideal was to wear flat-heeled shoes, if possible with Tyrolean stockings, you know, with tassels. And then we hiked and went swimming a lot. Today it's really shocking – fifteen- and sixteen-year-old girls already having affairs. It definitely wasn't like that in my time. The young people today are in a bigger hurry than we were – yes, you could put it that way. But they have a lot more worries than we did. When a young girl falls in love or goes astray, she has her troubles. You mustn't think that it doesn't leave traces in a girl when she falls for a young fellow who's always looking for something new.

We have friends with children, and they're all very unhappy about the way things are going.

The young people are always talking about one thing: sex, sex, sex, from every angle. Even the fifteen-year-olds are asked for their opinion. That's ridiculous. They take themselves a good deal too seriously, they grow up too quickly. I know for a fact that a good many fifteen- or sixteen-year-old high-school students have lost their innocence. I can hardly believe a lot of the things I know. The girls tell me the wildest stories. I know a lot of them and they like to come and see me when they're feeling blue about something or when they've quarrelled with their parents. I can only shake my head at some of the things they tell me. Very young girls are having affairs with boys or young men. Here's a story I heard not so long ago: A boy and a girl, the boy is eighteen, the girl sixteen – their parents had gone off hunting. The parents were hardly out of the house when the kids asked their friends of both sexes over, and believe me, all sorts of things went on. There was no bashfulness at all between the sexes. Three or four of them were 'on guard' in one of the rooms. All in all, it was quite a party. But then there was a bad storm, the young people didn't notice. And the parents come home sooner than they were expected because it was cold in the hunting lodge. It seems to me the young men wouldn't be the way they are if there weren't so many young girls they could be so free with. Sometimes a girl doesn't even want to, but then the boy says: 'If you won't do it, you're just a wet blanket,' or 'You're no fun. You don't have to come again. I'll find somebody else.' And you see, when that happens to a girl once or twice, she doesn't want to be left out of things and she does what's expected of her. I know of five young girls under seventeen who were definitely forced into it because otherwise they wouldn't have been invited to parties any more.

Right in front of their noses the young men pick somebody else. Of course the parents are a good deal to blame.

All perfectly decent people, but they make the mistake of getting angry right away.

They start yelling right away if the young girls are a little disobedient and don't help at home and spend hours doing their hair and putting on make-up and the apartment is full of hair. The parents start screaming and the girls run away because they feel they're not understood. You can read plenty in the illustrated magazines about children who aren't understood. 'Aha,' the young people say to themselves, 'now I'm a member of the misunderstood club.' At first I thought: It's really a wonder more things don't go wrong, that more girls don't get babies if they start so early. But now I know that quite a few of them do get babies. I know some myself. And there are still more, I'm sorry to say, that have abortions, and that's even worse. I have two daughters myself, we discuss everything. One is twelve, the other thirteen. We talk about everything, including the things we read in the paper. Recently there was a story about a young girl who drowned herself because she was unhappy in love. So I asked my daughters: 'Why do you think she did that?' And then I explain the whole situation and they understand that they'd better watch their step. And besides I mean to keep them so busy they won't get any crazy ideas. My husband discusses all the problems perfectly frankly with the girls. We're more like friends to them than parents. They like to have the feeling they can talk about everything with us. My husband is marvellous, though to tell the truth I wanted an entirely different type. You know, Germanic, tall and blond and slender, the way a real man should be. And what did I get? An easy-going plump little man. But he's tops. He bought a motorcycle from my father who had a cycle shop. Yes, a motorcycle, and I went for a ride with him. I had to sign the bill of sale and somehow he invited me out for a practice ride and we fell off the thing. But I didn't cry or make a fuss and that impressed him. So we got along very well. I've only once been head-over-heels in love – well, maybe that's an exaggeration. I was working in a bank and a customer comes to my window. He was a wonderful man. He looked so interesting, really marvellous. And he turned out to be the brother of the Shah of Persia. I couldn't stop raving about him. In the end the whole bank knew. I told my husband about it but it didn't hurt our marriage. It was just a crush, that's all.

I wouldn't divorce my husband even if he had an affair.

No, certainly not. Even if he had a regular mistress, I wouldn't get divorced. I especially wouldn't if that were the case. But I don't think he'll do anything like that. I keep him too busy. It's true, he said he'd get divorced right away if I did anything wrong, but I believe he'd think twice about it.

As a young man he was in the SA.

He liked it because he had friends there. Even today he often says: 'Oh, I know him, he was with me in the SA.' And then in the War, they marched and marched. I don't think they had time to think about what was going on. At least he doesn't talk about it. And I'm really not so sure the Nazis brought on the War all by themselves. It takes two to make a fight. I read that before the War the Poles wrote to the French: 'If France attacks Germany in the west, we Poles will attack in the east.' That gives me pause. What I think is this: 'One nation alone just can't be to blame for all that misery.' No, I can't believe it. I can't believe that the Germans were stupid enough to start a thing like that all by themselves. If leading politicians or generals actually realized before it was too late that Hitler was no good and wanted to start a war, why didn't they pull out a gun and shoot him dead? They didn't have the courage of their convictions. What they did years later on 20 July 1944 – you can't call that an uprising. It was just ridiculous. That's plain even to a little bookkeeper like me. Incidentally, I do bookkeeping because housekeeping doesn't satisfy me, I'm bored at home.

Just shopping and cooking and washing dishes and making beds and cleaning, day in day out, is deadening. I wanted to do something else.

So I went to work at an art publisher's, they sell modern art and I work half-time as a bookkeeper. I get to know the new modern art. I didn't know anything about it before. Now I really like it, but it takes a certain time to get used to it.

We have a nice friendly landscape here, no high mountains or that kind of thing. Real mountains are much too big for me. And when I go to the seashore, all that water frightens me. In general I like everything here: the city, the people, all the little theatres and the university too. Now and then I go to a lecture. For instance I saw Strauss at the university. You know, Strauss impresses me. There's a man who's always been able to assert himself. Well, when he lectured here, he was still Defence Minister. And I said to myself: This is going to be worth seeing. The students will certainly give him a piece of their mind. When I got there, I said to myself:

I wonder if he's got a revolver on him. He's got to have some way of defending himself against the students.

And then he talked with his hands and feet and then he buttoned his jacket and unbuttoned it again, and then he put his hands behind his back, and I could see he was wearing suspenders but no revolver. He really floored the students. There was no discussion at all. Nobody dared to say a word against him. The big auditorium was overcrowded and his lecture was broadcast over the loudspeaker in another big lecture hall. The whole place was jam-packed. I thought to myself: Man, is he intelligent! And so quick on the draw! He really impressed me. Maybe you'd say he was a demagogue, and maybe Hitler was that way too, but Strauss is an able man and we need able men.

BRUNO FRIED, OTTO FRIED

16, 17, members of a beat band

We worked in a wholesale egg business and then we bought an amplifier.

Bruno Fried: We often listened to beat programmes and that kind of thing on the radio and we liked them. We already played the guitar, so it was only natural that we should start a band, and anyway we're the enterprising type. Besides, beat is really in. First we played at a class party for fifteen marks. We didn't know exactly what we were doing but we had fun. Of course our equipment was lousy at first but then we, my brother and I, I mean, made money to buy more instruments with. We worked in a wholesale egg business and then on a construction job and then we bought an amplifier – secondhand for 500 marks – and a mike stand and a solo guitar, a rhythm guitar and a bass guitar. We ran the bass guitar over the radio with borrowed drums, and then three other fellows joined us and we got to be a real beat band. The two of us are in school, two of the others are in school, and there's one who works in a factory. He's our percussion man. That makes five of us. At first we didn't play in night clubs but at the Red Cross. But then when our technique improved, we played in the cellar of St Mary's Church and every time we played we got better. Now we call ourselves 'The Thinks'. It has to be something striking. There are lots of 'beat bands' and they all have names. There's another band that calls itself 'The Things', so we just put in a 'k' instead of the 'g'. So now we're 'The Thinks'. There's some connexion with the English verb 'to think'. Our mother supports the household all by herself. Father is dead, he was principal of the Goethe-Gynmanasium [classical high-school]. On account of him my mother gets a very good pension, and besides she gets her widow's pension from the government and her family allowance. It's enough to get by on. We're a big family, eleven brothers and sisters. Most of them are married. Otto and I have already got twenty-one nephews and nieces with more coming all the time. Anyway, we're an enormous family. Our oldest brother is thirty-two. What a guy! He's always racing around on a black motorcycle. He wears a black leather suit. Everybody calls him the Black Rider or the Black Death Rider. He always rides the newest and heaviest motorcycles. Right now, he's got a 750-pounder. That's a real heavy model from England. He's got motorcycles on the brain. He's had a million accidents. He goes dashing around the country with all sorts of hardware, but when it comes to music, he's only interested in classical. The others in our family only play the piano, the oboe and those kind of classical instruments.

They don't like beat at all, they call it an infantile disease. But they leave us alone.

Naturally our long hair throws some of the older people, even my mother, but she's fairly tolerant. She doesn't try to make us cut our hair short, because she knows there'd be trouble. She says when the time comes we'll have it cut of our own free will. She thinks the whole thing will pass. The people in the neighbourhood are fairly tolerant too because they think we're nice boys. And the priest of the church where we play in the cellar doesn't mind the long hair. He says he'd rather have us playing music than going wrong. We two are the only Catholics in the band. The three others are all Protestants. The priest doesn't mind. We play in his place, it brings in quite a lot of money, and it goes to the parish youth organization. We go to church on Sunday on account of our mother; we don't believe in it very much. The way we look at it, you don't have to go to church to be saved. About other things our priest is old-fashioned. In religious instruction he always used to threaten us: 'One day when you're in trouble, God will ask you where you were on Sunday. And you'll have to say: we were lying in bed, rolling our fat behinds around in the feathers.' That was the way he looked at it. If we didn't go to church, mother would be very unhappy, and our aunt would start in with: 'My goodness, what's happening to the children? Have they lost the faith?'

Not at all, we believe in God.

But we simply refuse to believe that God said people had to go to church on Sunday; he just didn't. He and his apostles didn't meet every Sunday. Otherwise the priest is okay, but the long hair drives our teacher crazy. Two or three of us in our class have pretty long hair. One time the teacher got sore about it, he said I should take my mane out in the fresh air. And the old crank that teaches us Latin gripes about my hair too. And one time the principal came in and pointed his finger at me and shouted that I should go to the barber, he'd supply the two marks fifty. And I said: 'I don't feel the need of it.' All that isn't so bad.

But in the streetcar some people once said: 'Look at those vulgar hippies.'

Or when we come into a restaurant: 'My God, that hair!' They go on and on, but it doesn't bother us when they call us hippies. We steer clear of the real hippies. You must have seen them, they're always standing around the market place. Hair down to their shoulders, ear-rings and filthy and unshaved. They always hang out where there's a big crowd. They need people to provoke, and practically everybody goes through the market place. The city people don't get very excited, but you should see the peasants who come in to shop. They're really upset and the hippies do their best to bug them. A lot of those guys get to be hippies because they can't stand the busy life today.

They can't stand people telling them to study and study some more . . . it makes them sick.

They drop out and run away and become hippies. Then they take it easy. No more school. They take an odd job now and

then when they need money, and then they bum around some
more. Until the next time they need money. But there's one
interesting thing: here in Germany and in France too some of
the hippy groups have members with higher education. They
think a lot, they're sort of philosophers, anyway they think so.
They meditate a good deal and talk even more. Naturally they
run down the bourgeoisie and talk about escaping from the
fetters of society. Well, if you ask me, there have always been
hippies. Some people have always been too lazy to work. But
today it's different. These hippies are a product of our time,
because everybody – especially the older people – is so pig-
headed and always in a hurry. A lot of us don't go for that, all
this hustle and bustle, you've got no time for yourself. Sometimes the way they load on the work at school, I sit studying
all day. I study, I have a bite to eat, I work some more, I have
another bite to eat, I work some more and go to bed. And next
morning it all starts in all over again. You can hardly get your
breath. But even so, I wouldn't want to be a hippie. No, I really
wouldn't. Most of the time they live in filth and there's a lot of
hardship. They practically sleep in the street, or in parks, or
they go to some flophouse for 30 pfennigs a night. No, we have
nothing to do with them. Fans like us use Churchill's old high
sign, you know, you spread two fingers to make a V: 'Victory'.
That's our sign. No, no, our models aren't the hippies. Not the
Beatles either, not really. Our favourites are the Pretty Things,
another band, not very well known. The Pretty Things are
hippie types.

They're not exactly beautiful to look at but their music is
great.

Our solo guitar is really hot and on the technical side everything is okay. The people go half crazy. Yes, I've noticed that
quite a few times. When we give a good performance of a
piece that just happens to be No. 1 on the Hit Parade, it's
always well received. The people shout like mad or hammer on
the tables with their bottles. Then we really enjoy ourselves.

Yes, our ideals right now are good beat bands, we don't really care so much about movie actors. The other fellows in our class are crazy about them. I read a lot too. We've read Bertolt Brecht – *The Broken Jug* – right, that's by Kleist, what I read by Brecht was *The Affairs of Mr Julius Caesar*. I didn't like it so much. My favourite author is Paul Gallico. He's written some really nice things, like *The Snow Goose* or *The Small Miracle*. He has a very impressive way of describing his characters, he has a lot of humour and he's very romantic.

In general we have a weakness for romantic things.

For instance, look at the lighting in our room. When we're alone, we turn the red bulb on. It gives a nice, muted light, and we also have tallow candles and stuff like that. That's the kind of night spots we pick too. Sometimes on Sunday we go to the Münchner Stuben. The whole place is divided into booths. You can sit there quietly and there are girls too. Most of them are about seventeen. They come around after we play and we strike up a conversation. Our playing gives us a terrific 'in' with the girls. If we wanted to take advantage of it, we could have girls by the dozen. A lot of guys do that. But it goes against my grain because it doesn't really give me a kick to change girls every day like my shirt. I don't see the point. Right now I'm a grass widower, but when I have a girl I usually go with her for a long time,

Until she goes off with somebody else or I'm fed up.

When it gets boring, I usually put an end to it. And another thing – naturally we make a big distinction between bags and girls. Bags – well, I mean the old wrecks you run into on the street or in the clubs. Girls are the kids of our own age. The kind we get along with, their heart's in the right place, and they aren't so easy to get. But there aren't so many like that. When a girl comes across so easily, I have no respect for her. Most of the girls are too willing. They're frivolous. If a guy says: 'I

love you,' even if he's only sixteen or seventeen years old,
bam! There they go. What love really is, nobody gives a damn.
Maybe they do it only because they're afraid their boy friend
will run out on them or say she's an old prude, or some such
thing. Probably it's just a matter of style. With this sex wave
they whip up in the movies and the illustrated magazines, you
can hardly see straight. Naturally the boys who see and read all
that stuff get enterprising, there's nothing to be surprised at.

They're always running stories about girls who give themselves and nothing much happens.

But it's not always true. There's a seventeen-year-old boy
living next to us. He's already got three kids. He has two different girls. One of them knew that he had a kid already. And
she took up with him just the same. That's beyond me. She's a
filthy old swine, that's all I can say. All that comes from the
movies and the magazines. I'd rather read the newspaper. Anyway, I always read the headlines to see what's going on.
Whether they've been bombing Vietnam again, or what's going
on in China or if they've bumped off a few more Negroes in
America. You know, sort of a bird's-eye view, not all the
details.

Our history teacher has a pretty strong clerical tinge, if you
know what I mean. He has a funny way of teaching history.
He's always reading us old plays, junk about the Romans and
Greeks. Most of it's pretty boring, I just sit there and doze.

They ought to tell us something about the Nazi period.
That would interest me, it would interest me a lot!

Otto Fried: Well, I'm in a technical high school, not the
classical high school like Bruno. We get to hear about it. The
Nazis, I mean. We have a young teacher, he shows us movies
of the Third Reich and tells us what different people had to say
about them, Jews and so on, people who were interviewed
after they'd seen them. Our teacher is very active politically.

He's running for town councillor. And we're only at the beginning. Actually, we're only up to Hitler's seizure of power. But we also get an idea of the Nazi period from our mother because she suffered a lot: she was bombed out and her brothers were killed in the War and our father was a prisoner of the French for five years and came home half dead and then he died. She was left alone with all the children and she's often told us about the Nazi days. It interests us a good deal, trying to figure out how a whole country could fall for such a thing.

My opinion is that Hitler was sick, mentally sick at any rate.

The orders he gave were completely insane, he simply didn't realize that anybody but himself was capable of thinking. And then this hatred of the Jews. Anybody normal would have aesthetic scruples about killing such an enormous number of Jews. And that system of violence! Nobody dared to say a word. I can't understand that some people are still Nazis. In the NPD, for instance. But when you go to an NPD meeting, it's all full of young fellows. That's bad. They don't seem to care about so many Jews being killed. I think it's mostly the fault of their parents who still approve of what the Nazis did, who were always in favour and still are. . . . They pass it on to the kids and that's why they're in the NPD.

WALTER BUSCHE

47, married, insurance salesman, former member
of the Waffen-SS

They didn't take the dumbest.

My father was a postal clerk and not very keen on the Third Reich. He came of a peasant family. But his eldest brother took over the farm. Nobody in our family had any connexion with National Socialism. But naturally I was in the Hitler

Youth, and at that time high-school students could graduate without an examination if they volunteered for the Waffen-SS before a certain date. So I reported with several of my schoolmates, and on 20 November 1939 I was assigned to the 'Deutschland' German reserve regiment of the Waffen-SS. In the Hitler Youth they'd made a good deal of propaganda for the Waffen-SS, and I knew that it was an élite troop. In those days Saturday was Youth Day. We had night manoeuvres with light signals. Actually all we had was ordinary flashlights. But we called them flash machine-guns and kept blinking them. We camped in the woods with tents. We had a lot of fun. And in school we had pre-military training with rifle drill and so on. They'd fixed up a shooting gallery in the cellar of the school and we fired air rifles. And then we worked for our all-round sports insignia, that meant compass reading, developing a sense of orientation, cross-country running, swimming, etc. It took in all that in those days. As a boy I was attracted by the Waffen-SS because it was selective. I mean, they only recruited men with a certain degree of intelligence. Anyway they didn't take the dumbest. I wouldn't say we felt like supermen in the Waffen-SS, but in a way we regarded ourselves as an élite. The selection was also based on Nordic racial characteristics and size. They didn't take anyone under five feet ten and a half. It was only during the War that they took anybody under five feet ten and a half, when they brought in all the Germans by race from the Balkans, from the Batschka and that kind of place, and put them in the Waffen-SS. They were the so-called 'liberated Germans', people who had never seen an automobile in their lives. They simply piled them into a train and brought them up to us. I saw them for the first time when I was in guard headquarters, I mean the guard detachment at the Führer's Headquarters in Rastenburg in East Prussia. That was the so-called 'Anna Office'. You know, where the attempt on Hitler's life was made on 20 July 1944. In the shack where they held the situation conferences.

Hitler was hospitalized in an insane asylum.

I well remember the day when Colonel Count Von Stauffenberg put down the briefcase with the infernal machine in it near
Hitler and then flew off to Berlin where they were cooking up
this uprising on Bendlerstrasse. Hitler was actually wounded,
he was hospitalized with us, I mean, in Karlshof Hospital near
Rastenburg. That was a former insane asylum and that's where
they sent all the men who were wounded in the plot. Yes, a
lot of them were wounded. They kept bringing out coffins and
we had to stand honour guard. One day they carried out Ber-
ger, Hitler's stenographer. He was dead. But then they found
out he was one of the 20th July conspirators. Yes, he lost his
life in the plot. He didn't even know the others were planning
the assassination for that day. That's why people accused
Stauffenberg of cowardice, because he played fast and loose
with the life of his own comrades. General Stief was also
killed in the plot, and he was one of the conspirators too. I saw
Hitler himself a lot of times. At that time I was an Oberscharführer,* I had access to Restricted Zone Three. Most of the men
were only allowed in Restricted Zone One. In all there were
three Restricted Zones around the Wolf's Lair, that's what they
called Führer's Headquarters. I saw Hitler out walking with his
dogs, big wolfhounds, and Eva Braun was there too. Of course
I'd often heard Hitler speak over the radio. I'd seen pictures
too, but when I saw him in the flesh, the man somehow fascinated me. He was the ideal of us young men. I never spoke to
him personally. But I saw him very close up, and then I saw
him again when he came out of the hospital and we were
standing honour guard over the coffins. When he was discharged, he had a plaster on his forehead. That was all we
saw. But it was only for a short time that I was on duty at
Führer's Headquarters. Actually, I was in the combat troops, in
the Viking Division. I was sent to Rastenburg only after I'd been
wounded near Rostov in the Ukraine. I was wounded in the

---

* A low, non-commissioned rank in the SS, approximately 'Corporal'.

leg. That was our last retreat. We had to fall back to Dniepro-
petrovsk, the Russian tanks had broken through, and I was
wounded by a flare fired from a tank. The Russians moved on
past us but that night our chief pulled us out of there. He was
a wonderful guy, a Hauptsturmführer,* by the name of Karl
Rann. He always used his name as a battle cry. He'd shout
'Rann! Rann!'† Well, anyway, he got us out of there. He
passed through the Russian lines with a tank and got the
wounded out. At that time we were still a pure Waffen-SS unit,
consisting only of Germans, I mean Germans from Germany.
But then Finns came in and pretty soon the Viking Division
was full of Dutch, Flemish and Finnish volunteers. They were
all real volunteers. At first we had trouble understanding each
other, but then we got along fine. But later on – those Finns
were really tough customers. Let's say undisciplined. What I
mean is that sometimes there was no holding them. They had
an unbelievable hatred for the Russians. That was on account
of the war the Russians had made on Finland in 1939 in Karelia.
The Finns all had daggers, they'd sneak over to the Russian side
all alone at night and come back with their prisoners. They did
a lot of things they hadn't been ordered to. They said it wasn't
the business of the German sergeant – Oberscharführer, I mean.
The Finns had come to us in an entirely different way from
the Dutch and the Flemings. They were sent to us by – what's
his name again? – oh yes, Field-Marshal Mannerheim. We even
had Swedes. One of the Swedes was always stirring up the Finns
against us Germans. You see, he was the Finns' interpreter and
he always translated orders wrong; orders came out that struck
the Finns as impossible to carry out, so they went on strike. So
they were put in isolation. Finally it came out that the Swede
was the cause of all the trouble. He was sent to a disciplinary
camp. Then we got scum who robbed their comrades and that
kind of thing. In the Wehrmacht, it was usual to keep the barracks locker locked, but with us, the Waffen-SS, it always had

---

* Another SS rank, approximately 'Captain'.
† *'Rann!'* – roughly 'Let's go!'

to be open. If a man had lost his rifle or anything, he was sent to a disciplinary camp.

Some of the men swapped their rifles with the Russians for food.

Yes, I'm ashamed to say, such things happened. For instance the 'Blue Division', those Spaniards, they'd hardly got through Poland and all their weapons were gone. They even sold artillery pieces. But at that time it wasn't that way in the Waffen-SS. It only started towards the end of the War. You see, we really were an élite troop, kind of like trouble-shooters. They sent us where the going was rough. That's why our losses were so high. In the beginning there were 900,000 of us, at the end there were only 300,000 left. 900,000, that was the whole Waffen-SS including the foreigners, 38 divisions in all. How many are alive today, nobody really knows. We get together at the big Waffen-SS conventions they hold each year. We're almost all of us in HIAG.* We also meet in beer halls, right here in our town for instance. Between 40 and 100 of us get together. Of course there are many more in town, but a lot of them don't show up, they think it might make trouble for them, especially if they're in public life, working for the government.

It was all Reichsheini's fault.

I was taken prisoner by the Americans. They picked me up somewhere along the Neckar. I'd made out my own discharge papers. But they looked under my arm and saw the blood-group sign that was tattooed there. So they knew I was in the Waffen-SS. That was how the the whole mess started. The Americans locked me up because they mistook me for a war criminal who was accused of shooting prisoners during the Ardennes offensive. My hard luck was that I was an Obersturmführer,† and my name was Walter Busche; the other guy was an Obersturm-

---

* Hilfsorganisation auf Gegenseitigkeit – Mutual Aid Organization.
† Another SS rank, approximately 'Lieutenant'.

führer too, but his name was Jochen Busche. So the Amis held me until they finally caught the other guy. Until then they refused to believe that I was myself. I wasn't exactly well treated by the Americans. It was like a jail and they knocked my teeth out. I really don't like to talk about it. No, I don't like to remember those things, but if there's anybody I hate it's Himmler, old Reichsheini. The whole thing was his fault. It was hard for the Americans to realize that there was a difference between SS and Waffen-SS. They put us all in the same boat. They got us mixed up with the Death's Head units and the concentration camp guards. We had nothing to do with those guys. Those guards in the concentration camps of Dachau, Mauthausen, etc. It was all because one day Himmler arranged with Hitler to have our blood-groups tattooed on the whole lot of us, from the police to the Death's Head units and the concentration camp guards. Well, that's how it was, and that's why after a while the Americans just said: 'Raise your arms!' No, Himmler, old Reichsheini, wasn't a commander of troops, we didn't recognize his authority. The men we recognized and respected were Sepp Dietrich, for instance, and Hauser, who used to be chairman of our organization, and General Gille. Himmler was never really active as a commander of troops. He only arranged to have all the SS units put under his official command and everybody called him Reichsheini. He wasn't the least bit popular with us in the Waffen-SS. And we were really angry later on when he was made Commander of the Replacement Army and Minister of the Interior. He introduced the Hitler salute in the whole army. We knew there were these SS guards in the concentration camps. They were mostly draftees, not volunteers. They came from the General SS or the police. They just shoved them into the concentration camps and said: 'Now do your stuff!' There was only one Death's Head Division that belonged to the Waffen-SS.

For us Dachau was like a red rag.

I saw the concentration camp once. That was in 1939 during

my training. The Deutschland Regiment's Hospital was in Dachau. It was separate from the concentration camp but you could see them marching around in there with their striped uniforms. I had no idea what happened to those people, I mean I didn't know they were killed. A lot of people didn't know. And that's why they don't want to believe what comes out in these trials. I was also in a motor-transport regiment, near the Buchenwald camp. We thought all the inmates of the concentration camps were offenders against the racial laws. There were actually 175 of those. There were all sorts. Criminals too. All mixed up: black marketeers, Reds and politicals. Then after the War when I found out what had really happened in the concentration camps, it was more than I could imagine. At first I didn't believe it. No, not at first. But then I met a man at one of our HIAG meetings who had been in a Death's Head unit, and even served as a concentration camp guard. He told me all about it, and then I believed it. But the man had only come to us by mistake. Otherwise we don't accept anybody in the HIAG who was a concentration camp guard. We don't take anybody from the Death's Head units. We don't want anything to do with those guys. That's what I have against Himmler, the way he mixed them all up so everybody gives us dirty looks too. It's changed in the last twenty years. You see, this is my home town, everybody knew me and everybody knew my parents and nobody would suspect me of being mixed up in such crimes.

Our enthusiasm lasted through our time in the prison camps and we've still got it.

All right-wingers feel pretty much the same way. But when you come right down to it, the reason we meet is that we began to help each other during the hard times. We helped the widows of the men who were in prison or dead. We gave them coal and potatoes. We helped each other, too. That's no longer necessary today. We only meet at our regular table in the beer hall. We don't talk much about the War and the old combat

days. That's all dead and buried. There's just sort of an old bond
between us, and it's good for business connexions. It's not the
dumbest who are back in good positions. We can help each
other up the ladder. I'm an insurance salesman now. But I used
to be in a wholesale house. Well, it's been a long time and
there've been a lot of changes.

A lot of us are members of some democratic party now.

That in itself proves their opinions have changed. And it also
proves they're capable of doing good work. Look at the mayors
of the German cities, for instance. A lot of our boys are among
them. The fact is they made a good selection at that time, and
it proved itself even after the War. In peacetime. We've somehow got to get over our past. The other side too. It's no good
that people should still be hacking away at us. It's high time we
got rid of the curse of the Nazi days. Oh well, we lost a war,
you can't change that. I'm not against democracy, I'm close to
the CDU. My three sons are naturally interested in knowing all
about those days. The picture they get in school isn't quite right,
I mean, they don't tell them how things really were, so they
come to me and ask:

'Papa, you were there. Are those things we hear about really
true?'

And then they ask me about the camps and all that stuff. But
I can only tell my children this: 'I was a soldier and nothing
else. If anybody tells you your father was a criminal, don't believe him. Yes, there were criminals, but I wasn't one of them.
The Waffen-SS was okay but it doesn't exist any more. That's
all dead and buried.'
    Everything has changed in the schools. I've told you that my
father didn't think much of the Nazis. But when I went into the
Waffen-SS, he had to give his signature; I was still a minor. And
later on when all those things happened and we were all

branded as criminals, he was sorry he'd given his signature. But he knew I hadn't been in a concentration camp.

After the War I joined the Church again.

My parents weren't regular churchgoers. Both Protestants. We had the usual religious upbringing, but no great importance was attached to it. Of course we were sent to church. The only question is whether we went in. Later, when I was in the Waffen-SS, I left the Church. We were all what they call theists. Yes, we believed in the existence of God, but we didn't want to be connected with any religious denomination. We weren't atheists. After the War I joined the Church again. For my children's sake. I still don't go to church, but I wanted my children to belong to a religious community, to be baptized, and so on. So as not to get dirty looks in school.

When you see Germans firing on Germans . . .

It bothers me a good deal that the papers are saying less and less about unification. I don't think the wedge they've driven between East and West is very big. But I don't think either that there will ever be a war between brother Germans. I can't conceive of it. Though when you see Germans firing on Germans at the border . . . , that's tragic. You see, those young fellows, they probably never hear anything else but Communist propaganda. Sermons of hate. They don't hear anything else, any more than we did in the old days. Today I'd accept an all-European government. Naturally we couldn't claim to be the ones who ought to lead or dominate Europe. That's out of the question. Even today, we're probably being manipulated by the others, the Russians and the Americans. We're not a real independent state. But when I look at the Federal Government, say for instance the three chancellors we've had: Adenauer, Erhard and Kiesinger. Adenauer went a little too far to please the Americans. He toadied to them too much. Yes, that's a fact. And Erhard came to grief because of his own party. I liked

Erhard all right. He was responsible for practically the whole
economic miracle. And now they've booted him in the ass.

Kiesinger is really a fine man.

He was locked up too because he was in the Party once. Now
I guess you're going to ask me about the NPD. I'll tell you right
away: I leaned in that direction for a while, but then I didn't
like it so much because elements that don't appeal to me were
making a big noise. When I think about what went on at their
meetings and the kind of people who were there ... the whole
lot of them angling for some job. And they haven't any real
political idea. To tell the truth, they're the scum of humanity.

STREETWALKER

middle 20s

I'd like to talk to you.
Talk? What about?
About you.
You don't say. About me! You must be nuts. What is there to
talk about? There's nothing interesting about me. ... You going
to pay me something?
For talking?
Sure, it takes up my time.
Not very much of it.
How much?
We'll see.
All right. Then stop your car right here. It'll cost less. What do
you want to know? There's nothing interesting about me. I
can tell you that right away.
But perhaps there is.
Think so? All right, fire away. I'm getting curious.
Why do you stand here?
You going to start preaching?

Certainly not.
So you think I'm interesting?
Yes. Why not?
You're really nuts!
What made you start doing this?
It started with a lover. Yes, you could call him that. I loved
him. He was the only one.
Where is he now?
Gone.
Where?
You know, up there, where all of us go some day. .... I'm not
doing anything bad. Or do you think it's bad? I don't hurt any-
body. I only oblige. Is that bad? I don't kill anybody. I don't
cheat anybody. I only do what the men want.
What do they say to you?
Hell, they always have a reason: a terrible wife, or no woman
at all. Practically all of them complain about something.
Do you believe what they say?
Hell no, I just pretend to. That's what they want. I just
listen and I always say: yes, angel, you're perfectly right. Just
have a good cry on my shoulder.
You said it started with your lover?
Yes. One day he got sick and was taken to the hospital. And he
didn't have any money. I paid for everything. And then
another guy came around, a friend of his, if you want to call
him that. And he had a lot of money. He said to me: Uschi, he
said, you haven't got any money, but you need some don't you?
Yes, I said, I sure do. Then he said: If you let me spend the night
with you, I'll give you all you need for Karl. That was my guy,
the one in the hospital. Hell, I didn't like it, but I needed the
money, and he wasn't bad.
Had you many men before?
No, only two. I was only nineteen. Only my Karl and then this
guy. Actually, I enjoyed it. After all, my Karl was in the hospital, and I was young. All the same, I had the feeling I was
cheating. Oh well, that went on for about six months.
And then?

Then Karl died. And his friend brought another friend and things went on like that, it was the easiest way. Karl never found out. I was able to pay for first-class and he had a good life. Karl loved me and I loved him too.

You never . . .?

No, I never felt I was selling myself for Karl.

And then a friend of his came and a friend of the friend's, and then some more friends . . .?

Yes, that's the way it went. But in the beginning I enjoyed it.

And now?

I can't tell one man from another and I don't enjoy it any more, but I've got to live.

So now you're standing here waiting for customers. Aren't there enough who come by themselves?

Oh yes, I have my regular customers. They come to my place. They call up. I only stand here when things are slow.

Are they often slow?

No, thank God. It's hard to hold on to a place here on account of all the others.

Haven't they their steady customers?

Only a few. Most of them only have a steady place to stand.

Have you always had to stand here on the outskirts?

No, we used to be in town, on the Hauptstrasse. But we're not allowed to stand there any more. They say it makes a bad impression on people from out of town.

What kind of men are your customers?

A few foreigners, but not many. Mostly businessmen, office workers . . .

Workers?

No, hardly ever.

Because they don't make enough?

Go on, a lot of them make more than one of these office workers. But I guess they don't need it so much, they're happier.

With their wives?

That too, probably. They're not so much interested in adventures. They've got better lives, I guess they're just happier.

Are men very different from each other?

The richer they are, the worse pigs they are. They pay more, but they want more too.

Do you prefer rich men?

The money, sure, but otherwise, no. I like to keep it simple, without too much bother. I don't get much fun out of it.

You could take up a different occupation. Must you do this? Didn't you learn a trade?

Yes, I worked in an office when I was with Karl. But go back again? Nothing doing. Anyway, everybody knows me. This town is too small. It's hard to change.

You could go to another city.

Yes, I could. But give up my nice apartment? Oh no. Now I've got it, I'll keep it.

And when you're older?

I'm saving up, I'll be all right.

What do you do the rest of the time?

I read a lot. I belong to a lending library.

What do you read?

Oh, novels. I like Hemingway a lot, I've read all his books. And I go to the theatre.

Alone?

No, with a girl friend, or sometimes a boy friend.

A regular boy friend?

Yes, I've got one, he loves me, he's a salesman, he lives somewhere else. But he comes here often.

Do you love him?

Kind of. I don't think I can really love anybody any more. But I've got to have somebody that gives me a feeling of warmth.

Does he know what you do?

He has no idea.

What if he finds out?

I'll be out of luck, I'll have to find somebody else.

Are you from here?

No.

What was your father? Is he still alive?

He's dead. Died when I was seventeen. He was a clerk in

the tax office. My mother remarried and went to Hamburg.
Are you in touch with her?
No, not at all. I don't like her husband.
Any brothers and sisters?
A sister here. She's older, married to a building worker. I see
her on the street sometimes or in a café.
Does she know what you do?
I think so.
Haven't you any desire to marry and have children?
If I really cared for a man, but men are all alike. He'd be bored
with me after a while and he'd leave. You know, I haven't any
confidence, I don't believe in anything any more.
You don't believe in anything?
Yes, there's Christ. That's the only man who is good. He
wanted something good but even he didn't make it. But I like
him. I'm telling you, I'm not doing anything bad, I don't cheat
anybody. I think he'd be pleased with me. That's the way men
are, they do all kinds of disgusting things themselves, then they
come around and look down their noses at us. No, don't talk to
me about that kind. . . . You know enough about me now? Do
you get anything out of talking with a girl like me?
Of course I do!
At least I tell the truth, you can take my word for that. But
just wanting to speak to me? You must really be a nut. You
hand me a laugh. . . . Oh well . . . here comes somebody. All
right, you funny man, scram. – Never mind, just scram, you
didn't make me miss anybody.

FRANZ WALDMEISTER

44, married, peasant

Some of the things that happened were so really cock-eyed
I just can't get them out of my head.

Well, it may strike you as funny, but – well anyway, I wasn't a
Nazi. No, you really couldn't say I was, I was too much of a
Catholic, I still am. I'd always been a member of the Catholic
Youth Movement. At first the guys in the Reich Youth Admini-
stration said they were going to work hand in glove with us.
Naturally that was for the birds. It didn't take us long to find
out. We thought we'd infect the Nazis with the good Catholic
spirit, we talked about boring from within. That was for the
birds too. The Nazis said they were going to hug us to death.
And that's exactly what they did. That wasn't for the birds.

Yes, I had a lot of trouble with the Brown plague.

Good God, when I think of those disgusting brown uniforms,
that idiotic cockroach-shit colour, that dog crap. It makes you
want to vomit! Well, we somehow had to live with the lousy
bastards. We thought up all sorts of tricks. On account of my
work in the Catholic organizations I wasn't exactly in the Gestapo's good books. They'd had it in for me for a long time. After
a while they started making things hot for me. They kept
calling me down to headquarters, and we 'Catholic Cyclists'
developed a special technique for dealing with our friends of
the Gestapo. They photographed the marchers in the Corpus
Christi procession and chewed people out on the strength of
the photographs. They called me in one day and gave it to me:
'Look here, you nutty Christ child, you go to church on Sunday. Don't you, you holy water guzzler?' So I said straight out:
'See here yourself, next you'll be asking me if I go to the
movies every Thursday or sleep with my wife every Tuesday.'

That put the laughs on my side and I came off okay. But our best man was chaplain Sulzberger. He'd trained his dachshund – who was brown to begin with – to sit on his ass and raise his paw as if he were saying 'Heil Hitler!' This chaplain Sulzberger directed all the Catholic youth activities in our town. They were really gunning for him, but the sly fox said: 'What's the matter? Anybody can see I'm not against you, look at the way I've trained my dog. Surely that must convince you, gentlemen.' And the dachshund sat fat on his ass, raised his paw and went 'Heil Hitler!' Those Gestapo swine laughed and the chaplain had to go from office to office showing all the Gestapo officials how nicely his dachshund could make 'Heil Hitler!' So that day the chaplain got off again, so to speak.

As a peasant I'm gradually dying out around here.

You see, my father was still a real peasant and my grandfather even more so, and so on. Every one of them. In those days the city was still far away, it took them a good half hour to get there on horseback or in the carriage. But then the place got bigger and bigger. Our village, I mean. And the city people started coming out more and more. But it really started with the streetcar, when they brought it out this way. And then came the War, and then after the War when the building boom started, the price of land shot up higher and higher and I said to myself: 'Why this lousy work in the fields? You can make a nice piece of money doing something entirely different and fatten your pocketbook.' So I bought up more and more land. All the houses you see around here are on my land. They grow like mushrooms. Farming went out like a fart out of a cat. I still keep a big vegetable garden and chickens and three cows and a few pigs. And my bank account is growing. Now I've got a nice thick gold watch in my pocket all covered with diamonds, that's right, diamonds, oak leaves and swords, like a Knight's Cross, so to speak. . . . I never imagined I'd ever have a sweet little Knight's Cross like this disguised as a gold watch. Not in my wildest dreams. It all sounds so romantic, the stories

you hear nowadays and the stuff the kids read in those cheap
'Army life' magazines. The real thing was entirely different. I
was a sergeant in Section 2 AO, that's right 2 AO stands for
Offiziersangelegenheit (officers' affairs) and *Ordensverleihung*
(the conferring of decorations).

2 AO was in charge of handing out decorations. It took quite
a lot of imagination.

You had to find a sufficient excuse for giving a decoration. As
the War went on, the decoration business got more and more
grotesque. It got to the point where we had to make out de-
tailed reports explaining why so-and-so still had no EK II* or
KVK II.† This had nothing more to do with the actual giving
of decorations, but it was actually our responsibility if so-and-
so didn't have the decoration he deserved, although he had been
on the eastern front for so and so long with such and such a
unit. Towards the end of the War it got to be really hard to find
takers for decorations. One day, for instance, Corps Headquarters assigned us a Knight's Cross and I was given the job
of making the rounds of the divisional staffs to pick out a suit-
able bearer. Wherever I went, they gave me the cold shoulder
and sent me off like a mangy dog. All the units had shrunk to
such an extent that nobody felt the urge to wear the Knight's
Cross any more. The so-called sore throat, that old hankering
for a Knight's Cross hanging around your neck, had evaporated.
If you got a Knight's Cross, it gave you a right to home-leave,
but it was usually your last. Because recovering from your sore
throat, you know what I mean, getting the Knight's Cross, made
you a Hero of the Fatherland. So the minute this hero gets back
to the front, it's his moral duty to distinguish himself by some
more heroic deeds. His CO says to him: 'My dear boy, glad to

---

* *Eisenkreuz zweiter Klasse* – Iron Cross, Second Class.
† *Kriegsverdienstkreuz zweiter Klasse* – War Merit Cross, Second
Class.

see you back. You're just the man we needed. In fact, I've been waiting for you. You see, we've been having some trouble, bad trouble. Ivan has broken through next door. I want you to run over and close the gap.' So it's our Knight's Cross bearer's duty and obligation to distinguish himself by a special act of bravery. Naturally he knew he wouldn't last long. And it wasn't long before our Knight's Cross bearer was one of the many brave heroes who had given their lives for Führer and Fatherland, so to speak.

Hell, the famous morality of the German soldier was pretty shaky by the last years of the war.

What do you think the Poles made the famous Warsaw insurrection with? They didn't throw candy bombs. No, they mostly had German weapons, from pistols to grenade throwers. Same with the Russian partisans. All right, and now I ask you: 'Where did those fellows get their weapons?' It's not likely that they went to the arsenal. No, our own men had simply traded them for bread, eggs, meat, schnapps, and so on. 'Weapon lost in combat.' That's what they reported. In those days you couldn't take a furlough train and put your musette bag in the baggage net. Soon as you started sawing wood, your bag disappeared into thin air. There was a very funny code of honour. It was dishonourable to steal anything in your own unit, but if there was something your unit needed, you could go and steal it from the next unit, sometimes in fact you had to. Motorcycles, trucks, cars, and so on were stolen. They were redecorated by the workshop company and the numbers were changed. If a pursuit squadron had a new type of plane, they had to watch it like a hawk. There were all kinds of dodges. You invited the boys over for a friendly little party and when they were stinko the planes suddenly roared away and some others were flown in instead, the old models belonging to the unit next door. We waited for weeks for three 'Royal Tiger' tanks that never came. They'd been loaded on the cars back home, fifteen of them. But when the train arrived, there were only twelve.

Naturally the escort team didn't have the faintest idea what
had become of the other three. Somebody had made off
with them. One party had the 'Tigers' and another had the
money. Yes, you wouldn't believe some of the things that happened. In the beginning of course it was different.

They all fought like mad, they were drunk as fools on the
idea it was for a good cause.

The New European Order, so to speak. Well, one day, for instance, the word was: 'A little trip to the front lines.' We took
a personnel carrier, known in soldier language as a 'tulip crate'.
My job was to escort the General and play Santa Claus, so to
speak. That meant that I took along a big market basket full of
cologne, razor blades, foot powder, pocket-knives, and so on.
Anyway, a lot of stuff that was supposed to make the front-
line soldiers happy. Well, the personnel carrier started off, and
the closer we came to the front line the more we came under
fire. Our General stood there as straight as a ramrod. You've got
to give him credit, he had great personal courage. But I really
had the collywobbles, so to speak. The General noticed it and
said: 'Well, my boy, the air around here seems to have a little
too much iron content for you, doesn't it?' I said: 'Yes, Herr
General,' and tried to press against the armoured wall, but
then the General snarled at me: 'As you can see, I am standing
and as long as I am standing, you will also stand. Understand?
You wilted sausage, you! You flabby potato!' At that moment
the Stalin organ started up with all its pipes, and we really got
the music first-hand. My General threw himself flat on the floor,
protected by the armoured wall, while I, in an access of iron
determination went on standing as straight as a ramrod. But
then my General really chewed me out: 'Listen here, you fire-
cracker! When I find it necessary to protect my life, it's your
duty and obligation, damn it all, to do likewise and not to start
playing the hero!

'You owe it to the Führer to preserve your life as long as it can be useful to him. Understand?'

I could only mutter a feeble: 'Yes, Herr General,' and crouch down beside him.

Well, we got to the front-line positions okay. The poor bastards had been there for days, up to their knees in mud, unshaved, nothing to eat, and no relief for days. Completely emaciated, so to speak. But then a whisper passed through the trench: 'The General's coming. The General's coming,' and they all tried to pull themselves together. The General – all very palsy-walsy – slapped a soldier on the back and said: 'Well, my boy, how's it going? How do things look? What's Ivan up to?' And then he looked through somebody's gun-sights and said: 'Aha! There are the Russkies. How about shooting one across their bows? Permission to fire!' etc. And I trotted along behind the General with my market basket. But just to give you an idea of our men's attitude: although the General kept asking them to help themselves to a bottle of cologne or a safety razor or some foot powder or a pocket knife, practically all of them said: 'I don't need it, Herr General. Thank you, Herr General, I've got all I need,' and so on. So I just handed out a few pieces of chocolate on my own hook. On the way back, the General's driver, a good friend of mine, got a crazy idea. 'Herr General,' he says. 'Would you mind if Sergeant Waldmeister issued me a razor for my own personal use when we get back?' The General damn near split a gut. He really chewed that driver out: 'Who in blazes do you think you are, you ridiculous nightshade, you blue-nose, you hoot-owl? I'm going to rip open your ass up to the tenth vertebra. You stinkers here at staff headquarters lounge around in felt slippers, and the poor boys out there don't even dare to accept a razor. If you ask me, you haven't got all your marbles. Are you completely nuts? It's high time you picked up a gun and went up front. My dear Waldmeister: don't dream of issuing this man a razor, or I'll send you up there too, understand?' Well, afterwards I got hold of my friend and gave him his razor. 'You nit-wit,' I told him. 'The next time you'd better come to me direct and not through the General. You dumb jerk, what makes you think you can bother the General in person about a razor?'

Yes, there was plenty of misery and grief, but somehow we had a lot of fun. That's a fact, I just can't seem to forget about those times.

When we sit in the bar in the evening, we tell each other about them.

Well, you see, we cook up kind of a special German stew. Anyway, I've never seen anything like it anywhere else. There's everything in it. There we sit evening after evening: a few peasants, a prosecuting attorney, a gardener, a building worker, a theatre director, a few rich businessmen – big shots in industry – and so on. We've got university professors too, a crazy mathematician, for instance, who's always working out some kind of figures on the beer mats. He really lives on a different planet. We have some students, too, some of them are Negroes. There's a little fat character, as black as the rear end of the famous Isabelle of Castille, you know, the one with the lily-white thighs. . . . We always call this coloured guy Lumumba. He doesn't mind. He's sure to be a cabinet minister some day when he goes home. Anyway, in our bar everything that breathes sits together.

Nobody wants to hear any more about the Nazi period.

We concentrate on the best part, we talk about the funny things that happened. If somebody brings up the bad things, we all clam up, we even stop drinking our schnapps.

KONRAD WERTH

40, married, director of a pharmaceutical research laboratory

My father took his life in 1938, on Kristallnacht.

When my parents met each other in Bremen, the inflation was at its worst. Somebody gave my mother half a dozen eggs for a wedding present and somebody else gave her a blanket. That was the kind of presents people gave at the time. Before the inflation my father had a trucking business and a warehouse in Bremerhaven. He lost almost everything in the inflation. Then he became a house agent and managed my grandfather's estate which consisted of a number of apartment houses. It might be worth mentioning that my father had a leg amputated as a result of an accident. When he was eighteen he jumped on a moving streetcar, slipped and was run over. He was never able to dance with my mother or to swim or to engage in any sport. The loss of his leg was his one big handicap, the other was that he was a Jew. In 1938, on Kristallnacht, he took his life to save his Aryan wife and his half-Jewish children. In his younger days he had never really felt himself to be a Jew. He felt himself to be a good German. Of course he soon recognized that Hitler was a dangerous man, but for a long time he didn't think it would be so bad. You see, he was one of those decent Germans who were incapable of imagining that such terrible things could happen. When he couldn't help seeing how bad it was in Germany, he wanted to emigrate with us, but the idea of starting a new life as a cripple frightened him. He wanted to go to America. You've got to understand the way he felt about America in those days. Before the Second World War the average German didn't know much about America. They'd been to Switzerland, they knew England, they'd taken a trip or two to Paris, but nobody went to America. People had rather strange ideas about America. All in all, the idea of emigrating to America was very hard for my father to take. He said:

If only I weren't a cripple, I could start in washing dishes, or some other physical labour. ... He just didn't think that as a cripple he could succeed in making a new life for his family in a foreign country. So on 8 November 1938, he took some veronal and never woke up. In his farewell letter he wrote: 'I want to try at least to save you. The business will be Aryanized after my death. You will keep the property and you will be able to go on living without the danger that I represent for you.'

He sacrificed himself for his family. If he'd been a bachelor, he wouldn't have committed suicide but have let things take their course in the hope of pulling through one way or another. Yes, my father died because he was a Jew. But he'd never been in a synagogue in all his life, he'd been baptized in 1926 and went to Catholic church with us. My mother was a Catholic. My father was what is known in Bremen as a reformed Jew. He didn't become a very strict Catholic, but he was surely a very pious Christian. He prayed with us children at table and at bedtime. My mother told me that she had once come into the bedroom and my father was lying there on the bed with his hands folded and his eyes closed. 'What's the matter?' she asked him. 'Is anything wrong?' 'No,' he said. 'I'm praying.'

For a long time as a child I didn't know I was a half-Jew.

I didn't find out until I went to school. When they raised the flag outside, they said: 'Werth, Eppstein and Reich will remain in the classroom.' At first that bothered us a little, but then we took it very calmly. I felt no different from the other boys. In spite of being singled out that way I didn't feel excluded. The other children didn't make fun of us. Children are very fair-minded about some things though they can also be very cruel.

After my father's death I was sent to an international school for boys in Switzerland. My mother went to Bavaria with my sister. Of the 200 students in the school, 60 were Germans and 20 of these were Jews or half-Jews. At the end of 1943 or the beginning of 1944 a regulation went into effect prohibiting the issuance of currency to Jews or half-Jews, because the

Germans needed all their hard currency to buy optical instruments for anti-aircraft guns and other weapons in Switzerland, from Oerlikon and other firms. We were told we would have to leave Switzerland and return to our parents. The German consul in St Gall said to us: 'If you don't go home, your parents will be subject to reprisals.' So one day I arrived at my mother's in Bavaria. I wasn't allowed to go to school but had to do 'war-replacement' work. First I worked as a hired hand on a big farm. That was all right until 1944 when the action against half-Aryans was started. I received an order to report to the Gestapo in Munich with food for two days. It was pretty obvious that I'd be sent to a concentration camp, but at that time neither my mother nor myself knew much about the camps. Nobody had heard of the gas chambers. We knew that people were imprisoned for being Jews, but not that they were killed. The people we knew had no idea of those things.

I can only back up the people who say that they didn't know about the concentration camps at that time.

So my mother took me to Munich to the Gestapo. She said later that it was hardest trip of her life. But I can tell you frankly that for me – I was about seventeen – it was very interesting to be shipped off somewhere into the unknown. That same night we were loaded into cattle cars. They locked the doors and brought us to a salt mine near Stassfurt where we were handed over to the Organisation Todt. We were put to work setting up a factory in an abandoned salt-mine. They were trying to move the production of V-2s and planes underground. The work was hard and we didn't get enough to eat. Probably because the Ukrainian women who were cooking sold part of the food on the black market. As manual workers we received the so-called 'Hermann Göring ration', which, if they gave you all of it, consisted of an enormous Lyons sausage and bread. There were also concentration-camp inmates in the salt-mines. They wore striped uniforms and their SS guards chased them wherever they went. They had a really miserable time. For us it was awful watching them. They went to work at five in the morning. If they were late, the story was: 'They had to bury a few again.' You see, they themselves had to bury any of their number who died during the night. All the concentration-camp inmates were bloated with dropsy. They were so fiendishly cold that they put empty cement sacks under their convicts' uniforms. But if they were caught they were flogged on the spot. The SS guards always carried whips to drive the prisoners with.

In March 1945 I got boils on my lips and was given permission to go to the doctor's in the city. I took the opportunity and went home. They didn't notice my absence right away. It was just before the end of the War and everything was in a muddle. When I got home, an aunt of mine who ran a sanatorium for fliers hid me in a farmhouse. The peasants thought I was a flier from the sanatorium. Nobody reported me. But Gestapo men came to see my mother and asked about me. I don't know how she talked herself out of it. In any case, I couldn't stay in that hiding-place and my aunt pulled a fast one. She showed me how to simulate appendicitis. She showed me how to cough when my right leg was lifted and to writhe with cramps. Then, in the middle of a snow flurry she sent for an ambulance from a military hospital. That same night I was operated. Nobody there knew I was a half-Jew. I had my papers from the Organisation Todt. Next morning my aunt went to the Gestapo in Munich and said: 'What can I do, the boy's in a military hospital.' The Gestapo called the hospital and the answer was: 'Yes, yes, he's been admitted here.' That got me through the last weeks of the War.

It was only then that I found out what had really happened in the concentration camps and my only desire was to get out of Germany as quickly as possible. I wanted to go to Canada because I had an uncle who had left Germany in 1932. In December 1945 I finally had all my papers. I'll never forget how our ship, stuffed full of emigrants, left Bremerhaven on Christmas night. The city was smashed to bits. I stood up on deck in the cold and thought:

'I never want to set foot in this country again as long as I live.'

My uncle paid for my trip and got me a small job in an insurance company, so I had just enough money to pay for my studies. Before leaving Germany I had quickly taken my high-school diploma. Now I was making 100 Canadian dollars a month and paying my uncle back 10 dollars a month. During the first years I didn't have quite enough to eat because every month I also sent packages to my mother and sister in Germany. I studied chemistry and pharmacology. I enjoyed my studies, but I couldn't really get used to the Canadian way of life. I tried to turn myself into a Canadian and to do everything the young Canadians around me were doing.

I tried to be 'one of the boys'.*

But I didn't quite succeed. I simply couldn't live up to the image of the beaming, optimistic young Canadian on the brink of a magnificent career. I was never easy-going enough, I just couldn't look at things from the light side like my Canadian fellow students. I tried to strike up friendships with Canadian girls. You always had to take them out in a 'white dinner jacket'* and buy them an orchid. All that seemed ridiculous to me. My whole nature was unsuited to this kind of life. My friends were Norwegians, Dutchmen and Englishmen, they were almost all Europeans, and all of them wanted to go back to Europe. They felt the same as I did. Perhaps my past weighed on me somehow. I just couldn't be as happy-go-lucky as I thought the people around me expected me to be.

'To be a first-generation emigrant'* is terrible.

The second generation has it much easier. People of the first generation are always hybrids. They don't know exactly where they belong. There's still something European about them.
I longed more and more for Switzerland or Germany, a coun-

---

*English in original.

try where my language is spoken. I had meanwhile completed my studies and was working in a pharmaceutical research laboratory. In 1953 I revisited Europe for the first time. I was still afraid of Germany, so I first went to Italy and then to Switzerland. I heard German again for the first time, and decided to come back to Europe. I also thought I'd have better professional opportunities in Europe, because over here, especially in Germany, anyone who speaks English fluently and has a practical knowledge of the 'American-management'* method is very much in demand. I saw that I'd have better opportunities here than in Switzerland, so I returned to Germany and started my own pharmaceutical research laboratory.

I have no regrets at having returned to Germany.

I did well in business and married a wonderful woman. But for a long time I had trouble with the conventional social forms of the Germans. Take an example: when my wife – at that time we were still engaged – introduced me to her uncle who was a district court judge, I took out a packet of cigarettes as I'd learned to do in Canada and passed them round. Thereupon the uncle stood up and said rather rudely: 'Here in Germany only the host offers cigarettes, not the guest.' Besides, I was wearing a sweater and sport shirt, which wasn't exactly what was expected on a Sunday morning visit. I noticed the glistening wine-glasses on the mantelpiece. Then we were treated to a very formal sip of sherry. It was all very stiff and wooden. In Canada we'd have been calling each other by our first names after the first two minutes and slapping each other on the back. A certain superficial contact would have been established right away. In Germany it takes longer to make contacts but then they go a good deal deeper. In North America they have nice expressions like: 'Good fellow',* 'come and see me',* 'have a drink',* etc. Europeans, of course, are much more reserved.

I had fled from a Germany overrun with Nazis and now I

---

*English in original

found a democratic Germany. I have the feeling that I will
never see a dictatorship here again.

I don't believe the Jews will be persecuted again in my
lifetime.

I have the impression that the people of the Federal Republic
are making a great effort to live in accordance with democratic principles, and I don't attach much importance to the
NPD. Of course the Germans set a good deal of store by authority, but I don't believe that will lead to a rightist coup. The
other countries wouldn't allow it. I can perfectly well understand that the younger generation who had nothing to do with
the Nazi period are developing more national feeling and don't
want to wear sackcloth and ashes forever for sins they didn't
commit.

It seems to me the younger generation should say: 'Yes,
we're Germans but what our fathers did has nothing to do
with us.

'We condemn all that, but that doesn't mean we should hang
our heads for the rest of our lives.'
   In spite of everything that happened in the Nazi period, I
don't think the Germans are basically unfair. The Nazi period
was an exceptional phenomenon. The qualities it brought out
were not typically German. I believe that such an appeal to the
bad side of man could bear similar fruit in other countries. It
all depends on the circumstances. In Russia, under Stalin, horrible things happened too. But today different men have come
to power in Russia and conditions have changed. I believe that
some time in the future the Soviet Union will change its foreign
policy, towards Germany too.

I believe that the Soviets are beginning to realize that the
division of Germany is a constant source of danger and
unrest, even for themselves.

Because a conflict with China is probably inevitable, the Soviet Union will need peace and security in the West. Along with America it will try to bring about a world-wide détente. This may give Germany a chance. Of course Germany will have to pay a very high price for reunification: recognition of the Oder-Neisse line and the payment of reparations to Poland and Russia.

And while I'm talking about the Soviet Union, let me say this: Out of traditional feudalism industrialization brought forth a new social class, I mean the industrial proletariat of the late nineteenth century, which really was exploited. It was necessary to put an end to the slavery of the working class. In this point Marx and Engels were perfectly right. Communism did the job very radically and a good deal of blood was shed. In spite of everything, Communism led to a considerably wider distribution of property. That has had its effects on the Western world too. The exploitation of women, child labour, the four-teen-hour day, etc., have been abolished in the West thanks to the pressure of the industrial proletariat under Socialist influence.

Many of the social achievements of Communism are worthwhile, though their methods are unacceptable.

You know, the practice of Communism nowadays isn't nearly so radical as the old propaganda, and in the next fifty years a lot more of the edges will wear off. The Communist world and the so-called capitalist world are becoming more and more alike. What does capitalism mean in America today? The worker drives exactly the same car as his boss, he has his home and his children go to the same school as the boss's. Private schools have almost all been abolished. Of course there are still certain class differences, in Germany too. Of course certain sections of the populations have blocks about associating with each other. But I was in North America too long. As I see it, class differences have been largely done away with in Germany as well.

I'm not interested in knowing whether the father of a member of my staff was a street cleaner or a professor.

And I don't ask whether someone is a Catholic or a Protestant. I judge people by their minds and characters. To me those are the only things that count and I know other employers who feel the same way. Our social life is not confined to any particular section of society. We choose the friends we like. We don't care one bit where they come from or whether they have money or not. All in all, we feel very happy here. This medium-sized city strikes us as a very attractive place to live in. We're not at the end of the world but we haven't the disadvantages of a big city. We're not suffocating in a treeless sea of buildings. From our house we can reach any of the main points in town on foot. And because it's a small town we meet friends and acquaintances wherever we go, shopping on Saturday morning, or in the theatre, or at concerts. At a concert there are always at least ten people we know, we wave at them and sometimes we go out for a glass of wine afterwards. We're great music lovers and have a fine record collection. Every evening we listen to a piece or two. Preferably Bach. In addition, my wife plays the harpsichord and violin. My children play the flute. We read a great deal. We subscribe to three daily papers and a weekly. We often make each other presents of books. I'm interested in historical literature, especially everything dealing with the last World War. For instance *Russia at War*. At that time I was not a thinking man yet. If you don't mind my using a slogan:

I want to digest our undigested past.

I want to know more about that period. For instance, I read everything I can lay hands on about the persecution of the Jews, I read books about the problems of emigration and books by Jewish authors, such as *The Victim* by Leon Uris, and everything Theodor Herzl wrote. The problem of the Jews in the world still fascinates me. I can't escape from my own fate or my own skin.

From a purely religious point of view I'm a Catholic Christian, but in the last few years I've gone to church very little. My wife is a Protestant.

I don't want my children to live with this religious conflict.

It's certain that at the beginning of our marriage I put too much stress on my Catholicism and offended my wife in a way. That gave rise to conflicts. That's why I go to church much less than I used to. I don't believe I'm the least bit less religious or less Catholic today, but it really isn't nice to leave my wife to eat breakfast alone while I go to church with the children, who are born Catholics. My wife thinks that Catholicism is outmoded and that the Catholic Church has caused a great deal of bloodshed. Why, she says, should a man-made dogma be followed so literally? But she's intelligent and she doesn't want to hurt my feelings. Of course, she prays with the children and sends them to religious instruction. Of course she teaches them the Old Testament, although Catholics don't care much for that. I'm tolerant enough to say: 'I want my children to become familiar with the Catholic religion so they can decide for themselves later on. All my life I've been kind of in the middle. As a child I was half-Jewish and half-Catholic. I don't want my children to live with such a conflict.'

HANS RANKE, CLARA RANKE
26 and 23, working-class couple

We're a real old working-class family.

Hans Ranke: Nowadays apprentice jobs are a dime a dozen; there weren't so many of them when we got out of school. My oldest brother was a machinist, he worked in an electrical equipment plant here in town. I often looked into his workshop. Those things interested me. Then I put in an application at the employment office and after a certain amount of waiting

I finally obtained a position as apprentice in the same factory as my brother. I learned to be a machinist. The apprentice-ship was three years. Then I took the journeyman's examina-tion and stayed on in the same place, now I've been there for ten years. Most of my work now is installing drills. I net about 630 to 640 marks. We get 4.58 marks an hour and we work forty hours a week. We're a real old working-class family, we're all from round here. My father is a mechanic, my grandfather was a locksmith, my younger brother is a baker.

Clara Ranke: My father is a plumber. But he doesn't come from round here. He's from the Saar, but my mother comes from here.

It was always my dream to become a hairdresser.

My parents were always against it, but in the end they said: 'All right, do what you want.' So I got through my apprentice-ship all right and I was very happy in my work. Then I met my husband. It was in Carnival time that we really began to click. We'd known each other since our schooldays. We went to the same school, only we were three classes apart, but our parents lived right next door to each other so we played together as kids. When we were married, at first I went on working full time, then half time, then only Fridays and Saturdays, and then only Saturdays, and now I've stopped. It was on account of the child. He got bigger and bigger and livelier and livelier, and my grandma who lived with us kept getting older and shakier. It got to be impossible. To tell the truth, it made me miss a good opportunity. They were going to put me in charge of a branch.

It might have been better if we hadn't had a child.

But now we've got him we're glad. And the grandparents are especially glad.

Hans Ranke: My grandparents were some of the first people to move to Teufelsgrund. That was right after they put up this workers' housing development because of the new factories

around here. My grandparents lived in Meisenweg and my
parents in the Market Place. At first the rents were very low out
here. It was really cheap then, twenty-three marks a month,
and now it comes to over eighty. But the apartments have
three rooms. Downstairs one room, kitchen and bath, and upstairs two rooms. It was a lucky thing for us that nothing was
bombed out here during the War. The factories, yes, and a lot
of other working-class neighbourhoods, but not Teufelsgrund.
Otherwise, things were pretty bad all over during the War and
in general under Hitler. I started school in 1946 and got through
in 1954. In all that time not a word was said about the Nazi
period and Hitler. Maybe they talk about it now. I don't know
exactly what they teach nowadays.

Our history course went from Old Fritz to the First World
War, that was all.

Clara Ranke: Yes, I can still remember those times. I was only
five years old but I know about certain things. I remember
the nights of the air-raids very clearly. Every night we had to
leave the house and everything was on fire. You don't forget
those things.

Hans Ranke: I'm three years older, but I don't remember
the War at all. Except that my brother was in the Hitler Youth
and they had to collect shell fragments and bones for soft soap.
I tagged along when I was a kid of five, I remember that much.
What my parents thought about Hitler I really don't know. We
didn't talk about it. I only know that my father went to War
in 1942 and when he came back I didn't know him. He'd been
a prisoner and he came home in 1948. But I do know one thing
– yes, I remember now: my father wasn't crazy about the Third
Reich. He was against it from the start. Yes, now certain conversations come back to me. You see, it's like this: we're a
working-class family and we've always been in the SPD. My
grandfather was already a member, my father too, there was
never anything else in our family. Maybe that's why my father
wasn't for the Nazis. My grandfather, it's true, had trouble after

the War. He joined the Party as a pure formality to keep out of trouble. I only know that after the War he had to do some kind of forced labour, cutting down trees, for instance. And he kept having to report to the Denazification Officer and then they wanted to put him out of his apartment and send him to the slums where they relocate asocial individuals. Yes, he had difficulties because he'd been in the Party.

But he always spoke up and said he'd been in and for what reason.

The others always said they hadn't been in, when they'd been right in the thick of it. But he always admitted it. He always said: 'Yes, I was in the Party, I admit it and that's that!' It wasn't right what the others did. It's not right to deny everything all of a sudden and pretend not to know anything about it. My father was only in the Choral Society. He's been a member for forty years. For thirty years he sang and then for a long time he was manager of the football club. But now he takes things a little easier. He's sixty-three and his health doesn't allow him to keep up with his activities. He has a few friends in town, but no great friendships. The friends they've got are almost all in Teufelsgrund. All working-class families. Actually, there are a few employers, for instance, the owners of the big food store on the corner. That's right, they really are employers, they have several people working for them. We know practically everybody in Old Teufelsgrund, but up there where all the new houses are, it's all full of refugees and we don't come into contact with them very much.

I personally associate almost exclusively with football players and bowlers.

Yes, I play football and I bowl, and besides I have a few old friends among my fellow-workers. Two years ago we went to Spain together. We took the train, it was an organized tour. I've often been abroad. With the football club we went to Belgium, Switzerland, Austria and Spain two or three times. I

liked it fine. The way they live is entirely different, especially
the Spaniards. In some ways better and in some ways worse.
In Spain, for instance, I found out there there's no middle class
at all. Only rich or poor. The businessmen are certainly well
off and now the tourist trade has made things better for a lot
of the poorer people too, even maybe for some of those who
had nothing before. You see unbelievable contrasts. On one side
big villas with fine grounds, gardens with fountains, and all
that, and on the other side you see gypsies begging. They beg
on the beach. That was what really bothered us. About every
fifty feet a little boy or an old woman would come up to us
and beg. You don't see that in Germany. It was very disagree-
able. They just wouldn't go away, they're funny people, really
insolent, they mumble something in their beards and keep
holding out their hands.

But otherwise I liked the people in Spain.

In fact I liked them a good deal. Especially their temperament.
They're such nice friendly people. Maybe it's only the tourist
trade that makes them so friendly, but I don't think so; I believe that they're really nice, they act the way they feel, they're
genuine. Our experience in Belgium was very good too. We
were treated like kings. A national team couldn't have been
treated any better. It was really tops. We never had the feeling that people were looking down their noses at us because
we were Germans. Only in Austria one time we ate in a
restaurant, and there was a man – he must have been drinking
– who spoke to us from off to one side and said we must be
Nazis and he was in favour. He must have been some bigshot
in those days. We didn't want to have anything to do with him.
We stood up and left and visited a church near by.

I was confirmed and that was the end of it.

Then came my job, and I studied on Sunday morning. My father
and mother never told me I had to go to church. You know how
it is, when you're fourteen or fifteen years old and just out of

school. You play football at ten o'clock Sunday morning, which is just when church is.

Clara Ranke: It was different with me. I had to go to church every Sunday, my father is pretty religious, the Catholics from the Saar are kind of special that way. They made me go to church every Sunday, and I actually went. It wasn't until later that I spoke up and said: 'Somehow it's not for me, I don't really get it.' And my father said: 'Oh well, you can be a good Christian even if you don't go to church.' He was right. I'm definitely a good Christian all the same.

Hans Ranke: Religion doesn't mean much to me, so I didn't mind being married in a Catholic church. It was mostly because of the child. My mother-in-law put her foot down. 'It's going to be a Catholic wedding!' she said. 'Anything else is out of the question!' Well, it was all right with me.

Clara Ranke: It was all the same to me, too. I wouldn't have minded a Protestant wedding, it was only to please my parents, why not? My husband didn't mind, so that's what we did.

Hans Ranke: You don't want any trouble. It spoils the whole atmosphere. My fellow-workers feel the same way.

It's best to steer clear of serious problems and think about hobbies.

Most of them drive cars or motorcycles, that's their hobby. They don't complain much. Why should they complain? They might as well be happy. They can't change anything anyway. Why should a machinist or a worker want to make more money? What for? Of course, if he's in the union, they stick up for him, but what can they accomplish? If wages go up a little, prices go up too. It's always the same.

Clara Ranke: And if somebody has a car nowadays, his apartment certainly looks worse than somebody's who hasn't got a car. The ones that have cars naturally drive them on vacation. That looks good on the surface but when you take a peek behind the scenes it doesn't amount to much. They all live too high.

Hans Ranke: That's something I refuse to do. We like an orderly life. We don't buy on credit either. We haven't got much luxury but all the same we have a very nice life and no debts. The others are always buying things on credit. Otherwise they couldn't drive cars and buy so many clothes. It's got to come from somewhere. One buys a TV set and pays fifty marks every month. What sense is there in that? At the same time he's got his payments on a car, and he has other needs besides. He's got to put something on his back.

He never gets through paying. I don't go for that.

I don't buy until I've got the money in hand. That way you're much better off if something goes wrong. Those other fellows suddenly find themselves cleaned out. If I had a pile of money, I'd drive a car too, but I don't need one. It's only a few hundred yards to my work. I leave the house at half past six and I start work at seven. I knock off at a quarter to four in the afternoon, and I'm home by four. Then I take a look at the paper, the sports page, and look after the kid. And then I have other things to do. I have a friend next door, we're building a bar in his cellar. There are five of us and we work every evening because we want to be done soon. Tuesday I have football practice, Thursday evening I go bowling. Sunday I play football and do some bowling afterwards, and on Monday I read the newspaper again. But so far I haven't taken much interest in politics. Oh yes, when there's a Bundestag debate on TV, I take a look. I know what I need to know but on the whole I don't care about politics. My hobby happens to be sports and not politics. On TV I mostly look at sports. What else do we look at? Oh yes, 'Report', 'Panorama', Professor Grzimek's animal programme, and naturally a few crime thrillers. No, we don't spend all our free time looking at TV. Sometimes on Sundays we go out together. Down below there's a bar run by an Italian. We go there with friends. When we come in everybody knows us. It's real nice.

T–C

Clara Ranke: When my husband goes out bowling in the evening or working on the bar, I read books.

Actually I read everything, for instance Anne Golon's *Angélique* books. They're about a woman in the days of Louis XIV who comes to the court in Paris, and all the intrigues that go on there, and all her experiences, really wild. Then I've read *The Tin Drum* by Günter Grass, but if you want me to be perfectly frank, that's the worst nonsense I've ever read. That book is really nuts. I don't see how anybody can say it's interesting. In my opinion it's pure junk, really stupid. Such things just don't exist. It's simply not normal. I just can't imagine such a thing. I can't understand it. I have a lot of friends who say: 'Oh yes, I see the deeper meaning.' But I can't see a thing. To me that book is absolutely worthless. But I like Louis Bromfield's books.

   Hans Ranke: Now we've taken out *Dr Zhivago* by that Russian, Pasternak, the one the Soviets didn't want to give the Nobel Prize to. We saw the movie and we liked it. It was about the October Revolution. It's very interesting. You see we're in the Book Guild, so we ordered the book.

We have to read a book every three months.

It's not so expensive. This is how it is: if I don't order any particular book, they send me a book automatically. They count five marks. If I take a book that costs fifteen marks, the five marks are deducted. We get a prospectus with descriptions of the books. We look it over and take our pick.

   Clara Ranke: Mostly I go by the authors. The ones we've heard of or read. Hemingway, for instance, he impresses me. The things he wrote have always appealed to me. He had something, he was somehow human. *Death in the Afternoon*, for instance, that's marvellous. Oh yes, we've also read ... that's it, Daphne du Maurier's *Rebecca* and *Desirée* and *From Here to Eternity* by James Jones and *Via Mala* by John Knittel. Then Joan Becker's *The Grapes of Tudonne*. I don't know how to pronounce it, it's about South Africa. Yes, and then there was Bromfield's *Bitter Lotus*, Graham Greene's *The Power and the Glory* and *The Story of San Michele* by Axel Munthe, that doctor – and a very interesting book, but really gruesome was *The SS State* by Eugen Kogon whom we've often seen on TV. He's a very interesting man. I think he was on that panel recently that discussed the NPD.

When I think about the NPD it makes me afraid that such a thing might happen again.

I mean like with the Nazis. It's true that I didn't live through it, but the pictures we see and the things we read make me terribly afraid. What frightens me most is what happened to the Jews. I just can't see how people can do such things. As it turned out later on, it didn't achieve anything.

    Hans Ranke: It was rotten. Hitler shouldn't have done that. It was a good thing he put people back to work, but he shouldn't have persecuted the Jews that way. Yes, the Americans dropped those atom bombs. They've done a lot of things too. I mean those bombs on Nagasaki and Hiroshima, but that was war. They had to drop bombs, but the way they tortured the Jews, that was inhuman. And it's hard to understand that it never came out. Most of the people who were in favour of Hitler didn't know about the concentration camps. You didn't hear anything about them. It was only after the War was over that people heard about Dachau and those things.

Among my friends we don't talk about it much. We almost always talk about sports, movies, what's been showing on TV, and so on.

We have debates about it. We have some pretty lively get-togethers. Sometimes we do dumb things. We sing and so on but we don't talk about politics much. You understand: one is in the CDU, another in the SPD, and if we talk about it there's an argument and that's what we try to avoid. We don't want fights. Those discussions usually degenerate and that's why we don't talk about it. Only when the mayor was up for election, we had a discussion. ... Here's how it is with me: on principle I vote for the SPD, regardless of who's running. I have nothing against the CDU people, but with us workers it's mostly SPD all the way down the line.

Clara Ranke: I vote the same as my husband but as a general rule I don't think much of women voting. A lot of them don't understand a thing.

If it were up to me I wouldn't vote.

If it were all right with my husband, I'd sooner stay home. But he wants me to go out and vote, so all right, I do what he says. He explains things to me because I don't know much about it. I don't think we can change much that way. Reunification, for instance, would be a very good thing, but I don't think it will ever happen. They've been talking about it for years, but those people over there don't want it, anyway not the leaders. Ours do. That's my impression.

Hans Ranke: One of our football players was over there a little while ago. He was in Bautzen. He says their standard of living doesn't amount to much. They can't buy anything decent. Every two weeks they put up a sign saying that there's fish to be had. Then everybody eats fish and after that there's no fish for a long time. And it's only once in a blue moon that you can get a piece of cheese or a lemon. They simply can't buy anything decent. They're all crazy to have one of those light nylon raincoats, because you can't get them. Our football player left his brother his coat. He was as proud as a peacock and other people looked at him kind of enviously. It would be very good if we had reunification and they were as well off as we are.

Altogether, that's the kind of Europe we should have, no boundaries, one currency and one government.

Like the United States of America. Maybe with a common

language, so in time everybody would speak English or German. We just ought to get together. We have a lot of foreigners at the plant, they're all nice, decent fellows. It seems to me they're the same as we are. In general people make too much difference between themselves and other people, they ought to be more tolerant. For instance, what people say about the young fellows who are growing up now, the hippies, the Beatles, and so on. If you ask me, they're no worse than we are. It's just a question of fashion. And morally they're no worse than anybody else. Maybe they grow up a little younger. That's the times. But most of the young people are perfectly decent, they all go to work, they have a job or they go to school. When you hear one of those beat bands playing and they all hop around, it's not bad. One man lets his hair grow long, the next cuts it short. What does it matter? What is there to get excited about? But the old people make a terrible fuss about it and exaggerate something terrible. I think it's each man's private business. They should let everyone do what he wants.

GÜNTHER PECHOW

42, married, manager of an electrical equipment factory

My father wasn't a worker or peasant.

I wanted to study medicine and become a psychiatrist. But later I gave up the idea. My mother was a trained nurse with a state certificate that she was very proud of. At our home in the East zone we entertained a good many nurses and a number of doctors. After the War I wanted to study medicine at Humboldt University in East Berlin. But they wouldn't admit me because my father wasn't a worker or peasant. So I gave up the idea and studied languages. Then I became a commercial apprentice just in order to learn a trade, but I wasn't very enthusiastic about it. In 1946 they were still very revolutionary. Only the sons of workers and peasants were admitted to the university,

or the sons of Party functionaries, but my father was neither.
He had developed a violent antipathy for the Nazis.

He didn't see much difference between the Nazis and the
Communists.

It was a terrible thing for him because he'd been in the opposition ever since 1933 and had been waiting the whole time for
the Nazi régime to come to an end. And now he couldn't help
seeing that conditions hadn't changed appreciably under the
Communists. My mother was different. She had no idea about
politics and in general no ambitions or interests. Actually, the
only impression she made on me was that she had an exaggerated sense of duty. She never did anything because she had
thought it over. It was always because of the feeling: 'Now I
must do this or that because it's my duty.' These duties were
limited to the family, the household and the business of daily
life. My mother wasn't very intelligent. She was a very average
sort of woman who had been brought up strictly, in a *petit-
bourgeois* environment. Her father had been an agricultural
worker. Come to think of it, I was influenced much more by
my father. He had a strong sense of duty too, he was a clerk in
a tax office, but he was an extremely intelligent man who
hadn't had much education and was probably rather unhappy
about not having gone to high-school or the university because his parents couldn't afford it. And now he was always
dealing with people who had studied at the university or anyway had a better education or background than he did. Little
by little my father filled in the gaps in his education, but he
never made up for a certain lack of background – anyway, that
was my impression. At that time my parents lived in a little
village outside of East Berlin. In 1953 my father couldn't stand
it any longer. His nerves were really shot.

So one day he took the E1 and went to West Berlin with
nothing but a briefcase.

My mother followed him a little while later. But in West Berlin my father wasn't granted refugee status because he couldn't prove that he had been in danger at home and would have been imprisoned. They didn't recognize his civil-service status either. In the Soviet-occupied zone at that time there were no civil-service ratings. Civil servants were all lumped together as government employees. So my father studied bookkeeping and worked as a fiscal adviser. But after a few years of transition and adaptation he became much more open-minded and I might almost say well-balanced. But then unfortunately he died. At the age of sixty-eight – it was a great loss for me.

I never had the Christian faith.

My father wasn't a very religious man, but I think he may have believed in God. We never talked about it. And my father never discussed religious questions with my mother. Perhaps because she herself was very religious and took it as a personal offence if anyone showed signs of doubt in religious matters. I myself didn't belong to any Christian denomination, or to any other for that matter. I never had the Christian faith. I had to take religious instruction, but even at that time it didn't convince me. All my life I've searched and struggled, and today – I believe – I'm a convinced atheist. A resigned searcher, if you like. But fundamentally it's the same thing. From a Christian point of view in any case, I can only call myself an atheist. I can't make myself believe in a conscious guiding power that has somehow made the world. Of course I see a certain physical order, but I believe, in fact I'm convinced, that human reason is incapable of grasping the concept of infinity. That, I believe, is why men invented their gods. In general I think that if men believe in God, the Prophet, and so on, it's only because they're afraid to recognize their own imperfection. Probably most men have to believe in God simply because they need something to hold on to.

Mrs Pechow: I've left the Church. It was probably under my husband's influence. On the whole, I'm the passive type and I probably wouldn't have done anything by myself.

Günther Pechow: No, you're mistaken. I never consciously influenced you to leave the Church. I never said anything of the sort. No, I'm sure I never did. On the contrary, it wouldn't bother me in the least if you were religious. I'd be more inclined to say that I'd like it. If you were religious, it wouldn't disturb our relations in the least.

I must tell you that we are expecting a baby. In my opinion he should grow up and form his opinion later. It's wrong to force those things on a child. He can always get himself baptized when he's big enough to make up his own mind. Being without religious convictions myself, I would regard it as hypocrisy to have my child baptized. To tell the truth I'd like to send him to religious instruction but you don't have to be baptized for that. It's allowed. We've inquired.

Mrs Pechow: My brother-in-law is a theologian. He told me that nowadays there's a certain percentage of children who aren't baptized and there are even a good many ministers who don't have their children baptized because they say their children should decide for themselves later on what they want. To have a child baptized I'd have to join a church again myself. That would seem like a funny thing to do, it would look as if I regarded the church as some kind of public utility.

Günther Pechow: There's still another question:

'How should we have the child baptized, as a Protestant or a Catholic or a Jew?'

Probably a Jew would be best, because if you're convinced that religion never accomplished anything significant as an instrument of ethical education, that the most it can do is give you a kind of anchor in life, the Jewish religion is better suited than any other to give a person self-confidence and support. So if you ask me what religion a child should be brought up in, I would certainly not exclude the Jewish religion. The idea of the Jewish master race, of the chosen people, may not be very pleasing to those of us who have grown up in the Christian tradition, but it seems to me that an individual who has this conviction has a very special kind of moral strength. I used to talk with young people who had been brought up under the Third Reich and were not at all convinced that what had happened then was wrong. They still expressed radically anti-Semitic opinions. Sometimes, in such discussions I'd stand up after a while and say: 'Well, gentlemen, I regret to say that this conversation is rather displeasing to me because I'm a half-Jew.' Of course I'm nothing of the sort, but the effect was crushing. In the last ten years, I must admit, I haven't come across any anti-Semitic remarks.

One day my employers insisted on my enrolling at the university.

First I was an apprentice in a big factory that makes electrical appliances. They did everything to encourage me. After only half a year's apprenticeship my knowledge of languages made them decide I was some kind of universal genius, and they asked me to help build up the export division. This was fine for me and I was delighted. It gave me a chance to improve my languages. I was able to travel a good deal abroad, but of course I had no time for studying. But one day my employers insisted on my enrolling at the university. I went on leave and attended the free university and took a degree in business administration. After that I stayed on in Berlin for a while and directed the sales end of the export division. Then the firm was reorganized and a whole group of us were transferred to southern Germany. I stayed there for three years and then I was offered a position as manager in a newly established firm in this city. It was an electrical engineering set-up. It was a marvellous opportunity for me. You know I've always been a big-mouth. As a general rule 'big-mouth' isn't a very flattering term here in Germany. But when I say big-mouth I mean that I've always had my own ideas and stated them and usually put them through. I had the good fortune to fall in with employers who recognized the fact.

Mrs Pechow: They were looking for the kind of man who gets what he wants.

Günther Pechow: Though I didn't know a thing about this firm's line of production! But in my old firm where I had been in charge of exports I had found out that as a salesman in a business run by engineers you can only survive and get ahead if you acquire at least enough technical knowledge to ask stupid questions intelligently or answer stupid questions intelligently. After a certain length of time I mastered this art as well as a certain basic knowledge, so I soon came to be respected.

One can no longer speak of a real indigenous population.

I've been here for six years now and I've become used to the life. The people here don't shut themselves off against outsiders, because strictly speaking there hasn't been any indigenous population since the end of the War. It's like many, in fact nearly all German cities. In our firm we have an incredible mixture of German strains. The personnel get along very well together. But it gives me a chance to cultivate my old interest in psychology. All sorts of human problems come up. In a human community of several hundred people, there's a good deal of friction between individuals and characters. If you're in a leading position and you want peace and order in the organization and fruitful collaboration among the workers, foremen, section chiefs, office personnel, etc., it's very important for the success of the whole organization that the boss should be something of a psychotherapist or a psychologist.

I call it psychological massage.

Almost every day I have to deal with people who don't get along together or who have developed a grudge against somebody and are suffering from depressions or fits of violence. The only thing to do is to pacify them or reconcile them by means of a three-cornered conversation. I know just about everything that goes on in our place. When I walk through the plant, I speak to twenty people in ten minutes. If you meet somebody in the corridor and you know what he does, you ask: 'How is it going? How did you ever manage to do that? How do you get along with so-and-so?' You make these remarks in passing and you notice very quickly if something is wrong. If I find out that there's some kind of friction, I step in. Then I say: 'Come to my office at six this evening for a glass of beer. Then you can unburden yourself.' That does wonders. I can almost always settle these things, you know, things like somebody saying: 'The section chief doesn't appreciate me' or some foreman who gets along fine with forty girls and then one of them sasses and insults him, or another man who has the feeling that somebody's taking his work away from him, or the story is spread around that one of the girls is sleeping with somebody or that some man has been seen with one of his female subordinates, and that won't do. A plant like this is like a little village.

You musn't forget that these people spend eight of their sixteen waking hours in the plant.

In those eight hours they not only have to work, they have to get along with other people. I'm convinced you'd find the same problems everywhere. But I believe that a business is more affected by them in Germany than in any other country. In America in case of a dispute, they would just probably pick the better man and throw the other one out. They move fast over there. They wouldn't try to turn the fighting cocks into peaceable fellow-workers with psychological massage. It's not their way.

As far as I'm concerned, a true friend is somebody who's prepared to make real financial or other sacrifices for me.

We have perhaps a dozen of those. Well, when I think it over carefully, when I tot up all the possibilities in my businessman's mind, when I really look at the matter critically, then I can only think of three real friends.

Mrs Pechow: Well I'd say there were six, you've got to count the wives too.

I've never been satisfied in all my life.

It doesn't go with my philosophy of life. If you have a critical mind and you're not satisfied with the traditional answers, a time comes when you look at things with a certain resignation and you stop asking so many questions, for instance, the question of war or peace. I don't regard war as impossible or as inevitable either, perhaps it can be avoided for a certain time. Man just happens to have a strong need for self-assertion and if individuals are given practically free rein for expressing this need for self-assertion, they will probably – if they happen to be in leading positions – end up making some kind of a war. Aside from the purely political aspect, that seems to me to be a basic principle.

As long as we have states that give individuals the possibility of power, there will be war.

It is not yet possible to conceive of reason ruling the world. It's out of the question. I don't regard the situation at the moment as very critical but we are living in a time of world-wide reorientation and reorganization, for instance, the differences of opinion between Russia and China. The Western alliance has largely collapsed. The Western countries no longer see the need of sticking together. As for the European integration in which I had some hope, de Gaulle with his tradition-bound, senile stubbornness has punctured it, and the political immaturity of the Americans who go lumbering through world history like elephants prevents any further consolidation of the West. I do not believe that the responsible American political leaders are even aware of it, but they simply seem to have lost interest in a strong united Western Europe – perhaps even united into one nation – such as the Americans themselves quite admirably demanded right after the War. If we had brought about a merger of the Western European countries, we would have created a genuine third bloc, economically as well as politically and militarily. You see, two big countries with a lot of little ones in between are certainly a danger for the world. But three big countries, each with interests of its own, would be more of a safeguard against war. What Europe lacks is some external pressure that might impel the European countries to a genuine sacrifice of their national interests.

I don't regard reunification as a serious possibility.

To tell the truth, I don't believe I'll live to see it. The great powers aren't really interested in the German desire for unification. They talk about it a good deal, but in reality they're not interested. The Americans certainly have no reason to risk anything for it and neither have the Russians. And there's no bargaining counterpart. The division of Germany is a fact that was created by Hitler's insane policy, and we will probably have to put up with it for a long time to come. I'm not very strong on history, but I tend to believe that such situations are possible in every country and every people. It all depends on the methods and the mood of the people and the momentary situation and the kind of propaganda that's used. In my opinion that kind of régime can be set up in any country. Look at the American election propaganda, for instance, the refined publicity methods they use.

I see no reason why they wouldn't be able to organize a dictatorship in America if they really wanted to.

I don't believe there has ever in human history been a democracy in the truest sense of the word, and I don't believe it's possible. In America publicity is an essential ingredient of democracy, the same kind of publicity that's used to sell toothpaste. Mass propaganda techniques are used to persuade the people to elect a certain candidate. And yet the Americans have a long democratic tradition. With us it's much more difficult, because we in Germany have practically nothing but a tradition of dictatorship and it will probably be generations before a true democratic consciousness develops among our population. Our young people have too much distraction. Their parents don't tighten the reins enough. People go from one extreme to the other. Yesterday, the frantic nationalism of the Third Reich; today, a really exaggerated national laxity in every respect. And our economic miracle has naturally helped to distract our young people from thinking. We are in a period of superficial intellectual interests. Beat music and cars and material interests are in the foreground. I might put it this way: they have freedom, but no one tells them what to do with it.

ELFRIEDA SCHULTZE

51, unmarried, flower-seller

I was fourteen, and I ran away with a circus.

I went to grade school here, but I wasn't much of a student. When I got out of school, my mother had died. My father was an X-ray technician and had meanwhile remarried. So then I had a second mother. You know how it is, so I ran away from home. I've always been a black sheep. I was fourteen, and I ran away with a circus. They took me along with them and I didn't show up at home again until I was nineteen. Oh, I rode ponies and then I was an usher when I couldn't find anything better to do. I had a regular boy friend, he was a ventriloquist. I was his assistant, I carried his puppet. You know, it talked, but it was really him that talked, down in his belly. Oh, I saw a good deal in those days. We were together about five or six years. Except for Russia, I saw pretty near every country. I had to get out, I had to shove off on account of my second mother. I couldn't get along with her. She always beat me and I said: 'You're not my mother,' and then she whacked me some more. So I packed my things and left. Later on I broke up with the ventriloquist and met a Frenchman, a guitarist. He played Hawaiian music, but I only went with him for a year and then I was offered a number: 'rag painting'. This is what it was: there were great big frames made out of flannel, the rags stick to the flannel, and every night I made four pictures out of rags. It was a big success. Yes, I've seen a lot, sometimes I had the blues, sometimes I didn't, you know the way it goes, but I made good money. I wasn't exactly a star but I was satisfied. I made 25 to 35 marks a night and then – the War was almost over – I went back home. I was fed up with the circus. I had it up to here. At first they didn't know me at home, I'd got so old. But only from the hard life. And then I stayed home for about a year with my stepmother, in the living room. I had to pay 100 marks. And then I worked a while for the French and for the Americans too.

It was a kind of 'strength through joy'. They called it something else but actually it was the same kind of army show as under Hitler.

It was like this: it was a performance for foreign soldiers. We danced and did a few tricks but we didn't get money, only food – whole sacks full – and cigarettes and that kind of thing, and then we traded the stuff for money. I was alone for about a year without a man, and then one night I went out. I had to find a new job. I was sitting in a bar and an old flower-woman came in with violets and I spoke with her: 'Tell me, what kind of papers do you need to sell flowers?' 'Oh,' she said, 'we need a pedlar's licence, that's all.' But she didn't see what I was getting at, so next day I went to the chamber of commerce and they gave me a licence. I bought an old potato basket and a few flowers in the market. But that night I was stopped five or six times by the police. There were three or four other flower-women, they didn't want my competition, so they turned me in. They wouldn't let me into any of the bars except 'The Golden Bear'. There was a waiter there who said: 'Listen to me. You've got to come three times, not just once. I'll help you.' Well, I thought, he wants something from me. But he didn't. So I went there two or three times and they didn't say anything, and after a while I caught on to the trick. Only I had no peace because the other flower-women were always running after me and giving me hell. 'We don't need any more flower-women!' It was a year before I was on my feet. Today it's entirely different. Today I have my steady customers. The flowers are sent me C.O.D. by a large grower.

I have no foreign flowers, only the German varieties because they're much more beautiful.

Every three days I get my shipment. It comes to about 100 marks. I start working at about eight in the evening. Sometimes I go on until twelve. But once in a while I keep on until half past two. I just go from bar to bar. I do ten or fifteen of them. When I'm really going strong, as much as twenty. That gets me 160 to 170 marks a week. I've been given as much as ten marks for a bouquet, but that's unusual. Sometimes they tip me fifty pfennigs or a mark. There are some places where the people are more generous than in the average bar. When a young fellow is sitting with a girl, he's more likely to buy flowers. There are also a few crazy people who buy flowers even when they're all alone. Actually, they're very nice. Yes, there are men who buy a bouquet even when they're alone. They say: 'I'll buy it because I want to buy one from you. I'll take it home and put it in my room.' Usually I put seven to nine in a bouquet and sell it for five marks. That's a good price. But do you know, when rich people go out with the family, they never buy flowers.

Rich people don't react.

I stand by their table like a beggar and the blood runs into my head, not from anger, but somehow from embarrassment. Usually it's only the women that are rude. Of course it all depends on what kind of a place you go into. Some places are first-class and then again there are others that aren't so good. And the women vary with the joints. Believe me, some weird things happen. One time a girl student was sitting there, and I could tell by looking at her that she wasn't exactly the nice kind of student. 'Look at the old goat!' she says. So I say: 'Haven't you any better manners than to call me an old goat? Student or no student, I've sure seen you with an awful lot of men.' So naturally she turned red in the face and said she hadn't meant it. So I said: 'I didn't mean it either, so we're quits.' But do you know, the flower business isn't what it used to be. About five or six years ago it was still good. There were times when I had to go home and refill my basket. That doesn't happen any more.

The young people sit around the bars and gab. It didn't used to be so bad that way.

The people have changed, you see. And the men aren't as attentive as they used to be. Sometimes they can't afford it or there's no need of it. They're too sure of themselves with the ladies. They say they're married though I know they're not. But there are also some who buy flowers every day for their girls until they get what they want. And once they get what they want, I never see them again. Then it's finished. I know my customers. Usually it's not the wife the flowers are bought for. I know all the girls who are on the make. Mostly they say to their escort: 'Yes, I'd like some flowers.' Just to see if he has any money. You've got to keep that type in mind. They stick to certain bars. I have two or three places where they hang out. I sell my flowers, and what they do is all the same to me. They can settle that with their confessor.

I saw too much misery in the Third Reich, over there in Leipzig and Dresden.

That's where I was at the time of the air-raids. You know, they were coming out of the shelters because the 'all-clear' had been sounded, and then the bombs fell. Things like that. I can't see where God comes in. God shouldn't have allowed it. Afterwards, they were all lying in rows with white or red tags attached to them. The white tags were for the ones who couldn't be recognized. All right, I ask you, where does God come in?

Maybe you'll have a bad opinion of me now. ... Only I think that when you get old you get to be afraid of death or something. But my father always said: 'When you're down under, it's all over. You're gone and nobody gives a damn.'

GERTRUD FERNHÄUSER

20, unmarried, student

Negroes have great difficulties when they go looking for rooms.

Right now I'm studying English and French at Interpreter School, but I'm planning to study literature. I'll probably become a teacher. My parents gave me the idea. Last summer I taught at a German school in Spain. That took away some of my prejudices against the teaching profession. My father is in the diplomatic service. He's a consul in France. Before that, he was in Africa for three years, and before that he was in Canada for thirteen years. I didn't go to Africa with him because there were no German schools. I was in a boarding-school in Canada, I spent seven years there in all. One thing I like at the University is that you meet students from every conceivable country. A great many foreigners study here, we have a good deal of contact with them: South Americans, North Americans, British, a lot of Africans, Persians and a great many Arabs. At first I thought we Germans were quite free from prejudice in our relations with those people but some of the foreigners have told me the contrary. They say there's a great deal of prejudice among the Germans, not so much the students as the townspeople. Negroes, for instance, have great difficulties when they go looking for rooms. They regularly have to pay thirty per cent more rent than a German. If a German has to pay 80 marks for a room, they ask 120 of a Negro. The professors too make a big difference between Germans and foreigners. A Negro chemistry student from Nigeria told me recently, for example, that the professors and students all smiled pityingly at first when they saw him working in the lab. They asked him if he was able to keep up and whether they could help him. Actually he had studied chemistry in Nigeria and when the German students saw that he knew just as much as they did – well, then they got really sore. What made them angry was that a foreigner should be able to do just as well if not better than they. Since then they've avoided him and have tried to make things hard for him in one way or another. When foreigners come here, they are surprised and disappointed at first because they run into so many prejudices they hadn't expected. I'm referring mostly to the Negroes, the Negroes from Africa. With the American Negroes it's different, of course.

They're very glad to be here because in America they're used to much worse.

But naturally it makes them angry when people on the street shout 'Lumumba' at them and such nonsense. But once they've got used to that and begin to feel that the people are really friendly at heart, they resign themselves to being called 'Lumumba'. A lot of them get invited to meals by German families and their student friends bring them home. Some of the African Negroes were in England before they came here, because they come from former English colonies. They feel much happier in Germany than in England. I don't know, perhaps there's some psychological reason, because England was their colonial power and that gives them an antipathy towards England.

Originally it was supposed to be like this in the Student House: one third students from the Federal Republic, one third from Central Germany, that is from the DDR, and one third foreign students. But that has changed. Now about forty per cent of the students here are foreigners, and I've never seen anybody from the DDR. We have six storeys for men and five for women. We get along fine together. Eleven at night is closing time. After that no men are allowed to be on the women's floors and no women on the men's floors. Of course there's a great deal of protest against this rule and I guess it's broken a good deal. The supervision is only theoretical. If someone's accused of breaking the rule, there have to be at least two witnesses. But they're not allowed into the rooms. That's regarded as an invasion of privacy. In your room you're safe. If they really wanted to convict somebody, two witnesses would have to wait all night outside the person's door. It's been tried. They piled up some mattresses outside the door and spent the night waiting for somebody of the wrong sex to come out. But we don't get excited about such things. We discuss them much less than religious topics. We have big debates about religion.

Most of the people I know say they believe in nothing.

A great many have more or less given up religion as they learned it from their parents or at school, because they find the outward forms obsolete, for instance the Catholic customs of going to church and not eating fish on Friday. But those are only the minor problems. The big problems are things like birth control, etc., ideas that the Church doesn't accept. The students would rather be free and think and act according to their own conscience. I'm a Catholic and I'm opposed to a good many of the outward forms myself.

What gets me especially is the church's opposition to birth control.

In my opinion it's simply wrong for the Church to compel people to have more children especially when couples want to go on living happily together. I don't see why the Church should be opposed to some kind of reasonable planning so the married couples can live decently with the financial resources they have. I'm for prevention, but I'm absolutely opposed to abortion. Perhaps all girls don't feel as strongly about it as I do, but a good many are basically of my opinion. Abortion can't be compared to birth control. Abortion is killing. If I expected a child by a student who wasn't financially in a position to get married, my conscience would certainly be very hard-pressed, but I'm sure I wouldn't have an abortion. I think that if I did, I wouldn't be able to forget it for the rest of my life. It's against God's commandment and I do think I believe in God. We've often discussed the question. I don't know exactly what the word 'believe' means and how it's possible to believe in something that's so entirely alien to us. Of course God need not necessarily be alien to people, but right now He is alien to me and to many others who think about it a great deal and who would really rather know than believe. It's very hard to believe in a vacuum. The trouble begins when you ask yourself why one Church claims to be the only true Church. And then you start wondering why every Church teaches that its God is the one true God. Why should this particular God be the only right one? Why can't God be a being or an idea that's the same for all men?

By what right does a Church claim God all for itself?

We discuss this a great deal. We've arrived at some very abstract definitions. A good many maintain that there's no God at all. One said recently: 'How can there be a God who suffers so much injustice and so much evil in the world? How can we believe in a God who is supposed to be good and righteous when we see so much evil around us in the world?' In a way it's pretty hard to believe. When you believe, you live on a different plane from the plane of knowledge and facts. When you believe, it's as if you were jumping over a boundary line and relying on something that you can't get a hold of. My parents are both Catholics. They have no doubts. They cling firmly to the outward forms and see much more content in them than I do or some of the other students. My parents can't really understand these problems we have. They don't understand how we can doubt something that they take for granted. I've got to the point where I'd even marry an atheist. But do without a church wedding? Yes, I've sometimes asked myself that question. If you reject the outward forms of religion, the

logical consequence would be to go without the marriage ceremony and the wedding too. It seems to be just a romantic picture we have, this thing with the white bridal gown and marching down the aisle with music. Of course I'd like to have that,
though it's not consistent. I realize that. Well, I'm sure that if I
marry a Catholic we'll have a church wedding just like our
parents and grandparents.

Formerly the first question about any new boy friend was
his looks.

That was always the first question. Now it doesn't matter any
more. Naturally I wouldn't want one who gave me the creeps
to look at. But who would? Anyway, I want one who's intelligent and good to talk to, and tolerant. Whether his tolerance
should include adultery, infidelity, and so on, it's hard to say,
because it's such an emotional topic. In a situation like that
you're guided more by emotion than reason. Even if your intelligence and your reason say: 'If he's faithful in spirit, is
physical fidelity so important?' – I'd make it my business to be
absolutely faithful. Maybe that would make things hard for me,
but when you get married you're taking a certain responsibility
for the survival of the marriage. After all, you don't absolutely
have to get married if you think a relationship is merely a love
affair that you can break off at any time if you find someone
better looking, more amusing and wittier.

Love, oh well . . . what is love? It's hard to say. There's pas-
sionate love and then there's another kind of love that's certainly very rare. That's the kind of love where all you want is
for the other to be happy. Where you don't think about yourself. I've only seen that once, between my girl friend and her
boy friend. I find mutual respect very important. I believe that
when you stop respecting each other love becomes impossible.
Because in love both parties have to be on the same level, not
one higher and the other lower. Love requires a certain willingness to make compromises. It requires understanding. Sex and
love can be separated completely.

You can have sex without love but not love without sex.

At school we didn't say a word about such things. I only went
to Catholic schools, and when you suddenly get away from that
atmosphere, it's difficult. In my last year of school I was away
from home. I had a room in Bonn, and under such circumstances you meet entirely different people. Suddenly I heard
people talk about those things with a frankness that really
shocked me. At first I was simply flabbergasted to hear people
talk about such things; at home I couldn't say a word about
them. I tried once. My parents were both horrified. My sister
had said she wanted to become an actress. So I said that most
actresses get their start by sleeping with the director. And my
parents – you just can't imagine! Since then I haven't opened
my mouth. My sister began to bawl and my mother sent me
out of the room. It was a real little melodrama. Since then
we've never spoken about such things. Among students we talk.
Some of them love to use wild technical expressions. Of course
most of them have read a good deal about it, in the illustrated
magazines and in books. There are frank, open discussions about
such things wherever you go. We seem to be living in an
enormous wave of sex; a lot of people are so affected by it that
they do things they wouldn't normally do without all this
hyperstimulation from outside. But after you've discussed
these things for a certain length of time, the novelty wears off,
everything goes back to normal and things seem a good deal
less strained and secret and cobwebby than before. Though less
with girls than with boys. It seems to me that in the course of
the centuries men have more or less convinced women that
they don't understand much about certain things.

But I don't see why girls should be less proficient than men
in any field whatsoever.

At the University I'm in a political study group. Of course we're
encouraged to read and discuss certain matters. Each week
someone gives a report on a certain topic and if it's something

I don't know much about I bring books home and read up to it.
The last report was about Cuba. The Revolution that brought
Castro to power, and from then on. The economic role of the
Americans. A young man attacked the Americans violently. He
took the extreme position of the Castro supporters. As usual,
there was an interesting discussion. This is how we do it: one
group has to be 'pro' and the other 'con'. First the different
aspects of the matter are explained, and then we discuss. But
we seldom come to any agreement. Certainly not on the war
in Vietnam. Two reports were made on the subject. I read a
book about it too. *The Ambassadors* by Morris West. It was a
best-seller in America. First my parents read it and then I did.
Of course it's very impressive when a man argues a thesis convincingly and backs it up with all sorts of facts. Morris West's
thesis is that the Americans want to stay in Vietnam in order
to have a military base in South-East Asia, in other words, that
they are carrying on this war purely for reasons of power-
politics and that all the ideological and ethical speeches that are
made in defence of the war in Vietnam are a lot of eyewash.
I've read other books about the whole development in Vietnam,
from the French colonization and the war of Indo-China to the
present American engagement in Vietnam.

I can't understand why the Americans have such a frantic
fear of Communism.

For one thing, the Americans' fear of Communism is incom-
prehensible to me because they are not directly threatened by
the Communists as we are here in Germany. I myself do not
entirely reject Communism. I wouldn't like to live in a country
governed by Communists because I don't want to give up my
freedom, but I believe that countries which have decided in
favour of a Communist or Socialist régime – the Americans
always lump Communism and Socialism together – I believe
that these countries should be left alone. One shouldn't attempt
to force an ideology on them. I know – but in the course of
time it will become clear whether the people of those countries

are satisfied with the régime. If they demonstrate any political decision, it should be respected. It would be better if free elections were possible everywhere, but those people, in Vietnam for instance, can't possibly have a viable democracy as we understand it – with free elections and free competition. The people must first be politically educated and have a certain training if they are to take active part in the government. Otherwise democracy is by definition impossible. We in Germany have no real democracy. A real democracy is an ideal that can never be attained, not even in the U.S.A. I don't know whether you could say that the Germans are very deeply interested in politics. I have the impression that what the citizens more or less want is a government that tells them what to do, that makes their decisions for them.

If it didn't interfere with their personal well-being, they would even accept a dictatorship,

because basically they're not interested in participating actively in a government and in certain projects. Basically they went to be left alone to muddle along in peace, and the government should muddle along too and find the best way of doing things. They think: 'What the government does must be all right.' I think most citizens would prefer such a state of affairs to having to vote and make decisions for themselves. I believe that when it comes to politics many of our people, including the young ones, confine themselves to grumbling. Especially a lot of the young people are resigned. They have the feeling that a lot of things are wrong and at the same time the feeling that their little voice is only a drop in the bucket compared to the mass of other voices and that consequently it's senseless to say anything at all, so they confine themselves to solitary grumbling.

I believe that students and in general young people of our age don't see why there's so much fuss about reunification, why we're always laying claim to territories that have grown totally foreign to us. I mean the territories on the other side of the Oder

and Neisse. But reunification is a different matter. Primarily
it applies only to unification of the two existing German states.
I think I can say that many others think as I do in the matter.
We see no possibility whatever of a reunification. We ask ourselves the question: 'To whom does it still mean anything that
Germany should be reunited?' Only to the people who have
relatives over there or to citizens of the DDR who have relatives here. It's of interest only to them. The only difference is
that over here we have democratic liberties that don't exist
over there. Of course, we have closer ties with Central Germany than with any of the other Communist-dominated countries in Europe. When you come right down to it, we would
be equally justified in waging a war of moral liberation for
all the others, for the Hungarians, Poles, Czechs, etc. The only
difference is that having a language in common creates a tie
between us and the Germans in the DDR.

To all intents and purposes the fact that we used to be one
State is history as far as we're concerned, and no longer a
living awareness.

It simply is not true that we have any particular romantic feelings when we think of our old Germany. Besides, the Nazis are
to blame for the division of Germany. We read a great deal about
the Nazis, we hear all sorts of opinions about them, but the
truth is that everyone washes his hands of the subject. In
school no judgements were expressed about the Nazi régime.
The facts were allowed to speak for themselves. When, for
example, someone delivered a report about the concentration
camps or about the Jewish question, no one was allowed to
express any opinion. The facts simply spoke for themselves.
The only thing that surprises me over and over again is that I
have never met a single German who was in favour. All of them
claim to have known what was what even then. All of them
knew from the very start what was going on and were secretly
working in the resistance; they were only afraid to say anything.

I would really like to find a single German who admits that he joined in the cheering.

You might think it's a lack of courage that prevents people from admitting it, but I'm afraid people really believe they were opposed from the very first. And I think that the attitude of the Allies after the War has a good deal to do with it. There were those questionnaires in which everyone who had anything to do with the Nazi régime, the NSDAP,* had to admit that this was the case. And if it was, he was excluded from all responsible positions. So people were practically compelled to make a 180-degree turn and deny everything in order to get a job. And then all the anti-Nazi propaganda that came over from the U.S.A., France and England. The Germans had it fired at them right and left. I believe that most Germans turned off their convictions from instinct of self-preservation and then actually came to believe they had never had them.

GUSTAVE MÖLLENDORF
25, unmarried, student

At the moment I work in a café-bar and my studies worry along on the side.

Because they're not really compatible with the café-bar. You can't work and study properly at the same time. It can't be done. At the moment I need money because I'm kind of on the outs with my parents. Because of my studies and my whole way of life. It's really my own fault. I'm in my tenth semester now. After five semesters I should have taken an intermediate examination, but I just took it easy from semester to semester until I finally decided I couldn't really bring myself to ask my father for money, so I said to myself: 'I'll just see if I can make it or not.' Pure laziness. I have all the certificates I need for a

---

* *Nazionalsozialistische Deutsche Arbeiterpartei* – National Socialist German Workers' Party, the official designation of the Nazi party.

degree in dentistry except for chemistry, and I kept postponing that from semester to semester. Then I registered for the laboratory course in chemistry and then something else came up, some kind of business with girls. Things got kind of confused, I wasn't able to attend the course regularly, I drank a good deal and bummed around in nightclubs, you know how it is. So I never did get that chemistry certificate. So right now my plan is to work seriously for the next few semesters. I'm determined to get my chemistry certificate and then try my general examination. The café-bar belongs to a friend of mine. We were in boarding school together and it was through him that I came to this university. We were in Hinterzarten at a branch of the Salem Castle School which was attended by Prince Philip, the English Queen's consort. At that time his name was still Battenberg. Well, anyway, since I needed a job on the side, he took me on in the café-bar. I make relatively quite a lot of money, about 900 marks a month. It varies. Actually, to leave myself time for studies I ought to work half or two thirds less but that's difficult when you've got used to having so much money.

You very quickly get used to bumming around. It's easy to see how it happened :

I like to go out and we had a very nice group. They were almost all Frenchmen, French girls and Italian girls. We all lived in a hotel that rented rooms by the month and then there was a club, the 'Laokoon', a private student club run by Greeks. So we met there, danced, talked and drank, and we got to drinking more and more, and then you're not so fit next day. You can't really concentrate so well. And when, in addition, you're a little unstable and easily influenced, there's a party here and a party there and pretty soon it gets the best of you. Little by little you start thinking it's the main thing in life. In every bar there are cliques and since it's a small town you keep meeting the same cliques in different bars. One day you meet in the 'Querschnitt', that's the name of one of the student clubs, or at

the 'Cognac Trist'. The night is long. A lot of students live that
way. Ten per cent may be putting it rather high but I'd say
there were a good many students who loaf like that. Now
there's talk of enforcing more discipline at the university
because they realize it can't go on like this. At the moment my
circle of friends doesn't include many students. One is a newspaper editor, another is a cartoonist. The friends I actually see
at the café-bar are the people I work with, mostly the girl
students who wait at table. But with them the work is only
a sideline, because they only work four hours a day and really
study. Even girls . . . well, all I want of a girl is that she should
have a clean character.

That she should have ten or twenty boy friends, that doesn't
matter. In my opinion that has nothing to do with morality.

No, there's nothing immoral about that. It depends how far it
goes. Every student has a girl friend that he goes steady with,
and if he goes with other girls on the side, there's nothing
wrong with that in my opinion. A lot of girls don't care if their
boy friend goes out with other girls. In general, girls are easy to
get. Some make things a little harder but there aren't very
many who make real difficulties. It all depends on the degree
of intelligence and whether they've had a good background.
But all of them like to go to bed if that's what you want to call
it, and with eight out of ten of them it can be done without
difficulty. Whether they come of a good family is something
you can only judge after you've known them a little longer.
But there are also brief acquaintances, in summer courses for
instance; a single evening does it, even with girls of good family. They're French or Italian or some other kind of foreigners.
They're kind of on vacation here and on vacation people are
always a little freer and forget the way it is at home and then
things go very fast. Swedish girls have a funny reputation that
isn't the least bit true. I've been friends with several Swedish
girls. It's not because they're Swedish, it's because they're taking summer courses.

My parents' marriage was broken up by the War.

I don't know exactly what happened. My father has a real-estate business. He's my stepfather. I'm in touch with my real father too. He's a druggist. As a result of the divorce after the War, I stayed with my mother. Then my sister was sent to boarding-school. The courts are crazy. They assigned my sister to my father and me to my mother. And because my mother had to work I was sent to my grandparents in Berlin. I lived there until 1954 when my mother remarried. Then I was able to go back to my mother, but I never had any real relationship with my stepfather, although he's very tolerant, but somehow a man who isn't the real father so to speak can't ever really understand a stepson. That's my opinion. Because he's a very different kind of man with entirely different tendencies. It's entirely different when I'm with my father. We have the same kind of humour, though of course we haven't got the same opinions. That would be impossible because I'm still very short on experience and he has a general view of life. But actually he's only my father on paper because he's never really performed the function of a father.

It seems to me that I'm the type who doesn't really enjoy things.

I don't know exactly what I want. I started to study – oh well, dentistry is very interesting, but it doesn't quite suit me. My parents, all three of them, I mean, are always saying that if I feel like doing something else I should do something else. But that's complicated. I can't change my course of study any more without being sent to the Army. That's a drawback. I'd lose two years that way. So if it's at all possible I'm going to try to wind up my studies and then I'll have a secure livelihood. Then I'll be able to work as a dentist any time I feel like it. Maybe I'll be in it so deep that dentistry will interest me after all. But if I don't make it, I haven't really decided what I'll do. I'll just have to try to stay in the restaurant business or do something

else. There are so many things. At present everything seems a
little boring because I'm always meeting the same people and
we haven't even got time to have a real conversation. When we
get together, we talk about politics or art. It all depends on who
you're talking to. And if there's a party some place we usually
drink a good deal, so in the end nothing much comes of it.
There's a big blah blah, sometimes on interesting subjects, but
in the end you don't remember what you were talking about.
I read a newspaper now and then, but current affairs don't
interest me. I listen to the news on the radio. That's enough for
me. I used to read a good deal. But unfortunately I haven't got
all my books here. That's why you don't see any here in my
room.

But sometimes my sister advises me to read some best-seller.

She's very much interested and reads practically every new
book that comes out. When I'm with my friends we don't actually talk about anything. We tell each other things to laugh at
or we talk about our plans with girls. . . . Yes, girls cost a lot of
money. I've got one girl friend especially who costs a fortune.
In the first place, going out is very expensive. And then the
presents they want. It really gets you into financial difficulties.
My girl friend, I mean my main girl friend, is very extravagant.
She lives a little beyond her means. She's Swiss. You wouldn't
think so. She's only twenty. She's easy to get along with. If you
met her, she could talk to you about everything under the sun.
But she's a bitch all the same.

She has coal-black hair, an oval face, sensual lips, brown
eyes, a tiny waist and pointed breasts. She's five foot five.

Not really my type. Yes, what I really like is kind of plump
girls with kind of full bosoms, and so on. But they've got to
know how to make themselves interesting. When I see that a
girl is all out for me so I could do practically anything I wanted
with her, I can't stand it. That's the end. She can love me

passionately, I'm not interested. There's always got to be a little tension. Girls are always very eager to hear compliments. Some like big, strong, blond men, others go for the more intelligent types. A lot of them like older men. A girl of twenty is sure to prefer a man of thirty or forty.

Most of them tell you marriage doesn't mean a thing to them, but you can't really believe it.

My main girl friend, for instance, keeps saying that after my exam it will be all plain sailing and we'll be able to think about our future. Actually, she's right. I've always promised it, from month to month and from semester to semester. We've known each other more than three years but we haven't been faithful to each other. I haven't and neither has she. But that makes no difference. Neither of us holds it up to the other. It doesn't bother us. I've met so many girls through the café-bar. You go out with them once. And then you go to bed. But mostly it's the liquor that does it. If they weren't drunk they wouldn't go to bed with me, and I wouldn't do it either because I'm always disgusted next morning.

Without liquor going to bed with them would disgust me.

I don't know what the girls think. We haven't talked about it. You see, people talk about sex so much but nobody knows what it really is. Of course there are certain pictures that emanate sex, like in *Playboy*, for instance. You look at the girls, bare bosoms, and so on. But what does it mean? You know, I really ought to get married because then I'd be forced to act responsibly. I need something to hold me up. Then I'd have more sense of responsibility.

HERBERT GRASMÜLLER, KUNO PEZET,
TONI LIEBLING

all in their early 20s, unmarried, fraternity students

Ethical training is a lovely idea.

Herbert Grasmüller: Here's how it happened that I joined this fraternity. A teacher I had in school told us how a fraternity is organized. It appealed to me and later when I came to the university, I joined this fraternity. I liked everything about it, including the members. So I decided to take an active part. What appealed to me especially was contact with men like myself, fellows with the same interests, who know how to build up a friendship. What I liked especially was the way they train young men so they can make their way in life later on. Our whole career in the fraternity is aimed at this. The different stages: cub, full-fledged member. The cub comes directly out of school, he doesn't know what's expected of him, and it's very good for him if he has someone who can guide him and really introduce him to university life. That's one of our main aims and another is ethical training. So far I think we've done very well with it.

Toni Liebling: You see, what we mean by training is not so much a continuation of childhood training as a means of helping the student adjust himself to a different kind of community. Most students come from families where they were kept strictly in check, and here at the university they're pretty much on their own. We try to help them and give them comradeship, friends to help them with their questions and problems and stand by them in difficult situations. Well, this ethical training as they call it doesn't make much sense to me. Ethical training is a lovely idea but I don't think it really applies to us.

Herbert Grasmüller: There I must disagree with you. In my opinion ethical training is significant because we try to give the men ethical training not only for the university but also for life, so that they'll behave properly. We try to bring out the

training that our fraternity brothers received at home. It's
perfectly possible that a man will forget his training. Then of
course it's up to us to call it to their attention and to strike
their sensitive spots with the punishments that are current
among us. For instance, we can impose some really painful
punishment on a man who has been putting off his examination for an unreasonable length of time and that puts him back
up front. We also admonish our members in questions of
honour. We have what we call the principle of self-accusation.
If something has happened that affects our fraternity or our
public life, we ask: 'Who did it?' And the guilty party has to
confess even if it means punishment.

The man is punished.

We have the punishment of so-called 'dimission', for instance,
loss of the ribbon, which means that the man in question isn't
allowed to wear our colours for a time. There are different
degrees of dimission. For instance, the punished party isn't
allowed to speak to his fraternity brothers for a certain time – a
week, a month, or as much as two semesters. He has only one
fraternity brother who informs him about the most important
things that are going on in the fraternity. Otherwise, he's not
allowed to have any contact with us. If he's sitting in a bar
and some fraternity brothers come in, he's got to drink up his
beer and clear out. Then there are other punishments, for instance, what we call 'recorded censure'. After certain offences
the fraternity brothers hand down a censure that's published in
our fraternity newspaper, which means it's read by all the Old
Gentlemen. A certain number of 'recorded censures' means
automatic exclusion from the fraternity. Then there are small
punishments that can be very painful though. There are fines.
Anyone who sleeps too much or cuts classes is punished by
fines from fifty pfennigs up to five marks. In our fraternity all
fines are imposed by the Convention. Aside from the usual
division into cubs and full-fledged members, we also have a
Convention which is the supreme organ of the active members

and decides on all important questions. That is our democratic forum, so to speak, in which all the fraternity brothers vote on matters that come up and officers are elected and deposed. The Convention concerns itself with everything. If someone has thought up an idea, if someone has difficulties either of a financial or a personal nature or connected with his studies, we try to help him. In addition, we have a General Convention that meets twice a year. All the Old Gentlemen are invited to this General Convention. It attends to important matters concerning our fraternity house or the wearing of colours or the number of obligatory duels. Our fraternity has 420 members. Germans and foreigners. Yes, we have foreigners too. We don't take all foreigners, because we have the so-called 'life-membership principle', that is, we expect our fraternity brothers to come back to our fraternity later on, to anniversary dinners, and so on. That's why we don't take anybody who lives too far away, in Thailand or Japan, for instance. Of course we haven't very many foreigners, because most foreigners don't feel the need of coming to us; because most foreigners have never heard of student fraternities, or because, like many Germans, they have wrong ideas about fraternities, because a lot of people associate fraternities with the eternal student or with students who do nothing but drink and fight, who never pass any examinations but have plenty of duelling scars. An idea which may be partly true but no more of fraternity members than it is of other students. It's an idea that's come down from the past and doesn't really hold good any more.

So I came into close contact with men of my own social class.

Fraternities are no longer, as they were a hundred years ago, made up of aristocrats who have a great deal of money and are able to live very high. Today, the members are sons of parents with very limited financial resources who can't afford to spend their whole time drinking. You see, my father was an Old Gentleman in this fraternity, a physician. But he died in 1951 and my mother is alone, so I have to be very careful about my money.

Kuno Pezet: My father is a police official in Münster, he's not an Old Gentleman. I met a few fellows in Münster who were in fraternities and when I came here I became acquainted with a few of my present fraternity brothers. We often went to bars together and talked things over, so I came into close contact with men of my own social class.

Herbert Grasmüller: You can say that by and large we come of the middle class. It's unusual to have the sons of workers in a duelling fraternity. Most of the fathers are professional men or businessmen, that kind of thing. I said to myself at the very start that duelling would do me good. I've watched myself carefully and observed that duelling has really given me something. It wasn't pleasant for me. At first I was afraid. But I knew that at some time or another I would have to fight my three or four obligatory duels, well anyway, three. So I said to myself: 'If the others can do it so can you', quite apart from the fact that it's not bad for the health. Duelling helped me, it taught me to overcome my fears, including the fear of examinations. Duelling can't be explained rationally, it's a matter of feeling. It reinforces the bond between fraternity brothers. And it teaches us a certain fairness.

Fraternity brothers can also take a political position.

Kuno Pezet: Besides, we try not only to keep the fraternity brothers politically informed but also to take an interest in university affairs, for instance to participate in the elections of the ASTA.* Fraternity brothers can also take political positions. We have no restrictions. It's all the same to us whether a member leans towards the CDU or the SPD or feels close to the NPD or whether he's a left-wing Socialist or has Communist ideas. That in itself means nothing to us. Actually that's the best part of it, because it gives rise to discussions. For instance,

---

* *Allgemeiner Studentenausschuss* – General Students' Committee.

we're on very good terms with two fraternity brothers who wrongly, in my opinion, but rightly in their opinion, are supporters of the NPD. Of course, very heated discussions start up because that party tries to appeal more to feeling than to reason. I've heard some speeches by NPD leaders on the radio and I saw how they trotted out the blood-and-soil theory that the Nazis were always harping on, though in a refurbished, somewhat modified form. This NPD makes us a lot of enemies abroad.

As far as the Nazi period is concerned, I must say that I personally am not conscious of any guilt.

I know on the one hand that a great many crimes were committed during the Third Reich and that we must be on our guard to prevent such things from ever happening again. We must also be careful in our dealings with other nations and try to practise a certain modest reserve. After what's happened it's easy to understand that not every country says: 'Aha! This is the new generation of Germans, let's forgive them everything.' Foreigners will scrutinize our behaviour and our political actions to see whether the old spirit still prevails. To that extent I understand very well that certain peoples especially in Eastern Europe aren't just putting the blame on Germany for propaganda purposes, but also have perfectly understandable and justified fears for their security.

Herbert Grasmüller: I wish to say that the constant accusations made abroad and the usually biased picture painted of the Third Reich make for resentment, and the result is that a lot of our young people are beginning to sympathize with the Third Reich again. Certain conversations have given me the impression that there are a great many such people, not only students but young people from other sections of society. Of course, fashion has something to do with it. People are simply expressing opposition to the existing order when they say: 'It wasn't really so bad in those days.' And when now and then they make some anti-Semitic statement that actually doesn't make much sense – they're just blowing off steam – it's just from a spirit of opposition. The bad part of it is in the first place that it gives a lot of people the wrong idea, and in the second place that such statements always leave a certain mark. If a lot of people start saying: 'Well, actually it wasn't at all bad in those days', it's perfectly possible that people who haven't really thought about it very much will incorporate these idiotic statements into their opinions. Of course there is such a danger.

Toni Liebling: This spirit of opposition may be wrong but often it's provoked by the way they teach history in school. My history teacher used to say, for example: 'Anybody who voted for the NSDAP before 1933 was either an idiot or a criminal.' Even that opinion made us pretty mad. My father voted for the NSDAP before 1933.

And I don't remember my father as either a criminal or an idiot.

I don't know whether I'm properly informed about the Nazi period because in my opinion the historical picture we have of the period is still rather distorted. But in any case there is still too strong a tendency to condemn the Third Reich and everything connected with it. I am convinced that especially at the beginning of the Third Reich a great many people were trying to do something positive that would have served the interests of our people. It's obvious that it degenerated later on, for instance we had all those crimes, all that business with the concentration camps, and those are things that no one can approve of. On the other hand, people are always forgetting that before the beginning of the Third Reich there were two possibilities: either Communism on the extreme Left or the NSDAP on the extreme Right, and I don't know whether Communism would necessarily have given us anything much better. It probably wouldn't have sent any Jews to the gas chambers and wouldn't have given us a war. All that has to be weighed in the balance. It's very hard for us to put ourselves back into those times, to judge why people voted the way they did.

We can't be so very proud of the Empire either.

Still, we can be proud that after the War our parents in so short a time turned all that dreadful chaos and discouragement into an economic organization which today permits us a certain standard of living and certain educational advantages. We also ought to be proud that after those days of terror our parents built up a political system that has brought us very great democratic liberties. There are phases in the history of our nation of which we can be proud and phases we can look back on only with shame.

Kuno Pezet: That is particularly true of the Third Reich. We can't be very proud of the preceding period either, the Weimar Republic, because though efforts were made to achieve a democratic form of government, they didn't come to anything because only a minority supported them. We can't be very proud of the Empire because the Empire brought us a war. Perhaps we can be proud of the period before the First World War, because at that time monarchy was the idea that sustained the State, not only in Germany but in other countries as well. But come to think of it, I don't know if there's any point in being proud of a nation. We would do better to think of the future and try to see to it with our work and our behaviour that the name of Germany is respected in the world.

HANS-GEORG KÖRNER
27, married, student

My father was a police officer in Strassburg.

One day he was shot in the heart in mysterious circumstances, but he survived. We have no idea how it happened. He never told us anything about it. All we know is that twice before he had been arrested at the Stuttgart railroad station, but that he had been released after about ten hours. And that he had connexions with certain police officials and officers of the SD* in Berlin. Later we heard from a colleague of my father's that he had somehow been involved in the Resistance movement against Hitler. Probably it was connected with Admiral Canaris, chief of military counter-espionage, because in his position as a police officer my father was in close contact with that organization. He recovered from the shot in the heart. The bullet had passed right through his chest but only grazed his heart. Then my father was transferred to Russia as an SD official, and one day he was reported missing. My mother had learned sewing as a young girl, so then she began to work at home as a dressmaker in a village near Pforzheim. She sewed for practically half the town and that way she eked out her pension. The pension was very small because my father was very young when he was reported missing, so he hadn't time to be promoted and the pension stayed at the same level. My mother had to take care of my sister and myself, but she managed to send me to high school in Pforzheim. In general, I was very satisfied with my school and I have the feeling that I received a very good education which stands me in good stead now at the university. Only I was very much disappointed by the instruction in History and German. I always had a strange feeling about learning poems by heart and reciting them; it bothered me, especially when my classmates put so much pathos in their voices.

When that happened, I used to unscrew my fountain pen and squirt ink.

I can still remember that well because I was punished by being made to learn some passages from Hermann Hesse's *Narziss und Goldmund*. Same with writing essays; I simply wasn't able to deliver the atmospheric prose poems they wanted. My essays always had remarks by my teacher in the margin: 'You with your eternal cynicism. With this kind of thing you couldn't lure a dog from behind the stove.' I also remember an essay on an

---

* *Sicherheitsdienst* – Security Service.

assigned topic: 'Things That Give Me Special Pleasure'. I wrote that it gave me special pleasure to squeeze out the washrag when I was taking a bath and to listen to the splash when the stream of water fell back into the tub. That was my way of kidding my German teacher because I regarded those atmospheric prose poems as just too highfalutin and hypocritical. The German teacher was also the history teacher. Even so, I always had the feeling that he tried to be neutral. He had been a major during the Second World War, and of course we all knew where he had stood during the Nazi régime. Up to 1900, history was taught in some detail. After that it was hurry-hurry and he dashed through the history of the last fifty years at a hair-raising pace. It may have been intentional. But I rather think it was simply lack of time. Even so, we touched briefly on the Weimar Republic, the rise of National Socialism, the postwar period and even Communism. There was even a question about Communism in the oral examination.

But if all I knew about Communism was what I learned in school, the truth is that I wouldn't know anything.

Later, I studied Communism in detail and at the university I was able to carry on discussions with students from Russia and Czechoslovakia. My contact with those students was very satisfactory. I still correspond with some of them. I write letters to Moscow and Minsk, for instance. Of course we had very different ideologies, but we saw eye to eye in other matters. When I had discussions with scientists, we dealt with questions connected with our fields. We also spoke about the organization of their schools and their scholarships. That interested me especially because for a long time I have concerned myself with social questions relating to students. The difference between the Soviet scholarship system and ours is that there everyone gets a scholarship. On the whole it's hard to judge whether that is good or bad. I would say that it's good if a government can afford to provide equal opportunities for all. How it does so is secondary in my opinion. The crucial matter is the equality of opportunity. There's no reason to give the students who are well-off to begin with additional help. That is definitely not right. And it's just what the Federal Republic was trying to do with its lump sum of forty marks for every student. We sharply criticized this 'watering-can' principle, by which I mean that a great deal of money was scattered around to no purpose. Forty marks is no help to the poorer students, and the others didn't need it. The Russians have a system which makes the distribution of scholarships largely dependent on the students' work. If their work falls off, the scholarship is reduced. That strikes me as a very good idea. We have that too. We have two kinds of scholarship, the one goes to the gifted and the other to the poorer students. The 'Honnef Plan' which regulates our distribution of scholarships is not supposed to benefit the highly gifted; it is supposed to encourage any student who has graduated from high school and is in a position to study. We combat it constantly because we think the students who do no work at all should not benefit by scholarships. Of course it's necessary to check on their work, but it shouldn't be done by additional examinations, but on the basis of the examinations which are already a part of the course of study. Up to now, according to the Honnef Plan all beneficiaries of scholarships must take additional examinations and produce two certificates of achievement every semester. Simply because they have less money these students are forced to bear additional burdens and the others who are financially better off can hang around the university for years, doing practically nothing and taking up space. Their activity is not checked at all. Only the students who are obliged to take money from the state are obliged to do this additional work and produce certificates of achievement.

We also read newspapers from the DDR.

But let me tell you something about the instruction in history and about the students who are interested in current events. Actually the problem affects only those students who come to it of their own accord, who read the newspapers, for example, on their own initiative. My case was like this: from the sixth grade on, I began to read at least one daily paper every day. Since then I have taken to reading three dailies and one weekly. I read the regional paper, two national papers and in addition, the weekly *Die Zeit*. *Die Zeit*, I have to admit, is very tendentious in its reporting about universities. It complains a great deal about the universities, calls them 'old swamps', incapable of reforming themselves. But since I am a member of the Senate Commission for university reform, I know from my own work that the professors at our university are making a real effort to introduce university reform. Of course there are some professors who cling to the old routines and want to preserve the old hierarchial principles. But that's by no means the case with all of them, and the members of the commissions are the ones who want to introduce reforms. We also read newspapers from the DDR. They come to us from various sources in sealed envelopes and we have to promise not to pass them on to other people. I also read these papers regularly and I've been in the DDR. It strikes me as really stupid that these papers shouldn't be accessible to our public. I believe that ninety per cent of our fellow citizens are perfectly capable of reading them, and then they would really understand what the system over there is like, because I believe that the primitive way in which they describe conditions over here would make it apparent to any common worker what the system in the DDR is really like. After all, he knows how he lives, he knows what's going on over here, and if he read what their newspapers write it would discredit the government of the DDR, rather than do it any good. I regard it as extremely unwise to go on barring these papers. It would do us much more good if they were obtainable here.

I don't think it makes any difference what denomination a child belongs to.

My mother was mostly responsible for my open-mindedness. She was active in several of the Protestant churches' aid organ-

izations. She has close connexions with the Liebenzell Mission.
That is a Protestant church organization that trains missionaries and sends them to Africa and Asia. That put us into close
contact with ministers and missionaries. My parents, though,
were not religious in the ecclesiastical sense. My father was a
Catholic and my mother was a Protestant. With me, it's the
opposite. My wife is a Catholic and I'm a Protestant. It made no
difference to me. I took the attitude that bringing up the children is the mother's business and it's much harder to bring up
children in a religion that isn't one's own. So our little boy is a
Catholic. But I don't think it makes any difference what denomination a child belongs to; to me it's much more important
to bring up a child so that he knows what's Christian and what
isn't.

A nursery school for students' children would act as a
stimulant.

I've often been disappointed in my life but so far it hasn't dis-
couraged me. I've been disappointed by the whole society in
which I live. As an officer of ASTA I have tried to improve the
social structure of the student body. I have tried to build
student homes, homes for married couples, nursery schools, etc.
And in the course of this activity I have observed that very few
other people in the university or from among the population at
large wish to commit themselves in this direction. Especially
in connexion with the nursery school a mountain of prejudices
had to be combated. The matter was discussed in the town
council, at the university, and in the *Landtag*.* All these discussions ended in a decision that there was no need to encourage
marriage among students. A nursery school for students' children
would act as a stimulant and help to increase student marriages. They contended that a student shouldn't marry altogether
because he was unable to support a family. We had to keep
pointing out that in our opinion a student marriage is a marri-

---

*The lower house of the provincial legislature.

age just like any other. Student marriage is simply a fact and we have to act accordingly. In the end I was able to put through a nursery school for students' children but it wasn't because those people had changed their minds. It was simply because the political pressure had become too great. We put pressure on the town council by going to the SPD and asking them why they as a social-minded party were unwilling to support such a project, and then we explained the issue to the CDU. Gradually the pressure of one party against the other became too strong, because each one thought the other was trying to exploit the programme for its own purposes. In the end all the parties and groups within the city council voted in favour. And so the nursery school came into existence. We employed five specially-trained nurses and we are very proud of our nursery school. We have heard pediatricians say that our children really thrive. The parents pay 100 marks a month per child and they are kept all day. For that the children are also given fruit and milk to take home. I, of course, do not send my own child to the nursery school because I never like my public actions to serve my own interests. But let me tell you something typical: my fellow-students didn't give me a word of thanks for all this. It was just taken for granted. But you've got to accept such disappointments. You've got to take them for granted.

Another constant disappointment is the really comical attitude of certain professors towards their students. There are some professors who still cling to the hierarchical principle, they behave like little dukes and emperors and are absolutely unwilling to let anyone else make a place for himself. I must extend this sense of disappointment to our *Landtag*. I have carefully followed the debates, especially those concerned with approving funds for the university or for social purposes. In personal conversations with members I was hardly encouraged, because I saw how much attention every member of the *Landtag* has to pay to his electorate or to certain pressure groups when it comes to taking a position on any question.

My main ambition for the future is to assume political responsibility. There's little doubt that I'll always take an interest in social questions and that some day I shall come into a position of political responsibility, that is, either through a political party or some branch of specialized study I shall try to carry out my social ideas. I am strongly opposed to this custom of herd voting in the party fractions; it's simply impossible for the individual members to have a mind of their own. The members are expected to submit to their party, which often means voting contrary to their own convictions. I consider that wrong. Perhaps I'm too much of an idealist. My wife, in any case, always says I'm not enough of a materialist and that I knock myself out too much for other people instead of looking after my own family. I know that her reproach is partly justified. But I just can't help it.

I regard it as a good thing that the students don't want to submit to anyone.

I believe that every man has the right to live as he sees fit. And I would not say that the moral attitude of the students was better before. Nor do I believe that the students are less moral than any other section of the population. The older generation often accuse them of being less moral, of recognizing no authority, of having no aim in life, of being nihilistic, of being negative, of having only material interests, or thinking only of themselves and never of the state or the people. Certainly there's some truth in that, but the percentage of students to which it applies existed earlier too. Ice was no less slippery in the old days. When I hear that the students today don't want to submit to anyone and recognize no authority, I say it's a good thing, especially as generally speaking we in Germany have an exaggerated respect for authority. It begins at the ticket windows where everyone bows and scrapes just because the fellow back there has an official's cap on. If the students have stopped doing that today, I say it's a good thing. Our parents were submissive to everyone and showed practically no initiative or moral courage. Today we often hear it said that the students are too radical and too far to the left. The reason for this view, I believe, is that the radical groups are very conspicuous while the liberals remain more in the background.

I would recognize the DDR as a state.

On the whole the students and the younger generation in general tend to take a much more realistic view of things than their parents. I believe it's high time that the German Federal Republic should try to look the facts in the face – in connexion with reunification, for example – and to admit that the DDR is a reality, that it exists. There's no point sticking your head in the sand and saying: 'We don't see you.' I would recognize the DDR as a state. I would try to maintain close contact with that state in concrete negotiations. That alone can improve the situation of the people in the other part of Germany and keep the idea alive both in them and in us that we are still fundamentally one people. Playing blind man's buff with each other only increases the cleavage.

In addition, the Federal Republic should concern itself far more with a united Europe, and not just with little Western Europe. It is definitely worthwhile to fight for a greater Europe, a Europe that will also include the Soviet Union. If this problem could be solved Germany could be reunited by way of a united Europe, because then our political divergencies would be less important. Naturally the possibilities will become still greater as China moves away from the Soviet Union. That will give the Soviet Union more incentive to lean towards a united Europe.

For a long time now we have concentrated too much on the past.

Despite all this Europeanization I wish that a healthy nationalism could become possible among us again. At present practically no one can afford to make a national statement. That is the reason for the rise of the NPD. I believe that if we had found our way back sooner to a healthy national consciousness, the rise of this new party would have been impossible. For a long time now we have concentrated too much on the past. As Herr Augstein rightly says, we are the world's blockheads. This eternal breast-beating: 'We are guilty! We must make amends!'

We must stop just accusing ourselves and instead show by our deeds that we have built up a new state in which such things are no longer possible. That alone can improve our reputation in the world. That alone can carry conviction. Mere self-accusation is senseless. Only deeds convince anybody.

ALBRECHT JELLBACH

64, married, professor of law

I am very glad that the political interest of the students has revived.

Until a few years ago practically all the students' energy was taken up by study. The reason, of course, was that the study of law – of course I can judge only by my own field – makes incomparably higher demands on a student than in my time. Anyone who studies law today must really do a great deal of work in his eight semesters. In my time one spent three semesters in a fraternity, dropping in on lectures only occasionally, and actually spent only the last two or three semesters preparing for the examination. That's the way it was, but God knows it's no longer true. Today, the student's intellectual interests and his whole process of intellectual self-orientation are in far higher degree determined by scholastic requirements. Immediately after the War our typical student was only relatively intelligent but always conscientious, interested in nothing but the study of law – a specialist, you might call him. He regarded the National Socialist period as a historical fact that lay behind him, for which perhaps our fathers were responsible but to which he himself had not been committed. He studied, he tried to secure a successful future by getting good marks in his courses and examinations. It was only around 1960 that a change occurred and now the National Socialist period is again becoming a burning issue. Now incisive questions are raised: 'What actually happened? How did people behave?' I regard that as a very good sign.

I speak quite openly with the students about my past.

I tell them that at first I saw a good deal that was positive in the new régime and also supported it in my writings. I know that all my colleagues who taught under the Third Reich thought just as I did. There aren't very many of them who come out today and say: 'Yes, that's how I was and if it doesn't suit you, you know what you can do.' Well, moral courage is definitely not one of the foremost German qualities. I have to tell the students over and over again: 'If you think of the people who were responsible then and of all the people who lived in those days, you've got to realize that the average man wasn't born to be a hero. Heroes are revered because they're something unusual. You can't expect every man to risk his life for his convictions. You've simply got to realize what men are like. The average man can only take so much.' I do not believe that there is any difference between the people of Germany and those of other countries. I have always described the modern state to my students as an extremely fragile body, dependent on an extreme degree of rationality.

Generally speaking, all attempts to impose philosophies of life are doomed to failure.

Of course the young people demand ideals, but I have none to offer them. One might perhaps regard as an ideal what Max Weber calls professional ethics. But the modern world offers no basis for what in my youth we regarded as ideals. Adenauer had his plan for Europe. It was a very clever idea based on the assumption that a German state can never throw off the taint

we acquired between 1933 and 1945. If we succeed in abolish-
ing the German state and integrating it with a united Europe,
then we'll be out of the mess. But after that came to grief it
turned out that we had buried the national consciousness too
soon. You only have to look around you in France, in Belgium,
Norway or Denmark, or anywhere where people have perfectly
natural national feelings. If today a party should attempt to
introduce something of that sort in our country, we would only
be putting ourselves on a level with other countries. The
young people want to be rid of their fathers' guilt, and of
course that could easily lead to a new kind of nationalism,
the wrong kind – yes, unquestionably. On the other hand I keep
thinking that a dividing line should be drawn between my
generation and the present younger generation. Take, for
example, the reparations payments to Israel. On political and
human grounds, I was very much in favour of these payments,
but there's a good two thirds of the population that can no
longer be held responsible for what happened.

We ought to say: 'We are willing to pay for the responsible
generation, but we cannot put these burdens on the generations that were born later.'

The question of guilt complex comes up time and time again
among the young people. I can see that by my students. In discussions, somebody always says that something should have
been done in the spring of 1933! I answer: that was too much
to expect of me. Though I was critical in matters of detail, I
was generally favourable to the development. In 1932 just before the National Socialist seizure of power I was not infre-
quently consulted by the government of the time and what I
saw made me feel strongly that the system had no future because it had lost all parliamentary support. Since the elections
of 1930 there had been no majority; the leaders had consciously
adopted an authoritarian course, they tried to weather the
period of parliamentary difficulty with the support of the two
existing power factors, the bureaucracy and the army. That

would have been possible if they had had even one forward-looking watchword. The bureaucracy and the army are supposed to be neutral forces. They are not made for political leadership. I believe they could have withstood the period of political difficulties if, in opposition to the wild propaganda from Right and Left, they had found a convincing watchword of their own, but that was not possible with Hindenburg at the head of the stage.

That was the situation in November 1932.

I remember it well: Hindenburg was an old man of eighty-two. Surely a very honourable man, no one would ever have given him credit for political genius. At that time Hindenburg was really at the end of his physical strength, surrounded by a body of advisers who kept coming and going, which resulted in an anonymous government. All those people did was to engage in tactical manoeuvres against the Right and Left, but what they needed was a powerful watchword. General von Schleicher, who was Chancellor at the time, attempted an alliance with the unions and the SPD. The attempt failed in December 1932. That was the last attempt to put through anything like an idea. Then something totally unexpected happened: the parties and the unions collapsed. It was a process of self-dissolution. In this situation I wrote an article for which I have often been criticized. It was a plea for a strong state. I would still come out in support of it. It was an attempt to prevent the state from being manipulated solely by the opposition, that is, the NSDAP. At that time one was bound to see things differently than they appeared later.

What I wanted then was pure wishful thinking.

I thought I could influence the course of events. Then came a shift in my thinking. First in 1934 the Roehm affair, then the laws of 15 September 1935, the Party laws and race laws. I was then staying with friends in Hamburg and we heard a radio

announcement about the laws passed at the Party congress,
the law for the defence of the German blood, etc. We swore
an oath to each other that from then on we would never write
a line for this shameful state. But what people are still holding
up to me today is that in 1933 I at first took a favourable view.
And then a few anti-Semitic utterances which in my opinion
were harmless. I had written roughly that Jewish influence
must be eliminated because if that were done the reckoning
between the German people and the Jews would be more or
less settled. That was all I said. I also used the expression 'to
render harmless'. Only a short time ago I was attacked for this,
and I replied: I've just been reading in Bismarck's memoirs
about his fight against the alleviation of the 'Socialist Law'.
The purpose of the law for him was to render the socialists
harmless. No one will accuse Bismarck of wanting to kill them.
That was exactly how I felt about it.

But since Auschwitz of course, we see these things quite
differently.

Yes, of course the question is in order, but it's not easy to
answer. During the famous 'golden twenties' in Berlin I looked
around a good deal and I had the impression that the Jews for
all their intelligence, for all the wit they displayed in the
cabarets, lacked something that I should call a sense of situation. My impression was that they didn't see what was going
on. In 1928 and 1929 I never missed a programme at the 'Humo-
rists' Cabaret' in Berlin. I always enjoyed it, but when I came
out and thought it over, my impression was: those people have
no sense of situation. They don't understand what's going on.
They just don't grasp the political situation. They don't realize
what's brewing among the German people, what kind of chaos
is in the making around us. Even in the elemental frenzy of enthusiasm which undoubtedly existed in the spring of 1933, the
German people did not shout 'Auschwitz'. They wanted something entirely different. They wanted to put an end to the domi-
nant influence of the Jews. I can only say that that was how

I felt at the time. It is very difficult after such a lapse of time to say anything more about it. But I own that that is how I felt then. I tell my students so, too. I say it in my lectures. I talk with them about it: 'That's how it was, that's how it was!' I deny nothing.

For the present generation all this is a purely historical episode.

Naturally they can't have any sound ideas about it. They look at it – they can hardly be blamed – from the standpoint of a later day; they imagine that a thing like Auschwitz was already planned in 1933 and that people should have known it even then. Well, when I tell them the real course of events as I see them and lived through them, there are always some who take my word for it, if only because I enjoy a certain personal credit with the students. Then some of them ask me: 'But Herr Professor, what should our attitude be now? What can we do to preserve our democratic state? What should we do in case of a new crisis?' Then I'm obliged to say: 'My present professional imagination does not allow me to visualize the situation that would then arise.' The fathers of the Fundamental Law of the Federal Republic of Germany believed that the Devil always comes in through the same door, and they barred that door with several articles. But history does not repeat itself in that way. I sometimes refer to these years as the halcyon years; I do not believe that the period of upheavals and seizures of power, of total defeats and new beginnings that has been going on for centuries is already at an end. We have no definitive solutions.

EDITH SOMMERFELD

61, unmarried, landlady

As for the students who live at my place, we talk everything over.

I always like that about the students. I had a really charming French girl, we used to discuss everything that was on her mind, especially her love-affairs. When she met a gentleman who lived in another neighbourhood and wanted her to move in with him, I said to her: nobody can tell you what to do in matters of love, you've got to think for yourself. So she thought for herself and moved in with the young man, but later she came back to me. That little French girl – her name was Monique – was crazy about Germany. She wanted a German husband. She had no desire to go back home to her country. At first I couldn't understand it. I said to her: 'Why, Monique, you're a French girl and everybody loves his country.' – 'Yes,' she said, 'but it's entirely different here in Germany, and much nicer. I just like it.' 'Monique,' I said, 'you've got to be fair.' But there was nothing I could do. She was just wild about everything German. One day I was wearing a lace dress that was almost thirty years old. I took it out of the closet, shortened it, altered it and started wearing it again. Monique saw me in it and said: 'Frau Sommerfeld, couldn't you sell me this dress? If I wear it, it will put Ferdy's eye out!' So I said 'It's all right if he looks at the dress and the figure, but he'd do better to look at the heart.'

But unfortunately a young man, especially a German, pays more attention to the way a girl's dressed . . .

I have four students living at my place, boys or girls, it varies. It's all right with me when a boy or a girl student has an affair and a lady or gentleman comes visiting. It's normal. I have no objection. They can stay until ten o'clock. Occasionally, they've stayed until twelve. Then I've protested a little and requested them to stop doing it. And they have stopped. Well, anyway, I don't mind the students' friendships. If they'd only wipe their feet and close the doors more quietly. But they always drag dirt over the floor and slam the doors like mad. They're young, that's all. It was different in my day. But what can you do?

They don't brush their teeth properly, they gad about with girls, they bang doors and bring in dirt . . . it's terrible!

They've become more demanding. They've changed a little. They care more about their comfort. In short, they want everything. All these modern things: running water, gas heat, light plugs all over the place. Take a look, there are eight plugs in this room. You can shave anywhere you like. Anyway, they're very comfortable here and as long as they have that, they're satisfied. See what I mean? Of course the young people vary a good deal. One works hard, another not so hard. One takes it easy, another's a go-getter.

But all the boys drink—sometimes you feel sorry for them.

There was a student from Flensburg; he came here to study medicine. He had five bottles of whisky with him and he drained a bottle every day. I wouldn't have minded if it hadn't made him drunk; it started right here in the house before he even went out. Then when he went out he drank even more, and he came home drunk every night. It went on like that for a few weeks. I asked him politely to cut it out. Then it got worse. He slept all day. He was out at night and came home at three in the morning. I told him again to stop. One night, it was three o'clock again, he came home singing 'The Argonne Forest at Midnight' beautifully though it was long past midnight, and he had three others with him. They brought him up the stairs. He couldn't make it by himself. Oh well, I thought, let well enough alone; as long as he's in bed everything will be all right. But the three others were women and naturally they smoked and laughed, and so on, and at half past five in the morning I politely asked the ladies to leave. But instead of answering me politely they were insolent and stayed. So I said: 'If you don't leave, I'm going to the University tomorrow and tell them all about it.' But they stayed and stank terribly of perfume. It made my head reel.

We weren't allowed to stink like that in my time.

I was trembling all over. I really wanted to go to the University and complain but then I thought to myself: it's no use slandering people right away. You've got to put up with certain things. After all, for that nice big room, almost 200 square feet, with warm water, gas heat, separate meter and toilet and separate entrance – I get 110 marks a month. All four rooms – the others are smaller – bring me in about 400 marks, and if I could lease my parents' lots, I'd actually be rich. My father went to work on the streetcar line although he had a small farm from my grandparents on my mother's side. He tended to it in the evening when he got home. My mother had about an acre of land when she married. Before that it was more, then when my mother married it was divided up. There were five brothers and sisters in all. That's where I got those lots. But as you might expect they don't bring in anything.

Nobody wants to work in the fields nowadays.

Until four years ago part of the land was farmed. But that has stopped entirely. The lots are going to the dogs. The weeds are four feet high. The peasants around here say farming doesn't pay any more. Seems to be because of the EWG.* Some of the peasants have sold their farms to housing developments. They themselves go to work in factories. Yes, that's how it is. You can't sell your land just like that. The government has to

---

Europäische Wirtschaftsgemeinschaft – E.E.C., i.e. The Common Market.

approve. Nobody knows why but that's how the government is. I think it wants the land for itself. But it pays only two marks a square foot, and a private buyer would give me four or five. So I'm biding my time until I can put one over on the government. Meanwhile I make out all right with the money I get from the students, though it means hard work. As you can see, all the rooms are kept nice and clean.

After all, I've had an education!

I went to grade school here, then I studied domestic science, oh yes, and I did very well! I loved school. Besides, they gave me a piano when I was six years old and I played the piano a good deal. My childhood and youth were wonderful. Young people came here to sing. And we played for them. Then I took quite a few trips to Switzerland and Italy. Yes, on my own. This year I'm going to Paris. I'm going to visit Monique. She invited me. I'm crazy about travelling.

If somebody came to me and said: 'Come with me to Chicago,' I'd just pack my bags.

I'd go to Hollywood too at the drop of a hat, or Mexico, it's all the same to me. Wherever I go it makes no difference to me what the people think and believe, or whether they're Christians or not. You see, I'm for tolerance. I was given a strict Catholic upbringing, but I believe in tolerance. Religion gave me a solid foundation. You've got to have principles to live by and I take my principles from religion. They are: open your eyes, stand fast wherever they put you, be just and honourable! And if certain people don't like my open-mindedness, I can't help it. The main thing is that I stand by the truth. That's why I've had quite a lot to put up with, but I always find some-thing to cheer me up. The world is full of things that can help revive your spirits. That's why I like to go to concerts once in a while when my heart lets me. Yes, I have heart trouble, had it for a few years. Sometimes it gets better and sometimes it gets

worse and worse. It gives me quite a lot of misery. Maybe I
won't last long, but the way I feel about it is: 'Thy Kingdom
come', which means, you've got to make what you can of yourself here on this earth. Yes, this earth. What a man makes of
himself, that's his kingdom. And it includes everything. My
great-aunt taught me that. She lived here in the house and at
the age of ninety she was still wild about politics. She followed
everything, she spoke a good deal, sometimes she said:

'You see, child, now the people are going to church again
and it's the others that make the politics.'

The right way is to go to church and think of politics too. I
read newspapers, I listen to radio commentators. In short,
I keep up with everything connected with politics. And I argue
about it with my friends. When we meet, we talk non-stop.
One says one thing, one says another, and each sticks to his
guns. Sometimes we sit in a beer hall and argue. It used to be
only peasants but today all sorts of people come. A peasant,
a prosecuting attorney, a lawyer; and then there's a mason that
comes and a couple of women like me – some married women
too, of course. I believe we're a rather special kind of group.
Anyway, we think so. That's why we get along so well even if
we stick to our own opinions, because we belong to the soil
here, and a lot of us used to be peasants, or at least our fathers.
Most of us still own some land. The people in the inner city
haven't any land any more.

A person with his own ground under his feet is different.
He's smarter from down below, it comes from the ground.

You could see that in connexion with Hitler. My father, for instance, was a smart, sober-thinking man. He soon saw what was
coming. A lot of people here knew. They knew that even if he
did away with unemployment he wouldn't be able to keep all
his promises about our not having to pay any taxes, and this
and that. I was arrested under the Nazis. It was because of my

religion. I was invited to a priest's twenty-fifth jubilee in a near-
by city. The celebration had been called off several times. The
mayor of the city at that time was a very young Nazi. All of a
sudden the celebration was authorized, and then they struck.
I went over on a Saturday and when I came into my relatives'
house they were all making long faces. 'What's the matter?'
I asked. 'The celebration has been called off again,' they told
me. 'And go take a look outside!' I went out and saw a lot of
signs: 'Put the Priests against the Wall!' 'Down with the Black
Scum!' 'Down with the Traitors to the Nation!'

And on the Church they'd written in big letters: 'Down with
you Calvary-Crawlers!'

That really wasn't nice. All the same we went to the church.
Afterwards, when I was back home and was just about to
leave for the city again – I had put my foot on the streetcar
step – someone called me by name. I looked around and saw a
young girl whom I didn't recognize at first. Until she said to
me: 'Why Edith, don't you know me any more?' 'Oh,' I said,
'You're Anne!' She'd been in America and now she was here
for a visit. She asked me: 'How are things going, what are you
doing?' etc. I told her. 'I witnessed a lovely scene yesterday;'
and then I told her the story about the black scum. That was a
big mistake. Anne went away and told the story around, and a
little while later I was arrested, taken to prison and sentenced.
They claimed I had made untrue, misleading assertions. If I
had said all that three months before, they couldn't have sentenced me. The law had just been made. They said the signs
had been put up by the Communists. Of course it wasn't true.
It was the National Socialists. It was obvious, and a lot of them
admitted they had done it. They even boasted about it. At the
trial they all laughed. I was sentenced to nine months. There
were a few hundred people in the prison and we were given
intelligence tests. The first question was: 'Who was Bismarck?'
I thought to myself: you'd better be on your guard, and I said:
'A statesman and a general.' Then came the second question:

'What does Hitler want?' 'To finish what Bismarck started,' I said.

The third question was: 'Where does the sun rise?' 'In the swastika,' I said.

At that time you kept seeing posters with the sun rising and there was a swastika in it. But a lot of people couldn't answer the question about where the sun rises, they didn't even know the right answer. There were smart people and stupid people, and some who were for and some who were against Hitler. ... Yes, many thought the same as I did, but a great many didn't. They were enthusiastic Nazis. My impression was that the people were simply dying for a change. The change was Hitler and the people liked him. The people didn't think enough. You've really got to think more. I'd been in Switzerland once. Those people are old democrats and they think a lot more than we do. I felt very good there. I feel good in all foreign countries, and then I remember my great-aunt who always said to me: 'Don't forget your home, remember you're living in a paradise.' I took those words very much to heart, so I always came home again. Now that the Nazi period is over it really is nice here. I was especially happy when the War finally came to an end and stopped costing human lives. That was the first thing, the second was we had to get a democracy, and then the Economic Miracle. It gave us a good deal and I can understand all the little people when for once they have a real opportunity and they make better money, and why shouldn't they take advantage? You can't blame a plain worker for that. And if he lives beyond his means, you can't blame him for that either.

All in all, I think our people have come to their senses and have sensible ideas.

The people are coming around. I always say: If you've got any sense, you won't get a swelled head. We've got to realize that

being German isn't everything and that we can't rule the world.
... That won't do! We've seen what comes of that kind of
wrong thinking. Now we're paying for it, we're divided and
there's Communism in East Germany. It's sad that Communism
had to come. Perhaps we weren't social-minded soon enough.
I've got to think of my great-aunt again. One time I went to
visit a castle with her and she said to me: 'Beautiful castle,
isn't it? But who built this castle? What hands? What kind of
people? They were all oppressed.' That's one thing about the
olden times that simply can't be glorified. Those slaves who
carried the stones and built the castle – how did they live? They
were poor devils, and the rich people gorged themselves in the
castle. In the old days there was no sign of social thinking.
That's what led to Communism over the years. People don't
think enough. The young biologist I have in the downstairs
room is very much interested in politics. The German philology
student up here not so much. I've got to rouse him up from
time to time. I ask him various questions. Sometimes he can't
answer them. Then I kid him a little and laugh at him, and that
get's us off to a good start. I'll teach him politics yet.

STEFAN STEIN
39, married, engineer

Everything was so nice and peaceful in Danzig in those days.

My father is from West Prussia. After the First World War his
home country became Polish and they were going to put him
in the Polish Army. So he went to the Free City of Danzig. As
a young girl my mother was a barmaid in my grandfather's
beer hall. He had a mill besides. All that was in the Vistula
Delta. The part of Danzig where my parents lived was called
Rabbit Bastion. A terrible name. When I had to say it in school,
everybody laughed. It was a former fortress, long buildings,
barracks-style. There were lots of children in the Bastion. I espe-

cially remember a little girl with big brown eyes. Around our house there were rounded concrete platforms covered over with grass. It was wonderful to play on them. Everything was so nice and peaceful in Danzig. Anyway, for us children. For my father, things were certainly different. I may as well tell you that he joined the Party in 1933 or 1934. The NSDAP was legal in Danzig. He didn't join the Party out of idealism, but for purely practical reasons. He had been unemployed for six years. And the Nazis had said: 'We'll see that you get work.' As far as I remember, you had to be a Party member to get any work with the municipality, and so my father became a petty official.

He joined the party in order to feed his wife and son.

We were never rich, but up to then we had lived in very straitened circumstances. For years my father made toys, you know, jig-saw work. And he sold them to a toy store. Of course the office that paid out the unemployment relief wasn't supposed to know that. I can still remember clearly: My father had a shelf with a curtain in front of it. He kept the toys and his tools behind the curtain. When the doorbell rang we had to take care that no one should come and see it. Once a supervisor came. She went around the apartment and we all stared in terror at the shelf, but she didn't open the curtain. You know, my father didn't think very much about where this Nazi business might lead politically. He's a simple man. During the War he distributed food cards and supervised the blackout. Little men are always needed. Let's say that he went along. I remember one thing, though: one day the Jews had to start wearing a yellow star and there was a Jew living in Rabbit Bastion. He was a very poor man, down and out. My father didn't know him well, he was just part of the street scene. He'd always lived there and I can still remember well that my parents were indignant. 'They really shouldn't molest the poor man like that. It's not right.' That's what they said. You couldn't say openly: 'Why must the Jew wear a star?' The people were afraid something

would happen to them. They always acted very mysterious
when such subjects came up, they always started whispering.
Anyone who was in the Party had to be especially careful or
they'd have arrested him as a traitor. I know myself how
strict it was. Toward the end of the War I was an anti-aircraft
auxiliary.

Günther Grass, the writer, was in the next battery

We're the same age. The front was coming closer and closer,
the teachers came out to us and gave us classes right on our
gun emplacements. Our school principal came out there too. He
taught Latin. We were reading something or other of Livy and
all of a sudden he said: 'We've got to hold together now, just
like the old Romans!' He tried to teach us the civic spirit that
had welded the Romans together. He was a very convinced
Nazi and a very hard man. Besides, we had a biology teacher.
He was a theology student who had gone wrong. He dragged
everything connected with the Church through the mud. He
knew all his Bible quotations by heart. He could start talking
about a radish and end up with some Bible quotation that he'd
reel off with a cynical twist; for instance: 'Let us make here
three tabernacles, one for me and one for thee and one for the
Jew Elias.' And then we had a history teacher, he was a
Himmler type. Always talking about the early Germans, children of nature. What men they were! Blond, blue-eyed, and the
muscles on them! He himself was just a little sausage. Physically he didn't exist. When he ran around in gym pants, oh my,
what a sight! And an insignificant face like Himmler. You had
to look at him ten times or you'd forget what he looked like.
And then – after we fled to West Germany, when the War was
over – I had a history teacher in Westphalia who was very sly.
He simply left the National Socialist period out of the programme. But naturally you can't dispose of problems by pre-
tending they don't exist. In my opinion we've got to look
realities in the face, for instance, the so-called problem of the
recognition or non-recognition of the Oder-Neisse frontier. I

believe that it's meaningless to keep talking about our legal rights. Being right won't get us anywhere. What good does it do us to maintain our claim to our Eastern territory including my native city of Danzig if it permanently impedes an understanding with the Eastern countries? It's perfectly obvious that if we don't drop our claim to the restoration of Germany's borders of 1937 we won't come to an understanding with Poland and the other Eastern countries before the next Ice Age. We can't negotiate over something we no longer possess.

As a refugee from Danzig I say we should recognize the Oder–Neisse frontier.

Of course it's easier for me to get over the loss of my homeland than for my parents who lived there longer. Not so long ago my mother was watching a television programme about Danzig. She recited the names of all the streets she saw. 'We used to go there often,' she said. 'And now we can't go there any more.' My father took it more calmly. My parents still remember the way they were driven out and the cruel reality of the Polish and Russian camps, and such memories affect them deeply. After the flight from Danzig my father had to start life all over again. He found a small position with the occupation troops in West Germany. I was aware of our financial situation and after graduating from high school I said: I'd better learn a trade before I do anything else, so I learned to be a mason. It wasn't until 1950 that I went to engineering school in Darmstadt. I studied construction engineering and took my degree. After graduating I soon found a job. First with a big construction company in Frankfurt am Main, then with a construction authority in Darmstadt, and then with a construction firm in Bad Mergentheim. But the small-town atmosphere made me feel terribly isolated and depressed. I was already married and neither my wife nor myself felt happy there. It was all so cramped. There was no intellectual stimulation.

A county town with 5,000 inhabitants. My God!

Of course there were also the resort people and now and then there's an orchestra at the Casino, but it's not very good. We felt that we were drying up intellectually. There were no interesting people to talk to. That's the main reason I left. Then I came here because I received an attractive offer from a firm of consulting engineers. I wouldn't go so far as to say that I'm happy on this job. I'd rather not speak too soon. I first have to see what life here has to offer that can supplement the daily grind of my work. Those are the things that give zest to life. My wife feels very happy here, the place suits her mentality, and I myself am gradually getting used to the city. There are many cultural possibilities. But it takes a while to get used to a town. You've got to get your bearings. That's what I'm trying to do now. You see, we have to build up a new circle of friends. We have to find congenial people. I've met a few people through my office and my wife has a few friends whom she knows through family connexions. My wife is from south-west Germany. The people there have something of a French tinge; they know how to live, they're not so beastly serious about everything. They take things more lightly. I mean, they're not always pondering, trying to get to the bottom of things and figure out what holds the world together; they let themselves live. But they're not incompetent, no, not at all. That's something that has always appealed to me in the Latin peoples, in Greece or Spain, for instance; those people know how to live. I myself am the deep-thinking type and in Spain and Greece I couldn't help noticing how very different I am from those people. I take too many things seriously that are utterly unimportant. One time a bootblack said to me: 'Well, now I've made so many pesetas, that will do for a while. Now we can live for three days.' And then he went to a tavern and drank wine. I could never be like that. I have a wife and two children. I'd never dare to say: 'Now I've made so much money, we can live for three months on that. Let's rest and take it easy for a while.' It's this planning mania, this constant thinking of the future. I'm not the only one, most Germans have it. In general, I think we don't adapt very well. For instance, we were travelling with a German tour. In Barcelona we went to a little restaurant and they showed us a Spanish menu.

Instantly some of the Germans exclaimed: 'What, no schnitzel?'

I felt like poking them in the jaw. You see, I'm divided against myself. Yes, I'm a German but I was really ashamed that those people were my compatriots. Yes, I've got to admit it. My first trip abroad was to France while I was still a student. It was to participate in a pilgrimage to Chartres organized by the Catholic Youth of Paris. We hiked from Paris to Chartres and I became very friendly with the young people in the pilgrimage. They weren't all French, there were also Greeks, Spaniards, Dutch and Italians. I've always enjoyed meeting people, on the lower level, so to speak, workers, young people, etc. I like to hear how other people think, how they live in their own country, their ideas about politics and so on. We had very interesting discussions and the whole encounter made a big impression on me. I've always tried to find out how other people live, to study their way of life and compare it with ours, and I'm firmly convinced that it's necessary to promote the idea of a united Europe, because it would be most fruitful for our continent. Because the qualities of the different European peoples could be joined to create a much richer European quality. I mean to do everything in my power to push this idea. What is the use of all the treaties between governments if such efforts are only made on the top level, and there's no real basis for understanding down below. A great deal of progress could be made if these things were pressed more intensively and the young Europeans of the different countries came closer together.

I should also welcome the inclusion of the Eastern European peoples in this Europe.

From what I've seen on television I feel that especially the Poles, Hungarians and Czechs belong to Europe just as much as we do, that they are really oriented towards the West. I don't believe that an all-European understanding or even the reunification of Germany is possible in the form in which we have thus far attempted – or rather not attempted – to achieve it. It won't work that way. The idea that our alliance with the West and the build-up of our power will convince the people in Moscow to give us back Central Germany strikes me as absurd. That is an insane idea. Absolutely unrealistic. I should say: we've got to recognize the realities of our frontiers for what they are and build up friendly relations with the Eastern countries. Only then can we realistically approach the idea of the reunification of Germany. I can conceive of it only in an all-European framework. I think de Gaulle has done well to bring up the all-European idea. He was the first man to say that Poland, Hungary, Rumania, etc., are also parts of Europe. Altogether, this question of reunification is a problem that can't be solved from above. In the last analysis our politicians ought to be the executors of the popular will, but here in Germany the people just wait for blessings to come from above.

In this country it doesn't even occur to people to do anything on their own initiative.

Take a small problem, for example. The streetcar line runs through one of the main business streets of our city. Trying to shop there is almost intolerable. For one thing, because the streetcar almost sweeps you off the sidewalk. For another, because of the terrible stench of gasoline. The sidewalks are barely six feet wide. If I were a businessman I'd play with the following idea: all the shopkeepers ought to be interested in closing this street to heavy through-traffic. Conclusion: away with the streetcar! Away with automobiles! All the shopkeepers ought to get together and raise this demand. I've never read a word in the newspaper about any shopkeeper suggesting it. In England or America that would certainly happen. People would join together for common action. But in our country each man envies the next the bread on his plate. And at the same time there's always so much talk about civic spirit. People keep saying that something must be done on the lower level but, as I was saying, in our country people just keep waiting for the blessings to come from above. This reliance on authority is a universal German quality. It can't just be a question of mentality, it must also come from our education. I believe that if the school system were changed and if parents began to be more sensible, there might be a change in the general mentality. But that's the whole trouble: with us there's no communication between the government and the individual citizen. Perhaps because our democratic institutions are not old enough, because participation in government power and positive criticism on the part of the opposition are things people just have to get used to. Perhaps it's also because up to now the government hasn't bothered to make it clear to people what rights they have in a democracy. Too little has been done to enlighten the citizen. Look at our elections. On the radio I always hear them saying: 'It was a beautiful Sunday, fine sunny weather.' See what I mean? That accounts for the big election turnout.

What kind of an attitude is that toward a basic democratic right if the election turnout depends on whether it's raining or the sun is shining?

At first we had a dictatorship and now we have a democracy. If it is to endure we must make an effort to turn it into a real component of our thinking. Take a look at this NPD, I mean the susceptibility of the Germans to extremist ideas without rational content. A little group of that kind can always create a stir and unfortunately the bulk of our people give them too little thought. This awful political apathy. The people just say to themselves: We voted for Adenauer, then we voted for Erhard, and then we voted for Kiesinger, so they could attend to politics for us. That's what I mean by reliance on authority. There's too little political commitment. All the people think of is their business. When I look at our political parties critically, I can perfectly well understand that a portion of our citizens are disinclined to vote for any of these parties, because they're not satisfied with the men who are offered. I can understand that, but even so, I think the citizens ought to realize that the things of this world are imperfect and that it's necessary for political reasons to make up one's mind in favour of one party or another. I can't see why so many people say: 'No, I don't care for any of them. That's why I vote for the NPD, though they have no programme, though all they do is shout, and they're incompetent.' That's a half-baked, purely emotional reaction. Those people simply don't switch on their reason. It horrifies me when I think how many of my acquaintances, even doctors and lawyers, say that it might not be a bad idea to vote for the NPD.

Human beings are imperfect. And not only the Germans.

You see, even Lenin failed to recognize human imperfection and to incorporate it in his thinking. He believed that man can be educated until he becomes a superman. That is not possible in this world. Marx already made the mistake of exaggerating the possibility of transforming man. By progress the Communists always mean an improvement, but the correct meaning of progress is motion from one place to another. But that does not necessarily mean greater well-being. Do you believe that people were less happy in the Middle Ages? No, they were not at all conscious of their situation, they took it for granted. Measured by present-day conditions, they would probably have said: yes, this is better. But how would we feel in comparison to what the world will be in a hundred years? We don't know. Perhaps if we knew and understood what the world will be like in a hundred years we should feel unhappy by comparison. But since we do not know, we content ourselves with the present day. I don't

believe that men have become better over the years. I believe
that they have stayed the same and if you look at the history
of mankind you always find the same weaknesses of character, regardless whether it's the Ptolemies, the ancient Egyptians,
the Greeks or the Romans or the Middle Ages. With the exception of the Communists, almost all men have believed up to
now that they cannot exist without a higher being.

I for my part in any case can't conceive of a man who could
live without religion, without some relation to a trans-
cendent world.

I regard the question of the spiritual source and aim of man as
the central question. With the answer to this question we establish, so to speak, the axis of our system of coordinates, from
which all values draw their relevance. In the Christian view,
only God can be this axis. If we decide in favour of a relation
to God, then we are under obligation to make a lasting effort,
to put all our energies and powers actively behind the fulfil-
ment of God's fundamental law, and that in the last analysis
is: 'Love thy neighbour as thyself!' This endeavour must not
be forced on us by the fear of fire and brimstone – though of
course we must take evil very seriously – but must result from
a free decision to subordinate our human will to the divine will.
When I think about it, I believe that here the circle closes between 'thy will be done' and 'thy kingdom come,' the connexion between which is evident. Only through a determined
struggle to affirm the divine will, harsh as it may sometimes
seem to us, can we come nearer to the kingdom of God. This
struggle, it seems to me, must last a whole lifetime – until, as
St Augustine said, the restless human heart finds its way back
to its source. A Christian must realize that his religion is sym-
bolized by the Cross, and the Cross is a stern symbol which
makes a claim upon the whole man. I seem to be talking like a
priest, but I believe that all this means nothing to the pietistic
souls who keep their faith burning low in the farthermost
corner of the sacristy; it can mean something only to men who

take the divine commandments seriously and declare the most relentless war on their own egoism. I believe that the endeavour to love our neighbour and the struggle against egoism are the most difficult tasks confronting man. All those human actions that are rooted in a basic attitude of love of others bear the mark of real human greatness. Without outgoing love man becomes entangled in senseless egocentricity.

DR WERNER PAULSEN

32, unmarried, chemist, member of the NPD

History has always been my favourite subject.

I come from Westphalia. My father was a regional *Landrat.** After the War he remained in office for a short time, then he was pensioned. My whole family both on my mother's and my father's side comes from Westphalia. My father comes from a family of civil servants, my mother of the lower middle class. Her father was a carpenter. As early as my school days, in high school, I had narrowed my choice of career down to two possibilities. I wanted to become either a scientist, as I actually have become, or a historian. History has always been my favourite subject. I still take an interest in it and have attended many lectures on history and philosophy. My main reason for not specializing in history was that even in school I recognized the extreme relativity of all views of history. That is why I turned to the opposite, namely to science, where I thought I would be dealing with the absolute truth. But today, after extensive study, I must say that in my opinion the absolute truth has become very relative in natural science as well. It was a mistake on my part to suppose that I could investigate the truth in this field and find out the truth about life. All the same I mean to keep on with my research. I am very much interested

---

*The highest rank of executive civil servant.

in organic chemistry. Besides, the field has a great future. Also, I make good money and am able to live decently. I am in roughly the same wage group as a school principal, that is, I gross 1,400 marks a month. I completed my studies here and have been here since 1958. Unfortunately! Oh, I like this town pretty well because of its great cultural opportunities. But I don't care for the mentality of the population. I happen to be a North German and North German mentality is very different. Anyway, I have that impression. I have few friends among the native population. And what with my frequent trips home I've kept in pretty close touch with the people back there. I'm sure I'll go back to North Germany in the end.

What bothers me most about the people here is that they're too expansive.

You make friends quickly but lose them quickly too. With us at home it's different. There you have fewer friends, it's hard to make them, but the friends you have you keep for a long time. Here everything changes much more quickly. You could say that the people are more friendly. Well, anyway, there are lots of North Germans in the institute where I work. That gives us a kind of compensation. I've found good friends among my fellow-workers. A number of them have the same ideas on many subjects and the same interests. But I also have close friends in other circles. I myself was in a youth movement, I still like to hike, and I know quite a number of people here from my youth movement. I'm also in touch with many of the youth groups here. They include both young people and people of my own age, former members of youth groups. In 1963 there was a big celebration of the fiftieth anniversary of the Federal Youth Movement, on the Hohen Meissner. The youth groups reformed and established an organization parallel to the Federal Youth Ring. But we take a rather different view of youth work. Our idea is not that the young people should be taken in hand by adults, but that youth work should be done by the young people themselves. As a rule the youngsters are led by men only three or four years older than themselves. The German youth movement is split up into innumerable small organizations, because a group of friends can only operate on a small scale. At first, after the War, the Federal Youth Movement took no political position. But in 1963 on the Hohen Meissner the word went out that the young people ought to take an interest in politics. They were told to engage in discussion but steer clear of party politics, and every effort is made to keep party politics out of the youth groups. I am speaking of non-voters up to the age of eighteen.

Students show far too little interest in politics.

At least they haven't got the kind of interest I should like to see. I should like to see the young people concern themselves a little with politics, form a picture of the political situation, read more newspapers and attend party meetings. I'd like to see them enter into political life earlier than they do and think more nationally than is the case today. The schools don't do enough in that direction. Most schools have instruction in current events and civics. But in my opinion this instruction is too formal. It's not enough to teach the formal aspect of government. That's no introduction to living democracy. They learn the forms of democracy by heart, but that is no real practical instruction in democracy and it doesn't appeal to children. I have the impression that the young people lack ideals and models to look up to.

What impressive figure is there among our leading politicians?

They concern themselves much too little for example with reunification in connexion with the Eastern states and our Western allies, with the question of how it might be possible for the nations to live together in a united Europe. But the young people are very interested in this question. I am convinced that there will be reunification, perhaps not in the next five years, but I don't think it will be more than fifteen. Very generally speaking, I believe that nothing is so changeable as the facts of history. We've seen that in Germany. In a short time the historical situation can change completely. It is possible, for instance, that a conflict will break out some day between Russia and China, and it seems to me that in this case the Russians may find it desirable to have peace and quiet here in the West and would be willing to pay a price for it: that price would be the reunification of Germany. Of course the Russians won't give in to the Chinese without a fight even though the Chinese are right about their territorial demands in the East. There's bound to be a conflict and if the Russians have to fight the Chinese they'll find it very inconvenient to have someone here in the West who has demands to make on them and is prepared to exploit any trouble the Russians are having, no, not by war, but ... well, the ways and means will be found. Today I can't tell you exactly what they will be but the future will show.

I know that the Communist danger in the West is very much underestimated.

In the last few years I've been in the East Zone several times and I've spoken with a lot of people. Including students in Leipzig, etc. The young people over there go along only because they have to. They're not a serious danger. The percentage of young people who are really convinced Communists is not very high and never will be. But the young people in the East Zone are much more national-minded than in the West. I definitely have that impression. By national I mean that they feel even more strongly about the division of Germany, that it's even harder for them to bear than it is for the young people in West Germany, who are hardly aware of the division.

They do much more over there to promote a national consciousness.

Over there, for instance, the War of Liberation and the Prussian heroes of the day are again being glorified. Over here you'll find such things at most in the youth movement, for instance in the Federal Youth Leagues with which I actively collaborate. Not as a group or youth leader, of course, but as an organizer of seminars and get-togethers. We discuss all the topics and problems of the day. The alliance between the SPD and the CDU, for example; the Great Coalition. This strikes us as unfortunate from a democratic point of view. We don't like the idea of two groups coming together which were vigorously combating each other only a short time ago. Many of us think that such a union is dishonest, dishonest towards the voters. Because what the SPD people really want is an SPD government.

But now we have a new party, the NPD.

The NPD is not a union of the former small right-wing groups and parties, it is composed of the DRP (*Deutsche Reichspartei* – German Reich Party), the *Gesamtdeutsche Partei* (All-German Party), the FDP (*Freie Demokratische Partei* – Free Democratic Party), the BHE (*Bund der Heimatvertriebenen und Entrechteten* – League of those who have been driven from their homes and disenfranchised), and many individuals who have never belonged to any party. Both in Germany and abroad the NPD is accused of being a Nazi party. This is not true. If it were true, I would not be standing before you as its representative. As a proof to the contrary I can say that many young people in the NPD belong to a generation who had not reached the age of reason in the Nazi period. It's these young people who do most of the party work. They couldn't have been Nazis. We're accused of having Nazis in our party, but the same can be said of the CDU. The Chancellor himself was a Party member. Our critics always forget to speak of those people in our party who never were party members. They forget to say that Herr von Thadden, for example, is one of our leaders, and that he was even persecuted by the Nazis. Most of our present membership never belonged to the NSDAP.

We can point out today that the percentage of Nazis in our party leadership is no greater than that in the population at large.

Besides, the younger generation who had nothing to with all that is strongly represented in our ranks. And another thing: the NPD is not an ideological party. The NPD points this out over and over again. It has no desire to provide an ideology. A political programme must be based on practical considerations. You've got to take one line today and another tomorrow. Politics is always changing. But the parties that have been in a leading position up to now do not recognize this. They don't work nearly enough for reunification. One of our main points of attraction is that the NPD comes out – and above all that it comes out convincingly – for reunification and recognition of the right to home rule for the Oder-Neisse territory. In my opinion, that should be the government programme. Of course the other parties still advocate reunification, but unconvincingly. Especially abroad we often hear it said that their declared policy is unconvincing because leading members of all the main parties have come out against it, and the population know it, or sense it at any rate. And today when the NPD says that it favours reunification and is also unwilling to renounce our claim to Eastern Germany and the Sudetenland, the people know it's the only party that means what it says. This in my opinion is one of the main reasons for the drawing power of the NPD. See here: the President of the Federal Republic said only recently that we would probably not be able to avoid recognizing the Oder-Neisse frontier. That in my opinion is a completely wrong statement. It shows what Lübke really wants and in my opinion such a man is out of place as a chief of state. The NPD is honest and objective and its objectivity is another thing that attracts a large part of the youth, especially when they see that a section of the press is not objective towards the NPD. From the very start the press has taken a distorted view of the NPD and the result is that every well-intentioned person gets a false impression.

Easy does it. Gradually we are overcoming the prejudices against the NPD.

We are beginning to win people to our cause. Big periodicals such as *Christ und Welt* and *Die Zeit* have now written very objective accounts and made it clear that the NPD is not fascist. We hope the general opinion will soon change. I have spoken with many young people who formerly tried to attain their aims in other parties, as I did myself. But the aims of the political parties are largely unconvincing. The energies of youth are simply led astray. They can't make themselves felt. For the first time the NPD gives us younger men the possibility of active participation. In the large parties the younger men have little chance of putting their ideas over. Our principal aim remains reunification. The CDU and SPD conception of reunification is unconvincing. If someone wants to come out for reunification in those parties, he may be able to gain a hearing in the lower party organs but this impetus can never carry to the top and will not be reflected in party policy.

Reunification is one of our political demands. The recovery of the East German territories on the other side of the Oder and Neisse is another.

It would be ideal if we could put through both demands at once. Probably a small reunification, that is, reunification with the East Zone will come first. No one is asking the Poles to leave the eastern German territories. No one wants the Poles to be driven out, the ideal would probably be coexistence. Today, considerably fewer people live in the eastern German territories than at the time of German rule before the War. Not even a third as many, I believe, if I am well informed; I am speaking of Silesia, East Prussia and East Pomerania. The same density of population could be achieved as before the War, or at least two thirds of it. In other words, perhaps six million Germans could settle there. With modern methods the country ought to be able to support even more people. I believe we might con-

vince the Poles that they can live with Germans without any
fear of our wanting to throw them out some day. Yes, I think
so. Our relations with France have also changed considerably in
the course of time, over the last twenty years. For a long time
France was a mortal enemy and now it is a friend. Through frequent visits and tourism the population on both sides have
found out that the other fellow is not as we imagined and as he
was described in propaganda. That's bound to happen some day
with the eastern European countries. It's already beginning
with Czechoslovakia. I was very glad when travel to Prague
was made easier. Many Federal Germans go there and the
Czechs have an entirely different picture of Germans than formerly. The same thing might happen with Poland. Of course
the DDR is a dam between the Poles and ourselves and for
that reason our first goal is to diminish the barriers between the
Federal Republic and the DDR. In my opinion far too little
is done by the citizens of West Germany to overcome these
barriers. Many more West Germans could go over there to
Leipzig, and so on. There are all sorts of trade fairs over there.
All these offer an opportunity to encourage visits.

The other parties only talk and that is why so many of our
people realize that those parties have no real interest in
reunification.

People will come to see more and more who it is that really
champions these interests, who really thinks and feels
nationally. Take it from me, all sorts of changes are possible in
history.

ELISABETH WERNECKE

29, divorced, telephone operator

When she was a baby they put schnapps in her bottle every time she cried.

My mother was an illegitimate child. Who her father was I don't know. My grandmother didn't want my mother when she was little and sent her away to foster-parents, though there was plenty of money because her father was a rich manufacturer. He made window-frames and things like that. The factory was in Hamburg. I can't understand my grandmother's attitude. My mother still mills over it. The foster-parents she was sent to were awful people. When she was a baby, they put schnapps in her bottle every time she cried. Finally the public welfare people interfered and took her to other foster-parents who were supervised by the public welfare department. They were very simple people. The foster-father was a cabinet maker. But they were very nice, they took good care of my mother. It doesn't make any difference what class people come from or what they do. There are good people and bad people wherever you look. My grandmother wasn't a real woman. Thank goodness, my mother's entirely different. She's had a lot of bad luck, with my father too. He's left us. He's on the Czech border now. Their marriage wasn't harmonious. My father's a sick man. He has atrophy of the brain, I think that's what it's called.

He flares up over every trifle. But he can sit in the corner for hours reading a newspaper.

I often thought: 'Good God, there can't possibly be any more in it.' But he just went on reading and reading and reading. He probably barricaded himself behind the newspaper to keep us from talking to him. He didn't want to have anything to do with us. Before the War he worked for the Public Welfare

Department. Now he's a customs inspector. He lives all by himself in a furnished room. He's been on the Czech border for
three years and doesn't want me to visit him. When I send him
something for Christmas or his birthday he hardly answers.
Since he left, my mother has been working. She's a secretary in
the Municipal Construction Office. Father doesn't send her
enough to live on. Thank goodness, we're all making money.
My brother's in the customs too, on the Swiss border. He's married. So is my sister. They're doing fine. They're getting along
all right, they have love, and they have security. . . . Pity, really,
what happened to my father. . . . You see, he had to change his
profession because he'd been in the Party. It made a lot of
trouble for him. He wasn't a real Nazi, anyway not 100 per
cent. He liked a lot of things about the Nazis but he was
opposed to other things. He liked the way from one day to the
next there was no unemployment. He liked the Party the way
it was then.

But then when the War broke out he thought it was too
much.

But otherwise . . . I don't know how to put it. My relations with
my father weren't very good. We never discussed such things
very much. He talked more with my brother. He's three years
older. He didn't talk much with us girls altogether. He was a
better father for boys. When the War was lost all I heard him
say was: 'They asked for it.' He had to leave the government
service. We had to move out of our apartment and after that
all five of us lived in one room. For a long time my father
couldn't find work. We all had to struggle for our daily bread,
for our bare lives. My brother went out to work. He took anything that came along. Odd jobs. As a gardener, or anything
that came up. It was all terrible. Before that, up to the end of
the War, we had a whole floor in a four-family house. I went to
kindergarten, and the teacher was a very nice lady. I always
called her Auntie Strotthodel. She had some funny name like
that, that I couldn't pronounce. I still think of her fondly.

Maybe she wasn't a modern woman; she was a little old-fashioned, the way kindergarten teachers are, but very sweet.

She lived only a block away from us. I went there regularly. Those were happy days. Until we moved to Beethovenstrasse. Auntie Strotthodel wasn't there any more, but the attic was fixed up for us children. We were able to play there in bad weather. We played with old clothes and old dolls, we built our own dolls' theatre. Oh, I can still smell the wood in that attic. I had a doll that I called Auntie Strotthodel and she always played the leading parts in my plays. That was my little fairy-tale world. Later in school I got very bad marks because I was always dreaming about it, and about my Auntie Strotthodel. Well, after the eighth year I left. There were only eight school years at that time. Then I looked like mad for an apprentice job. I wanted to be a hairdresser but it couldn't be done. At that time it was desperately hard to find work. That was in 1950, two years after the currency reform. I've always liked to fix people's hair. I still do. I sometimes do my sister's hair or my mother's. I can't really explain why I was so eager at that time to work for a hairdresser.

Maybe it was only on account of the customers, to be among people.

Yes, that may have been it. But when I couldn't find anything I finally went to work for a florist. It was a hard apprenticeship. I was only fourteen when I started in and I was very much underweight. My God, what I went through! I'd only been there a week when a man came around to call for some wreaths. My boss told me to give the gentleman a hand with them. So I carried two wreaths and the gentleman had another, and it was so far I thought we'd never get there. Finally we got to the East Cemetery and went into the mortuary. He opened the door and then he stood beside an eighty-year-old woman who was dead, and began to wail: 'There she lies, my darling, my angel.' And I stood trembling behind him, holding my two wreaths until he came and took them away from me. Then of course I ran away, straight across the cemetery. I had only one thought: to get out of there. I'd never seen a dead person before. It was a bad time.

We often had to decorate coffins.

After that my boss came along. I must admit he was very understanding. At that time I was very scary. At first he let me stand outside the mortuary and I passed the things in to him. I stayed as far away as possible, so I wouldn't have to look in. Then he said: 'Come a little closer. I can't reach so far.' So I had to come closer. Then I had to lay the flowers against the legs. And that's how it went. For years I didn't go into the mortuary alone. They're awful little rooms. Everything so cramped. Barely room to reach around the coffin. It depressed me terribly. Only one door and everything so narrow, and the smell! I said the Lord's Prayer over and over again: 'Thy will be done, in earth as it is in heaven.' And I thought that one day I'd be lying there like that, so cold and pale. And then I prayed: 'Thy kingdom come . . .' and my only consolation and my only hope was that the dead people would go to heaven and I would too some day. I felt that way especially when it was children. I saw dead children, of all ages. They all looked so sweet. And then I thought: 'Oh well, who knows what they had in store for them, and now they're up in heaven.' That was my consolation. A lot of my work was at the cemetery. It was physically hard work too. When I got home in the evening I could hardly move. I carried the big wreaths in an old hand cart with squeaky wheels. As an apprentice I was paid 45 marks a month the first year, 55 the second year and 60 the third year. After I had finished my apprenticeship it was 125 marks, I think. Then I went to a larger shop in town where I only had to decorate corpses very seldom. And when we did have to make wreaths it was great big ones that cost from three to five hundred marks. That was nice. We didn't have to skimp on the flowers the way we did for poor people, and we could work according to our own tastes. There was a big difference between funeral arrangements, depending on the class the people came from. If it was someone from the upper classes, they put a silk cloth over him. You didn't see any legs. If it was poor people, well, then they weren't covered. They lay in the coffin in their shirts or suits. It was so awful. Their stiff arms and legs stick out and you've got to cover them. As a makeshift to keep it from looking so terribly empty we used cheap pine branches. You know, the more you see of that kind of thing, the less afraid of death you are. A few years ago I was much more afraid. I couldn't even think of it without my breath catching. Maybe I cared too much about life.

But then with my divorce I went through so much that I realized life isn't worth so much after all.

Sometimes it's better to be dead. The divorce didn't seem necessary to me. It began with his kayak. That was his hobby. I didn't enjoy it, but I joined in. We'd been married over seven years. The kayak craze went on all through the years and got worse and worse. First we went out on little rivers that were really charming and nice. But then it got harder and harder. We shot rapids. It's organized in six stages according to difficulty. I managed all right on the first three stages. But after that I was scared stiff. My fear got worse and worse and finally I fell out of the boat. It was in a mountain stream in southern France. The water was full of rocks and I kept bumping into them.

My whole body burned and right in the middle of it fear sat like a lump . . .

I kept trying to tell my husband that I couldn't stand it, that I was beside myself with fear. But his kayak craze got worse and worse. I tipped over in the boat another time. I couldn't get out. I thrashed around desperately, it was in a mill-stream

full of whirlpools and when I was finally driven out of the boat
and came up, I was all blue. And every other colour. And so it
went on over the years until I couldn't help see that there was
no understanding. A lot of times he sat there writing lectures
about how to handle a kayak for the club he belongs to. He
sat in his room for hours and for hours I sat all alone. Take a
walk once in a while? Oh no! I felt very much alone and slowly
but surely we moved apart. Then came the divorce. At first, of
course, it was terribly hard, although we didn't part in anger.
Neither of us wanted that. I was really desperate at the idea
that we might meet on the street and not speak to each other.
It seems to me that people should forgive each other up to a
certain point. After all, we're all of us only human. Besides,
you've got to try to understand him. His home life wasn't good.
His mother is divorced and she's not the domestic type. She
didn't love him. She didn't even pay for his education. He was
only able to go to engineering school because his grandmother
gave him money. When his mother darned his socks or washed
his shirts now and then, she always faithfully wrote down how
much it cost, and I don't think a mother should do that. I have
no patience with such behaviour. In my opinion she was no
good. Those things make a big difference. Well, now it's all
over with. I've been divorced almost a year. First I went to
work in a flower shop again, but the work was too hard for me.
Always lifting those heavy vases. And then I got terrible chil-
blains in my feet because it was so cold, especially in the winter
when I had to handle frozen fir branches. I had abdominal
trouble and then I gave it up and went to work in a publishing
house. First I was in the shipping department but there were
too many women, I didn't like it. Some of them were so
common.

You can't imagine the way women talk when they're among
themselves.

The things they talk about! Who's sleeping with who, when
and how often. That kind of thing. You don't believe me. And

always bickering. I've often said that I'd rather work on a job with all men than with so many women. I couldn't stand it any more, and then my boss suggested the switchboard. It's very strenuous too, always so wild and hectic. But what I like is the contact with the customers and the people who call up. I recognize some of them by their voices. Some of them sing out 'hello', or 'hi', or 'it's me', and then I know: aha, it's Herr Schubert or Herr Waldorf, and so on. I have to keep accounts of all the subscriptions of the magazines and check all the books that are sent out, and sometimes it's too much. Some evenings when I leave I feel as if I'd been stepped on. I don't feel really normal until I've changed my clothes at home: slacks and sweater and the radio running. I don't want to see or hear anything else, I'm afraid it might give me gloomy thoughts, because I'm still gnawing on my troubles.

I've given up nearly all my friends because they were also friends of my husband.

It's true I've found a few new friends but not as many as before. Sometimes on week-ends I go to the theatre or to a concert. Usually I have somebody to go with me. The last few week-ends friends have taken me out. We've gone to different places. It's helped me a good deal to get out a little. Before that I went with a girl friend, she has a lot of problems too. She's a good friend but a little slow and right now I need someone I don't have to amuse but who amuses me. Of course that's rather hard to find among men. Usually they want more and you've got to put the brakes on. In such cases I just say: I've got someone. I'm not ready for it yet. There's no point in thinking about such things right now. Most of them don't take it very well. They come around again once or twice more and then it's finished. I hope I'll find somebody who had real understanding, somebody I can make a nice life for. It's not very easy. Maybe I'm too domestic for most men, not modern enough in my ways.

A lot of them want too much right away; they want everything so quickly.

In the old days maybe things didn't go as fast as they do now. Maybe you had a chance to really get acquainted. Maybe it all comes from the illustrated magazines, all this sex. That's the whole trouble. This sex frenzy is just as repugnant in women as in men. When a man can get anything he wants wherever he goes, he thinks it's got to be like that. I hope these things gradually get back to normal. There's been too much prosperity. Everybody wanted more and more and it got worse every year. But things will have to get back to normal some time. If only the people don't get dissatisfied and start voting for a crazy party like the NPD or some other extremists. Lately I've listened to election speeches over the radio, no one in particular, I can't tell you any names. But it was simply dreadful. Everything laid on so thick, so wild and hectic: 'I am right, I, I and nobody else!' Each one shouted his head off and argued his point of view. I thought – it's true I was too little then – but I thought: 'That's what the Nazis must have been like.' After I'd listened to those speeches on the radio I tried to talk about it to people but no one really reacted. They all clammed up. It seemed to me that they were all afraid of saying something wrong. That's something I don't understand. I can express my opinion, no one can punish me for it, I've got to be able to talk about it. But somehow it upset people to have me bring up the topic. So naturally I dropped it. It's funny, but I just can't seem to understand . . .

EDUARD BENDER

70, unmarried, officer in the Imperial Army, architect, officer in the Reichswehr, construction engineer, economist, bank official, officer in the Wehrmacht, financial adviser

In the course of the First World War I gradually moved pretty far to the left.

When I was young I wanted as far as possible not to be in the thick of the mêlée but a little above it. But the years that lie behind me have been very turbulent for us Germans and a good many things have turned out differently from what I originally expected. Just as I finished school and was planning to study engineering as my father wished, the First World War broke out. I had been in the Youth Movement, it was started before 1914, you know. Perhaps for that reason, but also because of the attitude of my father and grandfather who had both been soldiers, I volunteered though I was very young, and soon became an officer. I can tell you this much: one of my motives at the time was a certain enthusiasm that I shared with a great many young men. I felt that Germany had been attacked and that the Fatherland had to be defended. That feeling was very strong in me; it was a product of the ideas that were then inculcated in school and everything I had heard at home. I joined the Engineers because that appealed to me, partly from the professional standpoint. After being seriously wounded several times, the last time shortly before the end of the War, I realized that my military career was at an end, and after the War I took up the study of architecture. Probably because I must have had a hidden artistic streak and now suddenly it made itself felt. Then something happened. Because I had received a high military distinction they were determined to take me back into the Army. I was approached by the recruiting office and asked if I didn't want to put on uniform again. I let them persuade me, though I had become rather sceptical because I

no longer had the same attitude towards the Fatherland as in
1914. The Fatherland was still there, but I had the impression
that everything wasn't really as we'd been told in school and at
the beginning of the War. I was gradually losing the – let's say
the usual national attitude, and moving pretty far to the left.
Mostly it was certain conversations I had with the soldiers of
all kinds who were under me that convinced me that my old
way of looking at things was not necessarily right. Nevertheless I went back to the Army and I played a not inconsiderable
role in organizing the officers' corps of the 100,000-man Army.
After completing this task I went to work for the so-called
Office of the Inspector of Weapons and Equipment in Berlin.
My parents were living in Berlin at the time, though my father
was from the Rhineland and my mother had been born in
Schleswig-Holstein. I stayed in the Reichswehr until 1924. I was
one of the first seven officers to attend engineering school at
government expense. I shifted over again, from architecture to
construction engineering. I studied economics on the side and
I graduated before leaving the Reichswehr in 1924. But
somehow it came out at the Charlottenburg Engineering
School that this student in civilian clothes was really an Army
man, and that led to political difficulties which made me decide,
with the consent of my superiors, to resign from the Reichswehr. Perhaps it wasn't quite so radical in Charlottenburg in
those days, but still it was a little like the so-called Free University in Berlin today. The wind was blowing from the Left.
But a man has to live, so there was nothing else for me to do
but look around for a civilian job, and since economically the
times were not of the best, I first went to work for the muni-
ficent sum of fifty marks a month. First as assistant director in
an industrial concern, then in a bank and then in a commercial firm. If only to acquire some practical experience. Meanwhile, it's true, I was beginning to make better money. After
what I'd seen in the years from 1914 to 1924, I said to myself that it might be better to look for a branch where I could
make my way more quietly, and I also thought business would
offer me better prospects than engineering, and the future has

borne me out. Business gave me an opportunity to see the world and I can say without fear of exaggeration that I made ample use of the opportunity. As long as it was in any way possible I visited at least one foreign country every year in order to pursue my economic studies.

It is probably in the German character to attach more importance to appearance than to reality.

My first acquaintance with other people was through the War. But now I was able to see them under normal conditions. That probably caused another change in my way of looking at things. I discovered that we Germans are not the only people endowed with abilities, and I also learned that when we go abroad we shouldn't make a big noise as, I'm sorry to say, you still see Germans doing today. I hardly dare express my opinion on the subject, but it's probably in the German character to attach more importance to appearance than to reality. Probably even earlier, but certainly under the Third Reich, it was drummed into people, especially the young people, that we were the best people in Europe, if not in the world, which in my opinion is definitely not true. I can't say for sure whether the young people today still feel that way about it, but perhaps I can give you an idea of what I mean.

The young people today are interested mostly in a comfortable life.

After I'd been doing well again economically for a few years, I decided to take three sons of fallen war comrades under my protection and to provide for their future. I sent them to the university and I believe all three of them bring out my point. Well, the first came to me from the East Zone in 1947 at the age of seventeen and I saw him through his high-school examination. Today he has an excellent position in Switzerland and is married. The second is the one I had the highest hopes for. I sent him to law school. He's the most gifted in my opinion, but, I'm sorry to say, he has been a disappointment to me. The third is now in his fourth semester of law in Munich. What he will amount to I can't say. Strange to say, he is more interested at present in theology than in law. All I am trying to say is this: there's no doubt that up to a certain point the young people of today want to accomplish something in the world and are not merely interested in a comfortable life with a big car, a television set, and so on. Nevertheless, it seems to me that none of the three has any ideals. It doesn't bother them, but it does me. I've discussed the matter a good deal with them, because after all my intention was to set them an example and show them a course of life they might follow – of their own free will, of course. I personally have the feeling that a good many of the young people today feel rather abandoned. I don't mean that they are necessarily looking for ideals; I only mean that I feel they have a certain feeling of emptiness. From above, on the part of the government I mean, very little has been done in a long time to inspire any sort of ideals. Here's something that might interest you in this connexion. When my second foster-son was in the graduating class at school, all his class-mates were opposed to the Bundeswehr. About a year later, just before they came up for their examinations, I learned to my great astonishment that almost three quarters of them were in favour of the Bundeswehr. The reason for the shift seems to be that a teacher whom they very much liked had influenced them in that direction. As far as I can tell, nothing much had been done by their parents to arouse enthusiasm for the Bundeswehr, and none of my three young men had been a soldier for so much as a single day. The third intimated to me recently that he definitely wanted to postpone his examination until a certain date, after which they wouldn't be able to draft him. The first no doubt has been kept away from the Bundeswehr by the fact that he enjoys his job abroad and is making good money. In the case of the second, the main deterrent seems to be girls; he thinks he has to devote a great deal of time to them. None of the three or any of their friends has been deterred from serving in the Bundeswehr by the thought that it's the army of one half of Germany and that there's another German army in the other Germany. That might have been a reasonable argument. All three come from the East Zone and all three still have ties over there, and I myself lived in the Zone, in Jena, just before coming here. I served again in the Second World War, and I wanted to go to Jena when I was discharged, but an American officer who was friendly to me persuaded me not to go to Jena but to Giessen. He knew the Americans were going to pull out of Jena two days after my discharge and that the Russians were coming in, and he didn't want me to fall into the hands of the Russians. To tell you the truth, I had got to know the Russians well before the War.

In 1932 I wanted to see the Communist homeland.

At that time the Nazis put me on a blacklist because I'd taken a trip across Russia, from Leningrad to Moscow and on down to the Black Sea. I wrote articles about it which apparently displeased certain people. I wanted to see the Communist homeland. But I also wanted to take a look at economic conditions there. I went there camouflaged as a journalist. They let me in with nine real journalists, some of whom I knew, and under the usual supervision we managed to see quite a lot. We were among the first to visit Russia under the auspices of 'Intourist'. I remember that in every city we were met at the station or the boat landing by some male or female and weren't able to see much by ourselves, so it was difficult to make contact with the population. We only had one opportunity. In Leningrad we decided to take a trip out in the country and they gave us cars whose drivers were undoubtedly security guards. And just as we were in the vicinity of the Putilov plant, the enormous Russian Krupp combine, one of our two cars had a breakdown. The drivers weren't very good mechanics because they were really something entirely different, so they were unable to fix the car and both drove back to Leningrad in the good car leaving us without supervision. We went a little closer to the Putilov plant, and it wasn't long before some Russian children approached us and then their mothers, and soon we were surrounded by at least fifty or sixty people who stared at us as if we'd come from the moon. We had with us an editor of the *Berliner Tageblatt* who had been born in Leningrad and spoke Russian perfectly. But we had agreed that he shouldn't give himself away because that way, we thought, we'd have a better chance of listening to the voice of the people. Those Russians around the Putilov plant were shy at first, but then they got bolder and bolder. They came up to us, felt our coats, our jackets, our trousers and our shoes and were amazed at everything. They were really astonished at our clothing, and our well-groomed appearance. We had some chocolate on us that we gave the children to win their confidence, and that gave us a chance to look into the people's homes, which were gruesome. Such filth and confusion seemed utterly inconceivable to our way of thinking. At that time the housing shortage in Russia was even worse than today. In Leningrad an individual was entitled to no more than fifty square feet of living space. In other words, a family of four had only one room, and if there no children, two families had to live in a room and the dividing line between the two families was only a chalk line drawn across the floor. The Nazis really held that trip against me. When I went back home to Berlin, an SA man was already patrolling in front of my house. It was only 1932 but already the Nazis had their eye on me. The mere fact that I'd been in Russia was enough. Apparently they suspected me of being a Communist and then, to make matters worse, I wrote some articles about Russia. My reporting was as objective as I could make it. They didn't seem to like that. Luckily I lived in a police precinct where the chief commissioner was a former school friend of mine. He kept me informed and one fine day he said to me: 'I advise you to disappear.' So I decided to go back to the Wehrmacht to make myself invisible. There they couldn't do anything to me because at that time the Wehrmacht still had a privileged position. That was in 1934.

It was reported to me that they were opening a mass grave.

At that time most of the officers were old veterans of the Imperial Army. But a younger generation of officers was coming up. What they were like I can show you by an example. In 1939 the war against Poland started and at first the offensive was set for 26 August. But for political reasons it was postponed. At the time I was a staff officer in a so-called mobile corps and I was given the mission of informing the commander of one of our divisions that we would not attack on 26 August. That night when I drove up to division headquarters I was surrounded by a considerable number of young officers who actually took a threatening attitude towards me and began to shout: 'Is this going to be another flower war like our march into Austria and Czechoslovakia?' I hope you see what I mean. Many of the high officers in the Wehrmacht had, like myself, served in the Imperial Army. Later they were accused of serving Hitler for the sake of their careers and so betraying the ideals of an officer, although they could see perfectly plainly what Hitler was planning. I'm sorry to say that this accusation was not entirely unjustified. I can say this from personal observation because I served as assistant to a high-ranking general who in my opinion was too much of a Party officer. I don't wish to say any more. At first I didn't know what was happening in the concentration camps. It wasn't until 1944 that I came face to face with a crime of that sort. That was in the area of Borisov made famous by Napoleon's retreat across the Berezin in 1812. One day there was a pestilential smell. When I had them investigate to see what was happening, it was reported to me that they were opening a mass grave and burning corpses. But I wasn't able to find out who had been shot. The whole area was hermetically sealed off by the SS. Most combat officers were not put in situations where they had to carry out orders incompatible with their conscience. I myself was never given a mission that obliged me to act against my conscience. And for that reason the Americans treated me splendidly after the War. I was in Czechoslovakia at the time. With my commanding officer and the other staff officers I crossed over to the west bank of the Eger to negotiate our surrender. There we were received by an American staff officer who took us to the headquarters of an American artillery regiment. After we had all introduced ourselves they took us to the officers' club and invited us to a feudal banquet that we probably hadn't seen the like of in ten years. After those gentlemen had bidden us a friendly good-bye, we rode to the headquarters of an American general who lived like a prince in a requisitioned villa. The generals on both sides carried on an excellent technical conversation on military matters. Then we were informed of what awaited us. We were instructed to install a camp for the troops, whom we had already instructed to move westward to American territory as quickly as possible. We expected about thirty to forty thousand German soldiers to converge in this area. But the Americans were better informed. They had arranged to take care of at least 50,000 men. To our surprise the offices of a bicycle factory were put at our disposal. At least fifty typewriters had been set up. They gave us mounds of blank discharge forms for German soldiers that they had already had printed up and our job was to discharge the German soldiers and send them to their homes as quickly as possible. We received orders to take the trucks that were coming in and organize trucking battalions to transport the discharged soldiers to Aachen, Munich, Hamburg, etc., but under no circumstances to the Russian-occupied zone. With the help of the American officers we succeeded in sending 50,000 German soldiers home in about eight weeks. When they left, they were given American rations for three days and at least fifty marks each from the regimental treasury that we had confiscated.

And now in my old age I wonder: When will I have to change my profession again?

After my discharge from the Wehrmacht I tried, on the basis of my former practical experience, to find a position that would bring in enough for me to live on. It was very hard, because the Germans had classified me as a war criminal on account of my last military rank. As a colonel one was automatically a war criminal in those days. At least that's what they thought in the employment office. I had to fill out a questionnaire and when they looked at it they said: 'There's no point in your coming back. We have no work for you.' Then I looked for a position as an architect, but pretty soon I began to feel that I could manage without being employed. And I did in fact succeed. Little by little I found a few clients whom I advised on tax problems, legal matters, questions of management, and so on. I seem to have done pretty well, because today there are several millionaires among the men who came to me for advice, and they made their money through me. In my work I have had a great deal to do with jurists, and certain judges and lawyers haven't made a very good impression on me. I have the feeling that a great many judges live in the belief that they have to make reparation for something and that this obliges them to treat the so-called socially underprivileged with kid gloves. In this way they try on the one hand to cover up their past, but on the other hand they seem to expect certain advantages from being as friendly as possible to the working class. Their idea is that the Russians aren't so very far away and that they may as well prepare a landing-place for themselves. They see how former lawyers have been treated in the Soviet Zone and that by and large they only give positions to the ones who are far to the left. You see, people tend to think of tomorrow. After all it's a constant struggle for existence. I myself had to change my profession in 1918, 1924, 1934, and in 1945 for the fourth time. And now in my old age I wonder: When will I have to change my profession again? That's the thing that most worries me as well as the boys I feel I have to provide for. The financial problem. Because no one can deny that we've been having a creeping inflation for a good many years. The pictures you see here, it's true, have a constant value. Somehow I take an interest in art: in former days I was something of a Sunday painter, but in the last twenty years my professional work has stood in the way. At one time I had quite a collection of paintings, but unfortunately they were lost in the War. I never really wanted to start buying paintings again, but I thought it would be a good idea to have a few modern paintings to show one of my foster-sons. I thought it would help him in his art studies and arouse his interest, and indeed it did. I started buying pictures first by myself. Then we bought them together. We went to exhibitions and auctions, and in the end I let him buy by himself. His choice has been excellent. Here you see paintings by Heckel, Kirchner, Nolde, Pechstein, Schmidt-Rottluff, Kandinsky, Marc, Macke, Jawlensky, Klee, Kubin, Archipenko, Baumeister, Marcks, Bargheer, Barlach, Beckmann, Dix, Gilles, Grosz, Kokoschka, Hofer, Jannssen, Wunderlich, Bonnard, Braque, Buffet, Chagall, Dufy, Matisse, Mirò, Munel, Picasso, Rouault, Utrillo, Vlaminck, Za-Wou-Ki, etc. They are the friends of my old age.

CLAUDIA CRAMER

18, high-school student

Of course Schiller's *Die Räuber* appeals to young people . . . but Goethe's poems . . . I don't care for them.

I read a lot but it's hard to tell you what I read. My sister has just brought me a lot of books by Balzac from the Municipal Library. And now I'm trying to read them. I'm on the short stories now. They seem pretty long-winded to me. I like the American writers better. I like Faulkner and Thomas Wolfe a lot. But I like the classics too. I'm especially fond of Schiller. In the first place I like the subjects he deals with and especially the way he deals with them. Usually I agree with him. Of course I couldn't say I'd have thought or done exactly the same thing, but usually I feel in agreement. Of course Schiller's *Die Räuber* appeals to young people. Young people put it on too. The tensions between the two brothers – well, that kind of thing must still happen, especially when two men are running a business or that kind of thing. Some people criticize Schiller nowadays for being sentimental. I'm not of that opinion. I like Goethe's plays, but his poems, no, I don't care for them. I think maybe the taste will develop, maybe it's still too soon, I don't know, but for the present I don't care for them. First I read all the books that I found here in the bookcase and then I went to the library, and then all the things they tell you to read in school or at the bookstore. But at the bookstore you see so much that you don't know what to take first. I look at the latest paperbacks. And I buy what interests me. I also buy an illustrated magazine from time to time. But I read more dailies, *Die Welt* for instance; my parents have a subscription. And now and then I buy *Der Spiegel*. I think it's interesting but I don't always like it. Sometimes it's so exaggerated. I wouldn't exactly say radical, but I don't think you can accept everything it says sight unseen.

First I'd like to study medicine. When I was little I always wanted to be a veterinary surgeon because I'm very fond of animals. But three years ago it occurred to me that it's not the right profession for a woman. And then, of course, I want to get married.

No, I haven't formed an ideal conception of my husband. I couldn't tell you he's got to be tall and have blue eyes and that kind of thing.

I have no such conception. Of course he's got to have the same interests as me and especially he's got to love music. I've been playing the piano for seven years. Classical things and modern. Both. It began with Bartók because he's the easiest for small children to understand – Béla Bartók – and now I'm on Schönberg. I like him a lot though I really prefer the Russians, I've got to admit. Prokofiev, Kabalevsky and Shostakovich – those are my favourites. My husband would have to understand all that. He'd also have to understand that I want to practise my

profession later on, because now I want to become a doctor. I
think it's a very good idea, if only for the sake of my marriage,
because I think a relationship is always better if both husband
and wife have a profession. Then they can discuss it together.
It's no good that the wife should just talk about her domestic
worries while her husband talks about his profession. Of course
a woman shouldn't develop too much ambition about her profession and stake everything on it.

Well, yes, and besides, of course, I'd like to live in a world
without war – I'd consider any country, even the Soviet
Union.

Why not? Why shouldn't I live in the Soviet Union? I don't
really believe that the social order and the way they live there
would bother me. There's no reason to suppose that there's no
upper class or some such thing in the Soviet Union. They have
one too, only perhaps it's a little smaller than here. And Communism? I can't really judge that at the moment because so far
I haven't really studied Communism, but I don't absolutely
reject it. Living in the DDR would appeal to me less, because
you've got to be very careful not to say the wrong thing. And
that would be pretty hard for me. I've often been in the DDR.
My grandparents lived there and I've been there seven or eight
times. They lived in a beautiful neighbourhood in Dresden, but I
still remember that when I took the streetcar I wasn't allowed to
say a word. Once I shot off my mouth and there was a big fuss.
You know, my mother is a doctor and she was very well known
over there. Some officials were always coming to see her, wanting her to look at one thing and another, and the problem was
that my father never went there with her, and they knew it.
They offered him positions over there. He's a doctor too. He
should come over, they said. If his parents are living over here,
he should come too. But my father didn't want to go. 'I won't
go to the Communists, they're atheists,' he said. We're Protestants, you see.

But it's hard to believe in God.

Two years ago I was still pretty orthodox, as they call it. But today I'm pretty shaky in that connexion. I think it's because I've grown older. When you're older things don't look so simple any more and of course there are problems. Today I say frankly: it's not so. A few years ago I could have sworn to you that all the miracles in the Bible happened exactly as they're described, but today I can't be 100 per cent sure of it. If only for reasons of biology. How can a dead man be brought back to life? He wasn't just clinically dead, he'd been dead a long time. The Bible says so expressly. And it's not just the miracles but the whole Resurrection and the Trinity. I used to believe those things without any question. But today? I've discussed it with the clergyman who gives us religious instruction in school. He understood how I felt and we had a very nice talk. If you ask me, that is a miracle.

In general the old people say that we youngsters don't amount to much.

They say we're narrow-minded and impolite and boorish. I don't think that applies to my friends. On the contrary, I'm amazed how polite they are. My parents will back me up. I attend the classical high school here and most of the members of my class are the sons and daughters of university people. Then through the athletic club I have friends whose parents aren't university people. They all act about the same way. When one of my friends doesn't behave quite right now and then, it's more likely to be one whose parents belong to the upper crust than one of the others. The young people that don't come from the academic world have a much harder time of it, they realize that they need an education and try to get one. And in the end their education actually goes much deeper. I notice that particularly as a girl. I've often heard and I can confirm it from my own observation that most young men nowadays are in a big hurry to start affairs with young girls. But naturally it depends on how the girls act.

I must admit that I myself have met boys who wanted to start in right away, but if a girl behaves right there's no danger.

Anyway, I don't see any reason why I should give in the very first time. It doesn't have to be that the very first time. A boy and a girl can have conversation too. There are so many subjects, politics, for instance. It's been known to happen. Some of them are very interested. I myself don't claim to know very much about politics or to be capable of holding up my end in every discussion. But in the main I know what's going on; the Great Coalition, for instance, I don't like it at all. In my opinion there's a big danger in it, because now that the SPD isn't in the opposition any more, the NPD has become the new opposition and won a great many votes. The NPD has practically been forced into the role of an opposition. That's the worst thing that could have happened. Normally, the people who were against the government party and wanted to vote for the opposition would have voted for the SPD. But now that the SPD isn't an opposition party any more, it's only logical that those people should vote for the NPD. Especially now that there are so many malcontents who are only looking for something to carp at. Those people turn to the NPD. That's terrible because the NPD has so many members who used to have leading positions in the NSDAP. Yes, it's full of Nazis. I can only say that I'm glad I wasn't living at that time – under the Third Reich – because I'm afraid that if I had been a young girl in those days,

I would surely have been an enthusiastic member of the League of German Girls.

I'm positive. If only because I'm so crazy about sports. You see, I wouldn't have known what I know now about all the things that happened, especially all those things with the Jews. That's what bothers me the most. We studied National Socialism in great detail at school. Our teacher who is quite intelligent attached great importance to it. She illustrated her lessons with pictures, documents and phonograph records: speeches by Goebbels, pictures from the concentration camps and films of the Nuremberg trials. And then of course, Hitler's speeches. I can't see why the masses were so fascinated. Because in my opinion he wasn't a good speaker. I regard Goebbels as a greater speaker. I also think Goebbels was more dangerous, because he was an intelligent fanatic. Of course Hitler was a fanatic too, but he wasn't intelligent. Most of my classmates think the same as I do, but I also know a few young people who have different ideas, who say: of course the business with the Jews was bad but all in all what Hitler was aiming at wasn't so bad. But I don't believe they really mean what they say. I think it's a kind of spirit of opposition that makes them want to say something different from what other people are saying. No, I don't think they're so dangerous.

KLEMENTINE MEUNIER

69, unmarried, pensioned

You see, they had given me a bottle of wine and fifty marks.

The lady came on Friday afternoon and said: 'Fräulein Meunier, would you kindly make sure to be home tomorrow at half past one.' And I said: 'All right.' And then the lady added: 'But if I were you I wouldn't wear such dark clothes.' The next day our Mrs Machner who runs the welfare bureau came with the lady. They asked me certain questions and Mrs Maschner made a sign to the lady and she took notes. Then in the Christmas edition of our newspaper there was a picture of me and an article. The headline said: 'Need Has Many Faces'. If you'll wait a minute till I find my glasses I'll read it to you. Here it is – you see I have bad eyes. So here's what they wrote: 'In the last few days we have been looking behind the façade of prosperity into places where people go hungry and turn a penny over six times before spending it. What gave us access was the laudable generosity of numerous friends and readers who have laid coin upon coin and banknote upon banknote until the mountain of contributions exceeded the ten-thousand mark goal we had set ourselves. One of the many contributions brought great joy to an elderly fellow citizen in the Old City.' You see, they had given me a bottle of wine and fifty marks. Of course it gave me great pleasure, though I'm not so badly off. I'm an invalid and at present I receive a pension of 152 marks a month. Besides, I get supplementary relief which comes to a 100 marks. Any of the first ten days of the month I can get the money at the District Savings Bank. I don't really know how it came about but anyway I have my 252 marks and I'm satisfied. I have to pay 52 marks rent and then there's the gas and electricity. I get around. I was invited to a Christmas celebration by the German-American League of Women. There was coffee and cake and at the end they gave me a big bag containing a bottle of wine and a credit slip for five marks and cocoa and soap, chocolate and pastry and a *stollen*. You see, my troubles started sixteen years ago. A bad case of *arthritis deformans*.

I have pains in my joints day and night.

It started in one knee and a few weeks later the other started to hurt and then my ankles. I was in bed for months. Then it went to the hip and then I fell down and a piece of my coccyx broke off because my bones are so brittle, there's no lubrication. After that, uric acid set in and now it goes all the way up. Now my hip joint is bad again. It's lucky for me that I don't live all alone. It's terribly hard for me to move, but the lady helps me now and then – the lady I live with. Her husband was killed in the War and then she was completely bombed out. She came here with the clothes she had on her back and I offered her my home. She's seventy-six now. She lives over there in the room where I was born. My parents took this place. My father was a plumber. There was a boy and six girls in our family. The boy was killed in the First World War. Here's his picture. One fine

day Wilhelm rattled his sabre and he had to go to war. He was
sent to a Saxon regiment in Meiningen. On the grand duke's
commemoration day he had to put on his helmet and take a
wreath to the cemetery. He was with a friend and they said:
'Let's go to the photographer's. Then our folks at home will
have a picture.'

So now I have Rudolf here in a spiked helmet.

I was the youngest of the girls. The eldest is still alive, the
second is dead, she was a nurse with Professor Saurerbruch, the
third is over eighty, she too lost her husband in the War. In
addition I have a sister in Dortmund, she's seventy-nine, her
husband died only recently, just before Christmas. And still
another one is dead. That's my sister Gretel. She was married
in Berlin. And I took care of my parents for eight years. My
father had dropsy and in the end he had cancer of the throat.

I took care of my parents, because that's what God wants
us to do.

I'd given up my work. First I worked downstairs in the corner
bakery. Then I went to work in the pretzel factory. But when
both my parents were bedridden, I left. How else could I have
found time for the cooking and the washing? I had to stay
home, that's all there was to it. At that time we didn't get so
much from the war relief. It was very hard on my parents. But
not on me. It was my duty as a daughter and I did it gladly
because I thought to myself: they brought me up. Then when
my father died, I went back to the pretzel factory. I stoked the
oven – but not for long, because then I started taking care of
Herr Wendland's father – the house belongs to Herr Wendland.
He had calcification of the brain. Herr Wendland said: Klementine took care of her parents, she can take care of my father
too. And I said: 'All right, I will.' For the patient's sake. So then
I took care of him until he died, and then I went back to the
pretzel factory until an uncle of mine fell sick and then I took

care of him. He was a postal clerk and he paid for it out of his
pension. I was sick myself at the time, but I did it all the same.
In the end he was just barely alive, he breathed a little but he
wasn't conscious. I sat by his death bed for five days. Death
agony they call it. In all I've seen seven being sent off to heaven,
but God gave me the strength to bear it, and that's a blessing.
With God's help I can also bear the pain He has sent me. He
must know why. I'm only depressed sometimes when it gets too
bad, like last month, for instance. People are always leading
their dogs along the house front to do their business. I was
coming in the house door and I slipped on it and fell and broke
my walking-sticks. I had to buy new ones, they're expensive. I
no sooner had them than my doctor said: 'Klementine, I like
everything about you except those walking-sticks.' 'Herr Doktor,' I said, 'I can't walk without them.' 'I know it,' he said, 'you
need crutches.' And then he went behind his X-ray machine
and brought out two crutches. He'd used them himself after an
automobile accident. 'Here,' he said, 'you can take these and
keep them as long as you need them.' Most people you see
with canes hold themselves like question marks. Not me. I walk
erect. But my pains prevent me from going out too much. All
I've got to look at here is a fire wall. That's awful. Sometimes I
think: if I could only look out on a garden ... but I've got to
be satisfied. I read a lot to forget. The newspaper and books too.
They're brought me by a woman who guides big groups to the
Holy Land, pilgrims and people who are interested.

You ask if I have friends who look after me?

I wouldn't exactly say that. There's more chance of my looking
after them. And the young people in the house? Such things
don't occur to them, they have other fish to fry. It's only
natural, they're still so young, but Herr Stolze next door brings
me my coal. He's a salesman but he isn't away very much. He's
always very good to me. If there's something to be repaired
he takes care of it. 'Fräulein Meunier,' he says, 'you have it
coming to you.' Sometimes when he's going on a nice tour he

says to me: 'I'll take you along, you've never been where I'm going.' When he sees me on the street, which isn't very often, he gives me his hand and says: 'Well, how's it going? If you have any trouble come and tell me about it.' But I don't like to ask him for too much. It's such a burden. Of course I know that things are going from bad to worse with me. One day I'll have to go to the hospital. There are good people there too, like everywhere else. I'm always satisfied. What I'd like to do? What can I do? Nobody's going to come and take away my troubles. I'll manage and God will help me. I'm satisfied.

FRANK PETERSEN
68, married, toy manufacturer

I'm a self-made man.*

I can say that without hesitation and I'm proud of it. I always intended to be a businessman. I was cut out for it. I wasn't sold on any particular line. Today you see, I have a toy factory, but I started out as an apprentice in a textile factory. At that time I was seeing a good deal of a gentleman who travelled all over the world. I helped him to get up his sample collection and I saw the orders he brought home. I read his reports and envied him his success. I said to myself: 'You've got to get where he is.' That was my first goal. I began to study languages at an early age, and when I was only twenty-one I went to England as a salesman. That was shortly after the First World War. There were very few Germans in England and a lot of the customers hung out signs saying: 'Germans not admitted'.* Later the English became a little less hostile to the Germans and wrote: 'Foreigners not admitted'.* But by 'foreigners'* they still meant Germans. Even so – and that's typical of the English – they were glad to help a young man. I can remember that I used to ignore the signs now and then, but they never took it badly. They gave

---

*English in original.

me a friendly reception. Of course I was a German but they always said: 'Here is a young man, we must try to help him.'* The human angle meant more than the nationality. Yes, I liked it very much in England and I was very successful in my work. My parents were pleased with me.

I'm attached to the soil.

My father was a farmer in the Sauerland, a real peasant, he had a medium-sized farm. He died young. My mother inherited the farm. After her death I sold the land but I kept my parents' old house. I've added to it, put some money into it and taken in two tenants. The memory of my parents means a great deal to me. They had a great deal of influence on me. They were strict Catholics. A man's home and childhood always inculcate certain ideas which he adheres to later in life whether he means to or not. That is especially true in connexion with ethics.

He knows that one must always stick to the straight and narrow

and not get mixed up in shady deals, to try to be frank and honourable in his private life, to be helpful whenever he can. I've always followed those teachings and so has my brother. He's a house painter and has a business of his own. He's very able, though he hasn't done as well as I have. Well, to get back to my story: I happened to meet a man who was in the toy business. I took an interest in his line and went on the road with it. I did pretty well. But the business was so small that the man couldn't pay my expenses, my commission, and so on. One day he came to me and said: 'Herr Petersen, you realize I haven't got enough capital, I'd like to take a partner. I already have a prospect.' 'That's not a bad idea,' I said. 'But not without me. Either you pay me what the firm owes me in cash or I'll be your partner.' He decided to take me. I was still very

---

*English in original.

young, only twenty-three. Even at that age I was never afraid to speak up. I looked out for my interests. My mother loaned me the money I needed to go into partnership. Business soon improved and in a very short time I repaid my mother every cent. But I saw it was impossible to turn the firm into a big business because my partner wasn't a big businessman. Most of all, he was too timid

You need spunk if you want to do anything big.

One day a toy factory here in town went into bankruptcy. The goodwill was sold but I went in with the former owner and took over the factory and the machines. I became his new partner. The other one had left in the course of the bankruptcy proceedings. We founded the firm of Petersen & Co. My 'Co.' was Herr Pfundbrot, a considerably older man. I worked with Herr Pfundbrot for twenty-five years. We never had a contract in writing and in all those years we never had the slightest falling out. Our pleasant collaboration brought us a success upon which I can look with pride today. Herr Pfundbrot died sixteen years ago. For me it was a great loss. He was a workman of the old school, and a good old soldier. Every morning at ten minutes to seven he himself opened the factory gate, and he closed up punctually at seven in the evening. Anyone who arrived a minute after seven had to come back at one o'clock. That's how strict we were. Herr Pfundbrot was the fairest man I've ever known. He was on very friendly terms with his workmen. He was familiar with all their family circumstances, and when they were in trouble he always helped. I can assure you that our workers were well off even in the hardest times. In the late twenties and the late thirties when the situation in German was very bad I made big sales in England. Even then our factory worked overtime and our people made good money. Later, in the Nazi period, everyone did better. Our export business was so big that the Chamber of Commerce treated us with kid gloves. All through the War I made trips to Sweden or Switzerland on behalf of our export business. I wasn't in the Party.

They tried hard to get me in but I managed to sidestep it without their taking it amiss. I think they overlooked me. But they got Herr Pfundbrot. He was known in town, and among the small peasants in the outskirts where he lived – he himself came of a small peasant family – there have always been a certain number of enthusiasts. They drew him in in the early days when I was still something of a stranger here. The first few years after we came here to live they didn't even regard us as Germans. They thought we were English. I guess my name sounds a little English, but not really.

As a young man I said to myself: 'You won't get married until you can support a wife 100 per cent.'

I met my wife in Düsseldorf at the home of friends. Her father was a highly respected citizen. Very active politically. At any rate, he was one of the leading figures in the provincial diet in Düsseldorf. Every year it was he who reported on the budget. He was in the Centre Party, he was personally acquainted with Adenauer. My wife is just the right type for me. Yes, I can say that again. Fortunately, my wife is entirely different from me emotionally. More on the artistic side. I married late. And when I put my visiting card on my father-in-law's table he said to his daughter: 'Take him, he's a good man.' I could afford to marry a woman of good family and give her the kind of life she expected. It all went very well. Only it was hard adapting ourselves here. It's not so easy for outsiders to acclimate themselves in this town, and strange to say, as we can't help observing now and then, only a very few of our friends are local people. A lot of outsiders say the same thing: 'The people here are funny, they're really weird. They stick together. They only buy from their own people. A businessman from outside has a hard time getting ahead.' So there aren't many local people among our friends. Some of them are entrepreneurs, some are managers, and then there are my friends from the Rotary Club. They come of every occupational group, but the lower limit is very sharply drawn. It's an intellectual group, I can tell you that. We meet on Tuesday afternoon, and if I ever stay away for a week I miss it. I hear very interesting lectures at the club. Sometimes they give you ideas you can think about all week. The first years here were very hard on me. It wasn't so bad for my wife because she's a great nature lover. She thinks the region around here is very romantic and she's fascinated by anything romantic. Every day she walks for two or three hours. So it wasn't so bad for her that I was on the road for six or seven months a year during the first years. I didn't just go to England but all over Europe. My trips usually began in Cairo and ended in New Delhi. Or I started in Vienna and went from there to Budapest, from Budapest to Belgrade, from Belgrade to Sofia, from Sofia to Bucharest, then to Salonika, Athens, Cairo, Alexandria, Port Saïd, and then Jerusalem, Baghdad and Teheran. Wherever I went I sold toys. There are children all over the world and they all want to play. What orders I brought home, what beautiful big orders! I had to face American, Italian, French and finally Japanese competition, but we Germans were in the lead. I owed my success to my direct approach. I could always say: 'I'm the owner of the firm. I come direct from the factory. You can speak to me directly, and you'll always get a clear yes or no.'

No two ways about it: initiative and hard work are the makings of success!

Yes, it's true that a lot of Germans work hard and have a certain amount of initiative. Maybe courage isn't so common. But I was always willing to take a risk. An able businessman, I believe, must have three qualities: he must be intelligent, he must be hard-working, and he must have character. If he has all that he'll get what he's after. Of course luck has something to do with it, but the other things are more important. You've got to inspire confidence. I am absolutely certain that if I were in London tomorrow without a penny in my pocket, I'd only have to speak to five or six men, my old friends, and they'd give me anything I needed. Once you've gained an Englishman's confidence, you keep it. Once you've lost it, you've lost it for good. That's something everybody should know and understand. You could call it a political question. A businessman today can't get along without politics. He's got to know what's going on, what people are doing. Take the unions. Naturally in a factory that's been in existence more than thirty years you've got certain old hands you can rely on. But even they have been slightly infected by the unions. It's humanly understandable. Why should a worker say no when the unions tell him: 'You can have this and that, just demand it. We'll get it for you.' I don't condemn the unions. I've got along fairly well with them. I even sympathize when they say: 'Why shouldn't the men share in the success of the business?'

But it's high time that the union should tell its members that they've got to do something for the money they get, because otherwise it's theft.

I've often told my workers that. To no effect, I've got to admit. But I personally take the point of view that it does no harm if we have two or three per cent of unemployed. That way they're glad to get back to the old shop. The times have changed a good deal. A lot of the old German solidity has been lost. I'm over sixty and I well remember the times before the First World War, the society I grew up in: good solid little people, strictly Catholic, a certain national pride, German pride – they were proud to be Germans. When I came home from the First World War and began to see the world, I was forced to realize that what I had learned in school wasn't right.

In those days people thought there was Germany and outside of Germany, nothing.

Then when I went abroad and saw that the world was entirely different, I realized that was a lot of nonsense. When travelling in foreign countries I've always kept my mouth shut and my eyes and ears open. I walked, observed, and didn't talk much. Then in later years, especially in the Nazi period, when Germans started travelling again, especially to England, they were so loud-mouthed that they made themselves disliked from the start. The English don't care for that mentality at all. They want you to be quiet and wait for people to come to you. I can remember well when I came back from a trip to England in the thirties and I saw a red flag with a swastika flying beside our house. I was really dismayed and I thought: 'Is it starting up again?' And then in Aachen when I saw my old black, white and red flag again, my heart beat a little faster and I hoped there was still a little of the real German spirit left after all. But the Nazis came to power. I never identified myself with National Socialism. On the contrary, during that period I did a great deal for other people who were its victims. I won't go into details, several people owe their lives to me. After that we Germans proved clearly that

when the chips are down we are people who can work and get things done.

Because it was only by our hard work that we fought our way up again. The trade union people today talk as if they had done it all by themselves. But the fact is we owe it to our workers; without them it couldn't have been done. The unions demand a lot and give very little. They have no respect for enterprise. Altogether in Germany you find no respect for others. When I think of England – those people have real respect for others, and that includes their next-door neighbours in the small concerns of everyday life. It begins in the family and extends to the greatest institutions. Of course we have our qualities too. We know how to work, and even among the young people there are plenty who are willing to work. It's wrong to condemn all the Germans out of hand. You often hear it said that people have become too materialistic and live beyond their means. It's very hard to resist advertising and all its charms. I don't think it's bad when this stimulation makes people work and make money by their work, but the people really ought to learn to stop spending money they haven't really got.

I'm against instalment buying.

A man should only buy what he has the money to pay for. It's always cheaper in the end. All my life I've gone by that principle. When I made a mark, I never spent a mark, not even in the hardest times. Of every mark I earned I put thirty pfennigs aside. That way I always had reserves, something to fall back on. All my life I've had the same standard of living. I haven't bought any big cars, I've always observed moderation. Unfortunately, I haven't been able to teach my daughters the same way of thinking. They appreciate what I've done but they keep saying:

'Daddy, you're making a big mistake. Why do you go on working? Let yourself live!'

But I can't change myself. That's the way I am. I work as hard as ever. Absolutely. Maybe I'm a typical German in that way. Every morning at seven thirty I'm at my factory, I leave at five minutes to one, go back at two forty-five, and come home at seven fifteen. My daughters don't understand. The younger is twenty-six, the elder twenty-eight. Neither is married. The elder is in a research institute, she works on laser rays with an American engineer. My daughters and I have considerable disagreements. My younger daughter says, for instance: 'Daddy, you made a big mistake in not letting me go to the university. I should have studied economics.' I say: 'My dear girl, you're perfectly right, but just remember how I kept after you to graduate from high-school. But then your good mother came in and said: "Don't torture the child so. She'll get married some day, why does she need a diploma?"' Then my daughter said: 'Daddy, you should have forced me.' Ha, it's easy for her to talk. It was pretty much the same with my elder daughter. She went half-way through classical high-school. Then she transferred to business high-school and graduated. She was enthusiastic at the time, but later she said: 'Daddy, you made a mistake, you should have made me get my classical diploma, it would have been much better for me.' My oh my, it's rough. All the same, the elder one has a pretty good head, she always gets to the heart of things. The little one is the enterprising type. She takes risks, she charges right in. But the young people look at life in an entirely different way from us older people with our weight of experience. And there's a big difference today in relations with the other sex.

When we were young we had respect for our superiors and for older people in general.

Just get into a streetcar nowadays. When do you ever see a young fellow standing up for an elderly lady or gentleman? Never! In the old days it was drummed into us, we took it for granted. And the respect we had for young girls! It was wonderful compared with today. Never mind, we had our pleasures too.

We flirted too but in an entirely different way.

When they talk about their schoolmates nowadays and all the things that go on, I can only shake my head. My elder daughter has a close girl friend. She comes of a good family and she's a bright kid. Well, this is what happened to her: First the children were born, then came the wedding, then came the divorce. Nothing like that ever happened in my family. You seldom saw such things in the old days. Morality has degenerated. A consequence of the War. We had a similar lapse of morality after the First World War. But then we put a stop to it. But today? Remember, the last War has been over for twenty years. I'm supposed to be a pretty smart man, but I ask you: how is it going to end? I don't know . . .

ANTON FALLER

55, unmarried, worker

Anyway, I'm good at handling people.

My ancestors came here in 1552. They were all sorts: reverends, I mean Catholic priests, mechanical draftsmen, painters, etc. My father was killed in France in 1915, and my mother died in 1932. I was still very young and I could have used a mother. But I found a patron, he sent me to the Academy of Art in Munich. Then I worked as a free-lance painter, a few portraits, a few landscapes, and I made a living at it. That was all right for a while but by 1949 I was having a hard time selling my pictures. A man's got to live. I needed money. So I took up house painting. I'd paint an apartment, a staircase, an attic, a house front or a room. That way the money came in every week. But then I saw the drawback. Out there on the scaffold in mid-winter – you froze to death. It was inhuman. Even when I was painting indoors, they made me bolt my sandwich in an ice-cold stairwell. The people won't let you into their apartment, not even into the kitchen to warm yourself. People who spend their time in warm rooms have no sympathy for the others. In 1965 I was fed up, so I answered an ad that an electrical appliance firm had put in the paper. They were looking for a foreman, no less – a man to supervise twenty-five women. 'We want you to put those women in their place. Be tough.' That's what they said. Before me, they'd had a forelady. Very attractive. When she left the shop in the evening she looked like a model. But she had a devil in her. They wanted to stop her little game. So I saw what the score was. Anyway, I'm good at handling people. Because actually I'm a pretty cheerful guy. I can start shooting the bull at six in the morning and keep on until seven at night. I'm full of inner merriment and I like to share it with the other fellow. At first it was hard.

Those women were furies, the worst kind of women you can get in a factory.

One would tell the other how she did it with her husband. They talked about the most intimate things and if one knew some dirt about another she'd pass it on to somebody else. That made for endless friction. That's why they wanted a man for the job. And that was me. Well, in the beginning those furies sabotaged me in every way. They tried to get me so disgusted I'd walk out. But of course I had the boss behind me. For the first six months I worked hard to learn the work and all the nomenclature. Then those bitches played one more of their dirty tricks on me. That was a Friday. The following Monday I went to work wearing a white shirt and a tie, I only pulled my work smock over it. Suddenly the man standing in front of them wasn't a workman but a boss who meant business – a foreman. Before that I'd been just as filthy as any workman ...

And suddenly I come in all dressed up like a man who has something to say ...

You won't believe it but the women reacted in a flash to my change of costume. Then and there they knew the jig was up, that they'd lost. After that, relations between us were entirely different, human and comradely. I'd buy a pound of coffee or a few chocolate bars and give it to the hyenas, and they started making me coffee every day. We drank coffee together and they began to cooperate. You see, I'd learned about women in the course of my life; in church too. I knew how to handle them. I don't go to church much any more. My faith is only about average. Yes, of course I've got a religion, I'm a Roman Catholic. My parents had me baptized and I've got to respect it. I couldn't run off in some other direction, to Jehovah's Witnesses, for instance. I'm a Catholic and a Catholic I remain.

I recognize the Church as a building, but not the fashion show that goes on there.

That's why I spoke about women. Right now short skirts are

the thing, we know all about that. Besides, they show off their
new hats and their new coats in church and then the ladies
start whispering to each other: 'Where *did* she get that new
hat? She can't have as much money as all that. And look at
that one over there. Good God, she's got a new coat again.
Something fishy is going on. God knows who paid for it.' I
discussed it with the priest, and he said: 'Yes, unfortunately,
that's the way it is. Nevertheless, we shall go on preaching the
word of God, it's our duty.' That's the way he felt about it. And
he was more secular than clerical, he took a real interest in
social and political affairs. I've also discussed politics with him.
You see, this aid to underdeveloped countries sticks in my craw.
You can't just take the money the people have earned and give
it away to those underdeveloped countries nobody ever heard
of. It's not right. We have enough poor people right here.

Believe me, I can show you poor people, you've never seen
anything like it.

As a painter I get to see all kinds of apartments. I can tell you a
story: one day I'm coming home from work and I see two old
people holding each other by the arm. They were so old they
had to hold each other up to keep from falling down. The man
must have seen me in my white painter's clothes, so he asked
me: 'Are you a painter?' It was pretty plain that I wasn't a
chimney sweep, but I believe in being polite, so I said: 'Yes.'
'Well,' he said, 'we have a room at home that's so dirty it makes
us sick to go into it. Maybe you could paint it all black?' So
one evening I went to Wilhelmstrasse and when I saw that
room – the ceiling was as black as a coal cellar; my God, what
it looked like! – I said to myself, all right, I'll do it for them.
But white of course. I began at six Saturday morning and at
eleven that night I was through. The old man said to me: 'How
much do I owe you?' 'My goodness,' I said, 'give me a mark.'
He took out his purse and put one mark in my hand and he
was really happy to have his room looking clean and human
again. After that, I went to see a pastor who promised to look

in now and then to see that the old people had something to eat and that their place was in order. They had a pension, but not enough to do much with. They were really poor devils. That's where this development money belongs. Then it wouldn't be money thrown away.

When I read that some sheikh or some black Sambo has come to Germany and cadged five hundred million marks.

And then he goes to London and throws away three quarters of the money having himself a good time. When our good President writes out a cheque to some foreign country, he should remember all the poor people there are in Germany. But like every medal this one also has its reverse. Of the twenty-five women I have under me in the factory, twenty-four go to work only in order to keep up the car, to pay for gas and the taxes and insurance and buy a TV set and a phonograph and a refrigerator and a washing machine, and if possible a dish washer. For all those things the wife has to go out to work and bring in her 320 or 340 marks a month. In other words, it's only for reasons of status, as they say. They could get along perfectly well without a car. They could walk. It's much healthier. Christ walked. But no, they need a car.

The neighbour has a car, we'd be ashamed not to have one.

That's a fine attitude. Then if tomorrow the husband gets into financial difficulties, he has nothing to fall back on. But when people like that really get into trouble, they start yelling that it's all the fault of the government. There are a lot of people like that, they're swine, always screaming about the government. They want the government to do everything for them, like under the Nazis. Then supposedly everything was so wonderful. You won't believe what I'm going to say now, but it's the truth: In those days I wasn't interested in politics. You could say that politics just swept by me.

My interest began with Adenauer.

Of course I knew that Hindenburg and Ebert and Pappen and Schleicher existed. The names have stuck in my mind. But I didn't really take an interest in politics. I'd put it this way: the Nazi movement owed its success to the hard times – seven and a half million unemployed. I remember well that a great many joined the Party at that time, it was a mad scramble, they couldn't join fast enough. They all hoped they'd be sent right out on the Autobahn and put to work for fifty-three pfennigs an hour, because that's the kind of wages they paid then. They were happy. I remember. They wept for joy at the chance of going to work for fifty-three pfennigs an hour. Can you imagine? And another thing while we're on the subject of Hitler – if we'd had TV in those days, if we'd been able to see that little black moustache, I'm convinced he would never have got so big. When I talk things over with the workers in the factory at lunchtime, a great many of them feel exactly the same way. If only we'd had TV in those days we could have gotten a better look at him, the way he made his speeches with his mask and his gestures. A lot of people would have said: 'The man's nuts. Something's wrong.' You've got to remember that wages were very low in those days, you could hardly afford to go to the movies. You needed shoes, you needed clothes. People were really worn down by that long unemployment. And when you did get to the movies and saw the newsreel, you didn't get an over-all picture of what was really going on. Nowadays when something happens you see it that same night on TV. It's brought right into your home. You can form an opinion.

Most people were enthusiastic because they got work.

But today a lot of people see where it led. Today we take a much more objective and sober view, but most people have forgotten a good many things, they don't want to remember. It's amazing how much has slipped out of most people's memories. People who were in the SA or the SS. They just repress it. They were enthusiastic at the time, but now they don't remember.

Well, in our factory we hear certain conversations. They're willing to believe that bad things were done to the Jews, but not a one believes that six million were killed. The figure mentioned is always six million, and our people simply refuse to believe it. They refuse to believe that so many could have been gassed. Though in my opinion it's not a question of a million more or less. If one man is killed, it's really just as bad as if a million were killed, because a man's a man. When life is gone you can't bring it back. So, I say: let's not bicker about figures. As far as I'm concerned, Jews are men just as much as I am. I respect them and I want them to respect me. We have a sweeper in our factory. He's a Jew. He was expelled from Poland in 1959 and he came over here. I've had a lot of political discussions with him. He's such a German-hater, he'd like to give the whole of Germany a dose of E 605. So there wouldn't be anybody left, that's how much he hates every single German. A fierce indiscriminate hatred. I keep trying to straighten things out with him, because it seems to me that a time comes when you've got to forget, or at least come to an understanding. Of course the Jews suffered terribly and I don't know how I'd react in their place. I sympathize with them. I never get into a fight with that man and I try to treat him as fairly and objectively as possible. We're on good terms but when my fellow workers start talking politics with him they shout so loud you can hear them in the next town. But you know, in spite of everything, this government we have is a joke. Sometimes it makes me laugh. Hitler founded the 'Thousand Year Reich'. It lasted twelve years. That was Hitler's eternity. And then came Adenauer and he too preached eternity. You remember the way he said:

'No German will ever again put on a grey uniform'? And only six years later we got the Bundeswehr.

That was Adenauer's eternity. But when you come down to it, the man did accomplish one thing, and I give him credit. He went to Moscow and brought back thousands of prisoners,

prisoners of war from Siberia. That was an achievement! It
was worth having Adenauer as Chancellor for that alone. That's
my opinion. The other fellow, Erhard, I mean: I tell you
frankly, I feel sorry for him. Good-natured, upright character,
really a very decent sort. He didn't deserve to be persecuted by
a lot of political foxes, or you could call them swine. He wanted
to build something that would be of benefit to others. But
where there's a will there isn't necessarily a way. Chancellor
Kiesinger is shrewd, he has intelligence and wit, a typical
Swabian, and in spite of the Great Coalition there's still plenty
of opposition. The opposition is right inside the Great Coalition
government. Even if the outside opposition, the FDP* doesn't
amount to much. But in my opinion an opposition isn't necessarily on the left or right wing. It's not always possible to say:
this is the opposition over here and that's the government supporters over there. Oh no! It would be perfectly possible to
take the FDP into the government. Then all the parties would
be in it and we'd have an extra-Great Coalition. And inside the
different groups you could still have a very healthy opposition
that wouldn't be visible from outside, but would be all the more
effective inside. Better than all these shouters that we sometimes hear in the Bundestag. And I really don't approve of the
way some people have been behaving. But there's one thing
we've really got to learn: to get rid of our fear of everything
that smacks of Prussia. When I say 'Prussia', I mean uniforms,
I mean the policeman, even the postman. It's engrained in our
German nature, it's passed on from generation to generation,
it's in our flesh and blood.

The minute a German sees a uniform he's struck with awe.

We've always had this respect for authority, regardless of what
kind. When a German sees a person in authority he starts to
bow and scrape. See here, over there in England when a noble
lord goes for a walk and he meets a streetcleaner, he says to

---

Freie Demokratische Partei – Free Democratic Party

him: 'Good morning'.* Good God, why can't we do the same? Our greetings go by the social scale, we greet our superiors, not our inferiors. That's the difference, and that's connected with uniforms too, we have it in our blood. Even the young people. On the street they act as if they were freer, but on the job – in our factory for instance – far from it. They're always looking up, always up and never down. Maybe they're freer about sex, maybe they're freer in their love life. Fine, let them be, they mature much earlier than we did. But when it comes to the feeling for authority, to respect for higher-ups, they're just about the same as everybody else. When they see a uniform, they stop in their tracks. Maybe they think it's a policeman or a general, and then it turns out to be the postman. It's a disease with us. Democracy is a form of government that doesn't exist yet in our country. See here, I was in Switzerland for three months, in Lugano. It was put to a vote whether the oldest church in Lugano should be torn down and an Italian department store put up in its place. In the morning the people of Lugano went to the polls and that night it was announced: 'The Italian isn't going to build anything, the church stays.' In my opinion that's democracy. There everything is up to the people. Or take the gasoline tax, that's another thing I saw down there. The government wanted to increase it by eight centimes, and the people were indignant: 'We demand a referendum, we won't stand by and let Berne do anything it pleases and increase the gasoline just like that.'

They went to the polls and voted against it and Berne didn't add any eight centimes.

And now I ask you: Have we in Germany really the possibility of acting democratically, of saying: we're opposed to that, and we want a referendum? No, we haven't. We have a dictatorial democracy in which the people have nothing to say. The only chance we get to speak is at elections to the Bundestag or the

---

*English in original.

provincial diet. But in between all decisions are made at the top. Switzerland is better in that respect. In our country the government has neglected to give the citizen a political education, to make him politically mature. Bonn does nothing to enlighten its citizens. They never do anything about it. Up to now Bonn has shown no real desire to give the people political training, to teach them to think for themselves in political matters and to act responsibly. The unions have their dictatorial side too. Out of 100 shops only one really needs a union because maybe one employer treats his workers like slaves. While 99 employers don't need any union because they take a naturally human and social-minded attitude towards their workers. That's a good thing. On the other hand, of course, we have the unions to thank that the employers have become the way they are, so social-minded. The trade-union movement has done us a lot of good, but sometimes there's a really dictatorial touch. For instance, is it right that all union members should get extra vacation pay and the ones who aren't organized get nothing? I call that unfair.

BARBARA BAUER

26, unmarried, psychologist

My parents' marriage taught me that the female sex is the stronger.

My father died in 1956 of injuries received in the War. Before the War he was a newspaper man in Waldenburg in Silesia. In the War he was a plain soldier. In 1949 he came home from a Russian prison camp with heart and bronchial trouble and he couldn't work any more. My memories of my father are very vague. That is probably because little by little my mother crowded him out. He was the artistic side of the family and my mother thought it was up to her to wield the sceptre. She succeeded brilliantly in destroying the father-image in us. It was very interesting psychologically. I can't explain the situation in any other way. I was fifteen when my father died. I had been living with him all those years and nevertheless I have only the sketchiest picture of him. I can't remember a single conversation with my father. I only know that he was very good-natured and inclined to give in. When we wanted something, we didn't go to my mother, but to him. When we had bad marks in school, we had him sign our report cards, because then there was nothing to be afraid of. Maybe another reason why my father had no real opportunity to look after us was that we children were on our own from an early age and had to help support the family. We were refugees from Silesia and first we were in Schleswig-Holstein. We had a hard time keeping body and soul together. On my way home from school I was always trying to figure out some quick thing to cook because on account of my father being laid up my mother was training to be a welfare nurse. Today she's a maternity welfare worker in the Department of Labour. Maternity welfare sounds pretty awful. Her job is to see that the maternity welfare law is observed; for instance, that expectant mothers are given the maternity leave they're entitled to, because naturally a good many bosses try to fire pregnant women. Strangely enough, my mother pretty much collapsed when my father died, and I had to do everything. Though my parents had five children, I can't really say they had a good marriage. We are all supposed to have been wanted but I'd almost say it was irresponsible to have all those children. Because my parents both knew that their marriage wasn't happy. I believe my mother had her children for her own personal consolation. As a child I always thought my mother was the better and more honest of the two. But now that I look back I see that I was dead wrong. She simply succeeded in crushing my father. Some women are experts at that. Meanwhile I found out that not the male but the female sex is the stronger. Unfortunately! I've noticed that in a lot of marriages. Maybe it's that the man gives in more easily because he's more intelligent and the woman is stronger because she's more primitive. It's quite a common phenomenon.

Women have enormous possibilities and some exploit them to the hilt. They master the art of ruling gently. They combine strength with shrewdness.

Sex is eroticism without love.

Because I know all that and myself would prefer a marriage in which the husband is the stronger, I veer towards men at least fifteen years older than myself. In any case my husband must have a stronger character than I, so I can subordinate myself to him willingly. But first I'd like to practise my profession. As a psychologist I'd like to work as a consultant in an institution for abnormal children. Nothing could make me go into industry or advertising. Ordinary school psychology, educational guidance, vocational guidance, etc. – I wouldn't dream of going in for any of those. But if I marry some day I mean to give up my job. I don't believe a woman can do justice to two such big jobs as marriage and a profession. I've known remarkable women who had both children and professional careers but they neglected both. In all the cases I know of, it didn't work, and I see no reason to believe that I'll be able to manage my marriage better because I've studied psychology and know something about the human psyche. To handle a marriage properly all you need is good common sense and a warm heart. What I hope to receive and to give is lasting love, not just any kind of love but the self-regenerating love that's always new. And that kind of love springs from a constant fruitful understanding. You've got to be together in mind, soul and body. Eroticism, when you come right down to it, is wonderful only when it's connected with love. Sex is only eroticism without love. If people were really the way they're represented in our illustrated magazines, the magazines wouldn't sell the way they do. Anybody who's really so sex-conscious doesn't need any *Playboy* or *Playgirl* magazine, he's sexy of his own accord, he doesn't need outside charms to influence him. All this sex talk is nonsense. I mean, a person who believes in the value of loving eroticism doesn't need to have complexes about the sex wave.

But the illustrated magazines give a lot of people complexes; they make them think they're not sexy enough, that they're abnormal if they don't ride the general sex wave, even if they don't feel like it deep down. No, I don't let it influence me. I want to have a normal life. I want to have children and bring them up properly, and I hope to be happily married. That's my conception of the little world, but of course the little world is very much influenced by the big world. And when it comes to the big world, you can only take a political view of it, because politics plays a determining role in our lives.

So many Germans are afraid to take any political initiative.

You see, I'm glad to be living in a democracy but I'm not yet satisfied with this democracy. I keep hoping it will be improved some day. Our democracy is still very young, because I don't believe you can call the Weimar Republic a democracy. If you look at it that way, we have practically no democratic tradition. It's hard to say anything very complimentary about our present political situation. The union of the two big political parties in the Great Coalition has practically eliminated the oppositon. We ourselves ought to do something to change this situation. But as long as we sidestep all political activity we should keep quiet if we have any brains. So many Germans – including myself – are terribly afraid to take any political initiative. It's very hard for them, they feel that it's risky.

The Catholic Church meddles irresponsibly in people's lives.

I was baptized a Catholic but I don't believe in the personified God of the Christian churches. I agree with Feuerbach when he says that we created God in our image. If the personified God of the churches exists, there must be infinitely many Gods, because each man sees his God differently. No, there may be a higher being, but I don't believe in that kind of God. Of course if I have children, they'll have to belong to some religion on account of school if nothing else, because in our society a child is still bound to feel put upon if he can't take part in religious instruction at school. But if my children must have a religion, let them be Protestants, because I feel that the Catholic Church meddles irresponsibly in people's lives, for instance when it says that no Catholic girl can marry a divorcee. I know cases where both husband and wife suffer terribly because they're both good Catholics but one of them has been divorced. Where does the Church get the right to interfere in people's private lives like that? And another thing: until recently people who had themselves cremated weren't supposed to go to Heaven. And now suddenly they're allowed through the pearly gates. In other words, an amnesty has been declared in Hell: cremated persons are free to get up and go!

Why shouldn't there be two German states?

I've often been in the DDR, visiting my brother-in-law, who took a degree in theology here and then decided to go over there as a minister because he thought there weren't enough ministers over there and it was his duty to the people to go there. I usually stay with him for two or three weeks. I enjoy being with my family but on the whole, naturally, I don't like it. I always get involved in those so-called all-German conversations that they arrange when a West German comes over. The authorities invite him in for coffee and cake. Strange to say, all the people from the West that I've met over there were people of very average mentality. I've never met any university people or for that matter anyone who was intelligent or politically committed from the Federal Republic. I soon caught on to the technique of those politically trained functionaries. The first thing they usually say is: 'You see, we have coffee and cake over here too. Of course we know that everything isn't perfect over here yet, that certain things are still lacking.' It makes a very strong impression on a western visitor when those functionaries frankly admit that everything isn't as it should be. And then little by little, the conversation is brought around to political subjects. They start attacking the Federal Republic.

They say the Western powers began dividing Germany by dividing it economically and that we West Germans had let the Americans bribe us with the Marshall Plan aid. I pointed out that the East Zone could also have had Marshall Plan aid but rejected it. You see, I'm pretty well up on my history and I was able to refute almost all their arguments. Some of our people say that certain things are better over there, for instance the morale of the workers, but I know it's really a lot of nonsense. On both sides we have a pluralistic industrial society and on both sides it has the same drawbacks. I once worked in a factory here for nine months, just to see what it was like. I assembled electric switches. Well, I found out that the bosses didn't care who was working for them and that the workers didn't even know who the boss was or what the part they were assembling was for. No one ever explained it to them and the workers didn't ask. They were like brainless robots. I spoke with the personnel management. I told them that was an impossible state of affairs, that they should at least distribute a pamphlet to the workers explaining the function of the factory and its products. But they answered: 'Oh, the workers. They never stay long anyway. Why should we bother?' And then people wonder why the workers' morale isn't so good. I also worked in a hospital for a while and I can tell you that the morale of the doctors and nurses isn't much better. After all it's not enough for a doctor just to do his work. What I expect of a doctor is empathy and commitment. Nothing of the sort. The doctors just put in their eight-hour stint like skilled labourers. I asked a number of them: 'Why did you become a doctor?' But I only got answers like: 'Don't ask me. It comes in the family,' or 'I don't really know.' Or they answered with questions of their own: 'Why are you studying psychology?' Not one of them said: I became a doctor because medicine interests me, because I want to help people. No one ever said that. I'm not really in a position to judge, but I don't believe such things are very different over there in the DDR, though certain other aspects are so different that I can't really conceive of a reunification any more. They're not as badly off over there as people say over

here. The worst thing we can do to them is to give them the
impression that it's a paradise on earth over here. You still
meet a lot of people over there who think we get everything
for nothing over here, that everything drops into our laps. But
after all they've got to live there and most of them don't mind.
They get used to it. Habituation is one of man's most astonishing faculties.

Even if my father had killed a Jewess, I'm not responsible.

If I thought the people in the other Germany were almost as
well off as we are, then frankly the question of reunification
would mean nothing to me. Why shouldn't there be two states?
Why must we absolutely insist on a big united Germany? Of
course there are national motivations, but I don't think they
mean so much to us nowadays. In general my generation is sick
of the old saws about Germany and our eternal guilt. A good
many of us are fed up with all those accusations and all this talk
about reparations payments to Israel. Besides, we've had unpleasant experience with Jewish students. They were incapable
of social relations with us because of this obsessive idea that
we and only we were to blame. I once spoke with two Israeli
students and the first thing they said to me was that they were
Jews. 'My goodness,' I said. 'Why do you tell me that? Did I tell
you I was a Catholic?' They were so terribly prejudiced that I
couldn't discuss anything with them. I couldn't talk about Kennedy, or about the Negro problem or the war in Vietnam. To
them being a Jew was everything. I've never had such disagree-
able discussions. They were really insulting. 'Why should I talk
to you?' they said. 'It may have been your father who killed
my mother.' Even if my father had killed a Jewess, I'm not
responsible. But they simply wanted to cover all us Germans
with guilt. I don't see how we can ever come to an understanding on that basis. This blanket guilt that we've taken on ourselves gets on a lot of young people's nerves, and that's why
some of them vote for the NPD. They do it the way a spiteful
child stamps his foot or sticks out his tongue.

But unfortunately I find a good many young people who say: 'Why should I vote?'

They include a good many who have never voted before. Altogether it's sad to see how many students don't vote, how many professors don't vote, and even how many newspapermen don't vote. When an election comes up, I always take my little public opinion poll. And unfortunately I find a good many who say: 'Why should I vote? There's no point in it, it doesn't do any good. The minute they're elected they do something different anyway.' Those are people who have discovered that the SPD is no better than the CDU, that one's as crazy as the other. So who should we listen to? They neither of them have any programme or plan any more, they've become terrifyingly alike. And now with the NPD and the extra-parliamentary Left opposition we have something entirely new. New alternatives and new outlets have been opened. This pains me, because for me democracy is the only tolerable form of life. If only our politicians were better democrats and were able to make something better of democracy.

JULIA DÖRFLER, her daughter FRIEDEL

34, married, and 17, gas station operators

Our dad was a good man, you couldn't say he ever went drinking.

My father was a miner in the Ruhr. He was in an accident in the mine and after that he was 100 per cent disabled. He met my mother in the Ruhr and then he came back here where he was born. A janitor's job was all he was good for. We lived in the Old City. Oh yes, my parents had lots of friends in the city – you know how it is. They knew half the town. Everybody knows everybody else in the Old City. We always had a lot of visitors. All kinds of people. Sometimes they played cards. My father never went out to a bar, no, he always stayed home.

Our father was a good man, you really couldn't have called him a toper. Oh, maybe when we were still little, I don't know about that. Our parents were okay. They only lived for us. For us children. Yes, there were a lot of us. Well anyway, we couldn't have had better parents. We had a really happy childhood. It makes me happy to think about it. We played with all the children on our street and in our neighbourhood. But I don't see them any more. They're all married now. I went to public school as far as the eighth grade. I didn't go into apprenticeship because right after the War there were no apprenticeships open. You just had to have a paying job. So I did housework. Hell, there are seven of us. The oldest went to the army when he was only seventeen. And then he was a prisoner for six years in Russia. When he came home, he looked around for work and now he has a gas station. My oldest sister is married to an American. He was here as a soldier, she met him here. First they went over to America. They lived over there. But now they're back here. He left the army and now he's got a private job here, I mean as an American civilian. And then there's another brother, he's a bus driver. And then I've got a younger brother, he works in a gas station too. And then there's my youngest sister, we call her the Mouse. Her name is Maria. She's married too, over in America. And then I have still another sister, she's been working for an American firm for seventeen years. She lives with my mother. How my sisters happened to meet their Americans? Well, the youngest was coming home from school and she met her Ami at my brother's place, the one with the gas station. And the other one, the Mouse, was taking a walk with my daughter. Her husband was the chauffeur for an American general who has an office here – at Allied headquarters I think they call it. So the driver was standing around waiting for his general and that's how he met the Mouse.

Church? I really can't find time for it on Sunday.

Well, we're Catholic. Religious? Oh, average. My mother had no time to go to church. Once in a while when she was out shopping, on weekdays you know, she'd duck into church, but we children were sent to church every Sunday even after we began going to school. My father and mother always wanted us to learn something and go to church and everything that goes with it. My husband is a Protestant. But we were married in a Catholic church and the children are Catholics. Little Paul, he's five, and Friedel. Yes, she's seventeen. To tell you the truth, we only go to church on Christmas Eve, because on Sunday I really can't find time. My husband works and I have to cook the meals and do the things that don't get done during the week.

When I met my husband – goodness, it was in carnival, in the gymnasium. You see, my husband comes from practically the same neighbourhood and I was there with a friend from the Youth Club. Then my husband saw me and decided to get rid of the other fellow. In those days they didn't serve drinks, only some kind of soda pop that tasted like a wet window-pane. But my husband had a bottle of potato schnapps. He went over to the man who had brought me there and said: 'Have a drink.' And he drank so much that he passed out and they took him away in an ambulance. So then my husband said to me: 'Well, we got rid of him.' Then he asked me if he could take me home. And after that he kept dating me and pretty soon it was wedding bells. My husband was trained as an automobile mechanic, but later he changed over to the gas station, the one that belongs to my brother. In Paulheimerstrasse. Then three years ago he leased this gas station. We only moved in here a year ago. First we lived with my parents and then we moved in with his grandma. That was for the birds. Only one room. For twelve years I looked for accommodation, and got nothing. We signed up at the Housing Bureau; but no luck. We put ads in the paper. Nothing. Then we got this place because it belongs to Herr Spechtmeier who owns the gas station. There are five small rooms. With heat, garbage removal, etc., the rent comes to 250 marks. But we do the janitor work and for that he deducts 150 marks. We only operate the gas station, but we get a lot of business. Today, for instance, we washed twenty-five cars. We all help at the gas station. I mean my husband, myself, Friedel, the attendant and an apprentice boy. But we're satisfied and we like the work. You meet people, nice people and some that aren't so nice. But on the whole we have good customers, regular customers you know. They're really nice people. We're nice to them too. It's the only way to be. We have out-of-town customers too. When they come to town they get their gas from us. It's a real nice town. We don't want to leave. We know our way around and when we want to go some place we know where to go.

You think my husband is interested in politics? Oh no!

As I was saying, I don't want to leave here. My husband doesn't want to leave either. The only thing that gets me riled up is politics. The thing I can't understand is the rent policy. The way they've been raised. Supposing only my husband were working, we couldn't pay it. Otherwise I don't know anything about politics. Only this thing with the rent, that gets me riled up. You think my husband's interested in politics? Oh no! What I say is: You can't change anything anyway, they'll always do what they please. Yes, we vote. I ask my husband. He tells me what to do. The newspaper? Yes, that's the first thing he does in the morning, but he just skims over the politics.

It gripes me the way they huddle up and talk about everybody.

I always like it best when I have the apartment to myself. And I also say: never start up with the people in the building. It's always best to keep to yourself. Maybe that's a funny way to look at it. There are nice people in the building, but it gripes me the way they huddle up on the sidewalk and talk about everybody. I don't like it. I say hello to everybody, I'm polite. My brothers and sisters come to see me and sometimes business friends come in, salesmen, and so on.

Daughter Friedel: Yes, but the bar across the street belongs to Herr Filz and we have to go now and then to keep up appear-

ances because he's a customer. A lot of young people go there.
So sometimes we go when they have doughnuts and then
there's a big crowd of us.

Some people want to look bigger than they are.

Julia Dörfler: Most people are out to save money; all they
care about is saving money. They try to get off as cheap as
possible. They always want a reduction. They want this cheaper
and that cheaper and gas cheaper. Some people want to look
bigger than they are. They drive a Mercedes and they take five
marks' worth of gas. Yes, that happens. Sometimes it's two
marks' worth. And sometimes they talk you blue in the face.
Even about politics. Probably trying to distract our attention.

No truck with Communists.

Not so long ago we were talking it over with my brother-in-
law, you know, the Ami, the one that came back from America,
and he says if there's reunification we'll have to leave Germany.
We want no truck with the Communists. When you hear about
all the things they do. Nationalizing everything, so literally
nothing belongs to the people. All the same we'd welcome reunification because then we'd know there was peace. Until then
there won't be any peace and everybody's afraid of war. Yes,
I think everybody's afraid there'll be another war. No, I won't
have anything to do with the Communists. Dumb idea making
everybody equal. It's better over here. I say, anybody who
plays the game can make a go of it, and everybody has his
chance. We work hard but at least we have our private life.
And nobody comes around telling us to do this, that or the
other.

We never go to the movies. Or the theatre either.

Well, my husband plays the accordion and his passion is driving
a car. We have a used Ford. But it's in A1 condition. In the

evening we watch TV. We never go to the movies. Or the theatre either. Yes, we read. Various books and illustrated magazines. We're in a book club, they send us books automatically. *Gone with the Wind* was very exciting. My husband reads too but he usually falls asleep over it. You know, he works thirteen hours a day and Saturday and Sunday too, that adds up to more than ninety hours a week.

Friedel: I work in the gas station too. Maybe I'll manage to find a good husband. But I don't want to marry at seventeen like my mother. No, I think I'm still too young. And Daddy is very strict about those things. I can stay out until ten o'clock but if I'm five minutes late he gives me two weeks of house arrest. He always says: 'Better foresight than hindsight.' That's why he keeps such a close watch on me. Sometimes it makes me sore but he's right. Anyway, the man I marry will have to be good-looking. He shouldn't be poor either, I want him to be able to support me so I don't have to work. Most of the young men nowadays are kind of stupid. Hopping around with long hair, dancing the twist and the shake, and all that stuff. I don't care for it. I do those dances now and then but I don't like them. And the way they shout after me: 'Hey, kid!'—hmph, I don't even listen. But there are some nice ones too. Some of them come to the gas station, they look clean and decent, but there are some others, they drive a car and when they get out, the pants they have on make you want to throw up, and the way they behave is scary. They get out with a cigarette dangling from their lips: 'Quick, one gallon, I'm in a hurry.' And they run after me telling me to step on it. That's the way they are. But there's one I've taken a shine to. He's not bad. I'd go out with him if Daddy let me. Oh no. I'd better not take a Beatle in to see him. Actually I want a man with a tummy. My grandpa had a tummy and I liked it so much I've always said I wanted a man with a tummy. But first he's got to be like my father: his temperament and black hair. Daddy is terrific. The way he runs around and never gets tired and says what he means. He's very fond of me. My only complaint is that he gets so excited when I paint too much. Then he really bawls me out. One time we went out on Sunday. We were eating dinner, and I tried to keep my eyes very wide open all the time so he wouldn't see that my eyelids were painted. But finally he noticed and started yelling: 'Go wash your face this minute.' 'But, Daddy,' I said. 'It's not so bad.' So he took me out and scrubbed me with a brush and I started bawling, and he said: 'Never let me see anything on your face again.'

WILHELM GENSERT

40, married, Protestant clergyman

On the whole I believe a minister still enjoys the respect of his congregation.

Our congregation takes in a wide social range. Its members live in a new housing development on the outskirts of the city. The first buildings were occupied in 1962. They formed a compound serving the University and the Max Planck Institute. A number of young assistants from all departments moved out here with their families. Later on low-cost housing was built. The tenants were what you might call 'resocialized' persons, people who had been living in the Old City under subhuman conditions. In many cases a family with many children had been living in one room. Then some of the better paid white-collar workers moved into the upper floors of the big buildings. And in addition we have the class of people living in the bungalows: engineers, white-collar workers and doctors. In other words, we have workers, members of the middle class, and university people. The only class that's missing is the really wealthy. There's just a short stretch of street where well-to-do people can build houses in their own taste and style. All in all, there are five thousand people. Rather more Protestants than Catholics, I believe. We have a Catholic priest too, but neither denomination has a real church in the development. The Catholic congregation now has a community house where they hold

their services. Protestant services are still held in a kind of
shack. It's a prefabricated house with two rooms for kindergarten classes. I can't exactly say that services are well
attended. The hall is usually full, but in view of the number of
Protestants who live here it's a very small percentage. Of
course I should also count the children's services. All in all we
have somewhere between 160 and 200 people in church on a
Sunday. I feel certain that more people would come if we had a
real church, because a lot of people don't regard such makeshift
quarters as a real church. It doesn't give them the right feeling.
There simply isn't anything to give the visual impression of a
church. In town about seventy per cent of the Protestant
population go to church. By comparison we're not so badly off
out here. It came as a surprise to me to find that the women
of the academic community were more than willing to participate in the life of the congregation, visiting new arrivals,
helping in the kindergarten, taking up collections for the Inner
Mission, lending a hand in case of emergency, taking care of
children and so on. So far we have had no help from the
women of other sections of the population. In general it's more
the older people who go to church. Probably because the
younger people are too busy with their work, with building
their families and making improvements in their apartments,
and also because they like to keep their week-ends as free as
possible. The older people have quieter lives and have more
time to think responsibly. I believe that's the reason they are
more willing to participate in our church life. One of our problems is that most of the children have religious instruction
only up to the age of fifteen. Great efforts have brought in-
adequate results. Of course we can't abandon our efforts, but
on the other hand we can't expect them to lead to much. Not
only in connexion with the church, but also in other social
groupings, clubs, circles and wherever young people get together, we have found that by the time the young people are
eighteen they no longer wish to belong to groups. At that age
an inclination to individualism sets in, a tendency to throw off
all obligation to a group or an authority and live their lives as

they see fit. At the same time you might say that the young people lack ideals; they have no inner light. But I don't believe the young people regard this as a great deficiency. If a young man, a student or apprentice, wants to get together with others, he has numerous possibilities: popular education or vocational guidance groups, political groups, occupational groups, clubs centred on various hobbies, and so on. On the whole I believe a minister still enjoys the respect of his congregation. Especially if his dealings with them are more personal than official. When a minister speaks at a public meeting, I don't believe that the mere fact of being a minister will win him much sympathy or respect; he must gain them by his own personality, by what he is and what he says. But in the congregation, when he visits families and goes into their houses, a minister is still somehow a figure that commands respect. Even among the young people, but more among those that are over thirty. True, it's a very reserved kind of respect. They watch and wait. They don't bare their hearts. They wait to see what the minister is really after and what kind of man he is. Once he wins their personal confidence, the relationship is much better. Then a human contact has been established. It has little to do with his title. Nowadays human contact is a vital factor in community work, and a minister who has a hard time making human contacts will have a hard time in his community.

I just have too little time for house calls.

There are too many other things to do. Generally speaking, the most I can do is keep in close touch with the people who participate in our community work, that is, the older people, the trustees and committee members, and the young volunteer workers who take care of the showcases and do neighbourhood aid work. Otherwise, I concentrate on the people who need me, either because they are sick or because they have family problems. The new arrivals are visited by other members of the congregation. Often I don't get to know them until they have children to baptize. Baptism, marriage, and of course

confirmation offer opportunities for talks. I take a great
interest in the parents of confirmees. I invite them in groups
to my home because I have no other place to receive them.
As a rule, about two thirds of them come. The other third don't
seem to want any direct contact with me. I haven't been able
to find out exactly why. I believe they regard it as an obligation and that's distasteful to them. I've called on some of
them, and then it turns out that they really don't want to have
anything to do with the church.

They only want their children to be confirmed.

They say: 'I don't want the children to miss anything and to
reproach me later on.' But they themselves want nothing to do
with the church. Often there are deep-seated problems. I start
by saying how difficult it is to preserve one's faith in these
times. The things of faith are invisible things that speak to a
man in his heart of hearts. In these times, when everything is
measurable, demonstrable and tangible, where external life
with its magnificent achievements makes so heavy a demand
on man's thoughts and aspirations, the invisible, imponderable
things, for which a man must give of himself, are neglected. To
these things people no longer have any real access, and so they
develop a certain indifference towards them. They doubt
whether there is really a God, because He does not make himself very noticeable and they doubt whether the Church still
means anything. Many people have had bad experience of
ministers or other ecclesiastics. And many feel that the Church
and its services are simply out of date. The hymns, the prayers,
the vestments, the Bible, the sermon no longer have any real
appeal for them. All that doesn't really touch them. Somehow
it doesn't fit into their lives any more. One class of people you
don't see in church nowadays is the successful ones, the ones
who get ahead and make careers for themselves. Successful
people pass the Church by. Formerly it seemed that people in
distress, people with worries, would tend to seek the help of
God through the Church. But I don't believe you could say

that today, because there are many people who even in affliction turn neither to the Church nor to God. They doubt everything. Even those who do their bit, who do church work and
try to help me, who really participate in the life of the congregation can't – when you ask them – give a clear explanation
of why they do so. I could only give you the theological reasons,
that God has moved these people's hearts, that these people
have not evaded God, that God has answered their prayers and
told them what to do. Something has happened to them of
which they themselves are probably unaware. It's not something religious in the usual sense. No, it's something connected with the reality of God, who works on men and makes
Himself known to them. And men respond – or else they fail to
respond.

A certain resistance sets in with puberty.

If from the first to the sixth grade religious instruction is given
in such a way as to arouse the children's interest, if we open
their hearts with friendliness, they follow willingly. But in the
seventh grade problems arise. Puberty sets in. For reasons
unknown to themselves the children become unsteady; sometimes they get silly and talkative. They are unable to concentrate and little by little they show a certain resistance. The
first sign is a loss of interest. Of course the family background
has something to do with it. Children who come of families
for whom faith and the Church had lost all meaning have a
hard time taking interest in a subject that isn't part of the regular programme. But there are some cases of children from non-
Christian families who are so moved that they stay on. They
start going to church, they join one of our youth groups and
help as much as they can. Those are exceptional cases. But a
clergyman has to think about every single soul.

Our family was reasonably Christian.

My father is a dentist. We were sent to church at an early age.

The War and the postwar period affected me deeply. I spent the last two years of the War as an air force auxiliary, in the Labour Service, in the Volksturm, and in an American prison camp. The physical conditions in the prison camp couldn't have have been worse. It was a hard experience. But it was good and it was necessary. I think it was good for me because I learned about people's religious reactions in an extreme situation. Thousands of us were living behind barbed wire in an open field, without barracks or tents or any sort of shelter. We slept in the open. When it rained, we huddled together and tried to sleep standing up. We ate coffee grounds just to have something between our teeth. We stood around all day, idle and stupefied, completely in the dark about our future. Some of the men were looking for a New Testament or a Bible to read. Luckily I had a New Testament in my pocket. That was something to sustain the heart and mind and when there was someone to discuss it with, those were the bright moments of our intellectual life. All of us were very shaken, it was something more than the general misery after the First War; this was total collapse. People had lost their bearings because everything they looked up to had collapsed and no one knew whether the German people or the German state would continue to exist. Our philosophical foundations were shattered. So we looked for new foundations. We needed a new orientation – and that's where the word of God came in. Here was something that could straighten us out, something that applied to all things human, to all man's acts and deeds, his undertakings and transgressions. In the first months after my return from the prison camp, I belonged to a Christian men's group. A number of men's groups formed at that time. They met on their own, without a minister and read the Bible. They tried to fortify themselves for the battle of life and to pave the way for a new community life in Christ. These were important, fundamental experiences. Men of all ages and walks of life took part. It became clear that we all had one common drive, we all wanted something very definite that was connected with Christ, a direct, personal bond with him. And later on there were youth groups from my home town who wanted to participate in Christian youth work and formed prayer circles. All those things moved me and led me to form a personal bond with Christ. I still had no definite desire to become a clergyman, to lead others to the faith or help them find the way. Sometimes during services I felt an urge to tell many people the things that seemed so clear and plain to me when I was in church. It was very strange. I felt: 'These things ought to be plain to every human being.' But I still didn't make up my mind to study theology. Actually I wanted to study medicine. The idea of being a minister repelled me, anyway it didn't appeal to me, because a minister is a prisoner in a big organization and has so many obligations that have nothing to do with evangelization. Actually, when you get down to brass tacks, a minister's job can look like quite a monstrosity.

Many of the younger theologians are very reluctant to become ministers.

Most of a minister's dealings nowadays are with so-called card-file Christians. He's become a kind of Christian functionary. People bring him their children to baptize or they want him to marry them, and he has to comply even though they are not real Christians and their interest is purely external. When I think of the masses of children we have to instruct in the schools. It's an enormous effort and a real torment. But we have to do it because if we want to build something new, we need young people. But it's hard to do justice to the traditional conceptions of the Church. There are traditional ideas of what a minister should do, how a church should look, what the life of the Church should be. These traditional conceptions can come from the church and they can come from the congregation. You can't separate the church and the congregation. They go hand in hand. Of course the institution is important, but the congregation is also an important organism.

People have a strange repugnance to innovations in the Church.

If anybody proposes new ideas such as: 'Let's try an entirely different kind of church service! Let's have a different seating arrangement and let the service be conducted by a few other people in addition to the minister' – quite a lot of people will be hostile to such suggestions and some will be dead against them. It's surprising when you consider that so many of these people are mere card-file Christians. Actually they ought to be open to modern ideas because tradition really means nothing to them. But that's not the case. In these troubled times when man hasn't sufficient inner clarity, when he isn't sufficiently filled with the presence of Christ, he expects the Church to provide him with something stable and solid to hold on to. And he associates this element of solidity with the familiar traditional forms. If the slightest change is made in the form of the service, if the confirmation ceremony or even the date is modified, such people jump out of their skins and say 'It's never been that way. Why the sudden change?' It's a strange contradiction. But perhaps it's because people, and especially the young people, are shaken by so many outward impressions. That makes them feel uncertain. There's the same kind of uncertainty in the field of sex.

Films, illustrated magazines and any number of periodicals exert an undesirable influence on the sexual consciousness.

They are sources of psychic affliction. The mass media are largely responsible for all these changes from the speed cult to premature sexual activity and the wish-fantasies of boys and girls. Where else would it come from? People's minds are subject to constant visual bombardment. Their nervous systems are stimulated by sound, image and word. Illustrated magazines, advertising, movies and television are mass media that affect people, especially young people, in their very depths. It troubles me a good deal. But there's nothing we can do about it. We can't even resist. But we see that these influences are entirely bad; we see how hard it is for the young people to get their bearings. It's no wonder that some of them ask for rules of conduct when everything they see is an encouragement to let their animal drives run riot. What should we do? That is the question. When we address young people in school or in a youth group, these questions always come up. The topic is inexhaustible. But here again you need human contact, confidence between man and man: without that you can't tell them anything because they won't listen. To begin with, the Church is suspect to many of them, they regard it as an ethical institution from which you can't expect help but only commandments. Probably the best way is to give the young people we meet the literature on the subject and then try to discuss it with them. Today there are excellent little books by well-known authors about growing to manhood or womanhood, the problem of betrothal, training for marriage, etc. Parents are very behindhand in giving their children such things to read. And often they shirk the task of enlightening their children. I've discussed the matter at length at parents' meetings with the parents of confirmees, and the general opinion was: 'Yes, it's best if the minister does it.' Educational psychologists have told us that a group conversation on such topics is often better than an individual conversation. If we do it in a group and manage to provide a frank, open atmosphere, a group conversation with children of that age is more profitable than trying to draw individuals into a conversation. I can't say that I'm happy. I don't think that's possible for a minister. He's drawn in too many different directions by all the business a minister has to attend to. Our work can't be really satisfactory because the field is too enormous. We're always dealing with problems we can't solve properly. In a way we are slaves. Even so, we shouldn't complain, because we know how important our work is.

ALFRED KRASKE, HEINZ NICKEL, REINHOLD SCHLANDER, JOSEF WALS

42, 44, 39, 41; Catholic priests

Nowadays the cities provide more recruits for the clergy than the country.

Father Kraske: Even during our student days our group of friends felt that it would be necessary later on to work in a team because we saw that one man by himself would never be able to accomplish all the tasks that confront a priest in a large urban congregation today. Later on we took our request to the bishop and he agreed at once in principle. Because of the shortage of priests, to be sure, he could only give us a congregation that had previously been served by three priests. Undoubtedly fewer men go into the priesthood now than before the War. At that time a good many of the young men in our diocese wished to become priests, but some were turned down because there were plenty of candidates. Unfortunately that has changed today. In those days the majority of candidates for the priesthood came from rural districts, from the villages. As our investigations show, there has been a drastic change. In that light, the sociological development in the villages, the change from a closed-in backwoods mentality to a modern urban view of life, is not so fortunate. The villages are in the midst of a social upheaval; consequently, we shall probably have to wait for some time before they produce a new generation of clergymen. Nowadays the cities provide more recruits for the clergy than the villages. This transformation, the end of the bourgeois social era and the rise of a new civilization is more concentrated in the cities. I have taken a special interest in this phenomenon because I myself come from a village, and I have been able to observe at first hand the revolution that has been going on in the villages. At present along with the other priests on my team, I am in charge of an urban congregation. I had no difficulty in establishing contact with this urban congregation because I had previously worked as a vicar in big cities.

Our community here numbers roughly 18,000 souls, about 8,000 Catholics and 10,000 Protestants. The two denominations are pretty well mixed; they live side by side in the same houses. In our congregation older people predominate. About a quarter of the people in the parish are over sixty, for the most part civil servants, office workers, persons of independent income and students; not so many workers. A part of our parish is situated in the Inner City. There is a constant migration from the Inner City to the suburbs. A common phenomenon. Especially the active younger people move out of town.

Be that as it may, I find the work here very stimulating and fruitful, and I am glad both denominations are represented. We have excellent relations with our Protestant brethren. We often meet in schools and hospitals. We strike up conversations and discuss our common problems.

It's a good thing for a clergyman to hear the views of the other denominations.

Recently we have begun to arrange meetings with the Protestant vicars. At our last meeting, for instance, each man present spoke about his youth work and his personal experience. We found that the problems and tasks on both sides are rather similar. Perhaps the Catholics are more church-minded than the Protestants. A Catholic tends to be more church-minded because of Sunday observances, receiving the sacrament, and other duties connected with the Church.

Father Nickel: But it is open to question whether more church-mindedness means more Christian conviction. We've given that question a good deal of thought. In our congregation we have members who take a very active part in church affairs and others who participate less in religious life but probably feel just as certain that they are leading a Christian life. We cannot be sure that church activity means more faith, more Christianity.

In any event we have come to the conclusion that church activity does not necessarily imply Christianity and a life in the faith.

One can only judge that on the basis of individual cases. Blanket judgements are not in order.

Father Kraske: According to our latest parish statistics, roughly three hundred members of our flock attend Sunday services. Not a very high percentage. The others of course are Christians in the sense that they get married in church, have their children baptized, send them to communion, have them confirmed, ask for the sacraments on their deathbeds, etc. You might call them nominal Christians.

Father Nickel: In connexion with nominal Christians, I should like to speak of my experience over the last eight years as a hospital priest. A good many nominal Christians do not refuse the sacraments *in extremis*, I mean when they think they are going to die soon – at any rate not if they are asked. Baptized Christians who say no to the sacraments are very rare.

Father Kraske: I should say that the big problem for Catholic Christians is this:

When we were children our parents put the Christian religion on us as if they were dressing us.

In religious instruction at school we are always learning answers to the ultimate questions of life although existentially those questions had not yet arisen. Young Catholics are stuffed full of religious questions and problems. When a young person comes out of school and has his religious instruction behind him, he thinks he knows all about religion and Christianity. He regards them as more or less finished business, and the teacher of religion is largely to blame for this mistake. When our young person enters the adult world, he thinks he knows all the answers to the questions of life. It doesn't occur to him that he learned these answers a long time ago and has given them no thought in the meanwhile. He doesn't realize that there is no connexion between the religion he has learned and his real life. Some never find out. If it never dawns on them, if they don't assimilate existentially what they learned in religious instruction, they will drop religion altogether. A person who receives no further religious guidance after leaving the sheltered sphere of his catechism class is almost automatically headed for a crisis, for a situation in which he will really need the support of a priest. In view of the present state of the secular world, we are therefore convinced that we must re-learn our trade, because adult education in secular life is something new to us. For a long time it was believed in the secular world that a man who had passed his journeyman's examination had mastered his trade for life, that as far as his work was concerned he had achieved maturity once and for all. Now we know that this is not true.

A man in secular life who does not continue his education is done for. The same is true in the religious sphere.

In the religious sphere we are forced to recognize that a man who does not maintain his dialogue with the Church in every new life-situation cannot claim to know what he should about religion. We must accept the fact that in this day and age no one can exist for himself alone. That was still possible in the age of individualism, but not today in this age of collectivism. The Church must keep abreast of these modern sociological developments.

If for example a man has learned in religious instruction that the Bible is to be taken literally and then, on the basis of television programmes, illustrated magazines, books and newspaper articles comes to the conclusion that the Bible cannot be taken literally, he is simply heading for a crisis. We still – it's a hangover from our traditional ways – do far too much work with children and fail to take an active enough part in the lives of young people and adults. When we speak of missionary work today, we mean essentially that it is not enough to guard our flock but that we must go out in search of souls.

We must go to people where they live and work.

We can't wait for them to come to us in the church or rectory.
We must carry our message to them in their homes and places
of work. But missionary work is not primarily the business of
priests; it is up to the faithful themselves. The popes have been
right in saying that the worker's apostle must be a worker, the
businessman's a businessman, and the professor's a professor. It
is physically impossible for the priests to perform this missionary task alone: there simply aren't enough of us. The most we
priests can do is to induce the believers in our midst to set their
fellow men a shining example by the account they give of
themselves at their places of work. A priest has his task, his
mission, and a true believer in turn has his task and mission
towards outsiders. Too few believers are aware of this. Most are
still living in the times when the supreme watchword was:
'Save your own soul.' In those days no thought was given to a
mission and responsibility towards others, to the need for
carrying the Church into people's lives. Today priests and faithful alike are in the midst of a transformation, and it remains
for us priests to inculcate this new manner of thinking, this new
attitude in our believers. Too little has been done but at least
we can claim to be moving in the right direction. One indication is the new apostolic efforts we have been making in Germany since the War. I have in mind the family groups and
clubs and especially our working-class youth movement, which
was impeded by the Third Reich and has only gained a foot-
hold since the War. I also have in mind the general Catholic
youth movement with its various branches – the Scouts, for
instance.

But only ten per cent of the young people in our community
belong to Catholic youth organizations.

The aim and purpose of this movement is to teach young
people a kind of Christianity that embraces the new missionary
thinking and is no longer restricted to the old principle that

each man should save his own soul. However, we keep reminding ourselves that seventy per cent of the people in this community do not take part in the life of the congregation. Nearly all the children in the age group come to First Communion, but a month or two later only a third are attending church services. The ones who go to church are those whose parents go to church. This shows you how little is accomplished by religious instruction in school. I find any number of boys who are enthusiastic about serving as choir boys during their first years at school, but when they see the duties involved, the need to be constantly present, a lot of them drop out. One reason is that so many families go to the country for the weekend.

A great obstacle to missionary thinking is that people today are so preoccupied with purely materialistic concerns. Most of them concentrate on the thought:

'How am I going to make money and organize my life in the spirit of the new prosperity?'

I believe that this consideration crowds out all others and that it is not beneficial. Of course, when you talk things over with these people and pass their lives in review, they often see the light and recognize the need of reshaping their lives. But unfortunately we ourselves can speak with only a few of them. And where nowadays will you find a man who spontaneously concerns himself with his neighbour and tries to explain what is going on in the depths of his soul? People are so caught up in the rush of life that they have no time for one another. It's only when a crisis arises that they feel the need of a kind of psychotherapist who will listen to them and throw some light on their lives.

Father Nickel: In cases of psychic disorder a priest alone cannot suffice. But when a man's crying need is an interlocutor who can help him to find meaning in his life, I believe he needs a priest and that this has always been and always will be the primary function of a priest. From my own experience I can assure you that occasions arise in the life of every man when he *must* find time to talk with a priest. It's astonishing, when people are sick, how easy it is to strike up a meaningful conversation with them. I regard a routine visit to the sick as only a first step. It gives the sick man the feeling that he can have more if he wants more. The most I can do is make a discreet offer. To insist would be to take advantage of a man's illness, to exploit his helplessness. If I pressed my services on him at such a time, he would feel that I had infringed on his personal freedom, and no dialogue would be possible. But many take advantage of my discreet offer. In a situation of illness they feel that total commitment to economic success is not the right thing.

'Yes,' they say to themselves. 'I have money, I'm a success in business, but what does it all mean?'

Father Kraske: It's the same in other encounters with people. A man's reaction depends on whether the priest behaves like a decent sensible human being. If he does, he'll be accepted. It's no good to start right in with the question: 'Do you go to church on Sunday?' You've got to meet your parishioner as man to man, to inspire confidence. You've got to give him the idea: This is somebody I can talk to. The older people still respect a clergyman. With the young it's a question of personality. They judge a clergyman like everyone else by what he says and does, by the way he acts. To the young people the clergy are no longer a special class, deserving of respect as such, but neither are they people to be met automatically with hostility. If a clergyman can inspire human confidence in young people, they come to regard him as their friend and often discuss their problems with him. Many young people feel their parents don't understand them. They feel restricted in their freedom. They would like to leave home, for instance, but their parents don't understand. This lack of understanding in parents often gives rise to sexual problems.

The young people often say : 'I can't discuss sexual problems with my parents. It's out of the question.'

When they get the idea that they can discuss such matters with us, they do so without the slightest restraint. The problem of sexuality is made very hard for young people today by their environment, by this whole sex-charged atmosphere. Just think of the conception of love and marriage that is constantly set before the young people in the movies and the illustrated magazines. It's a conception that has no relation to reality, but the young people try to follow these wrong ideas about love and marriage, which leads to terrible disappointments. But if you help a young person to discover the hidden meaning of sexuality he will come to appreciate sexuality and love at their true value. Often they have no idea what love really means. They drift into a relationship. Perhaps they occasionally sense its shallowness, but there's no one to speak to them and explain the hidden meaning of sexuality.

Father Nickel: The basic difficulty is that the people of today have grown up in a tradition that does not prepare them for personal relationships. To quote the rather extreme formulation of a psychotherapist, the family was formerly a patriarchal institution; today marriage and the family are becoming a partnership.

In the future love marriages will be the only kind.

I mean to say that a marriage will be regarded as successful only if it is successful from a personal point of view. This situation has been brought about by the disappearance of the old family ties and of the rigid old bourgeois customs. Nevertheless sexual enlightment is a problem for most parents. Probably because until very recently these matters were surrounded by an absolute taboo. Recently an eighteen-year-old girl came to me and told me about her sexual problems; she had good reason to. She asked me for literature that would help her get things straight. I gave her a book about the marriage partnership and asked her if she couldn't discuss the subject with her mother. That is impossible, the girl said. A few days later her mother called me up and expressed her gratitude at receiving help from the Church. She said it showed that the young people were no longer left so dreadfully alone in these questions. It never occurred to her that it was she who had left her daughter so dreadfully alone.

The Catholic Youth feel perfectly free to vote for a non-Christian party.

The political commitment of the members of our congregation doesn't amount to much. Only a few are politically committed. Probably for two reasons. One is that people in general are sick of politics. The other is that a good many of our bishops tend to believe that the faithful should vote for a party that is Christian at least in name and a lot of our people have their doubts as to whether the Church should really be equated with the CDU or the CSU. But recently the political dividing lines have been very much blurred, especially since the Great Coalition between the Social Democrats and the Christian Democrats.

The young people who are active in the community also discuss political questions. They think very differently from the older people. They recognize that a Christian cannot disregard his responsibility for the world. The modern Christian has a world mission. 'World mission', 'responsibility for the world', etc., have become topics of present-day theology.

Chaplain Wals: Another thing to be considered is that our town is very mixed from the standpoint both of religion and of politics. Our mayor belongs to the SPD but is a practising Catholic; he goes to church regularly every Sunday and even takes the sacraments. Ten years ago this would have been very unusual. We also note that our young Catholics do not necessarily agree when they attend a lecture by a representative of the CDU. They feel perfectly free to vote for a non-Christian party. In our opinion it is not an error if they come to such a decision after mature consideration.

Chaplain Schlander: I believe there are also Communists in our congregation. In general people hesitate to label themselves as Communists. It would probably be different if the Communist Party were legal here in West Germany. Some time ago a middle-aged man who had not yet been baptized applied for baptism. He attended the required course of religious instruction. The day before he was to be baptized he suddenly came to me and told me that baptism would probably get him into great difficulties because he was a secret member of the KPD (Communist Party of Germany). I asked him if he personally was disturbed by the contradiction. He replied: 'It's only that I would not like to be bombarded with questions and reproaches by my political friends because I have been baptized. For this reason please let me postpone my baptism a little, don't make me hurry.' Naturally I understood his reasoning and consented. I believe the man has become a good Christian.

ALIX GALLOCK

70, unmarried, actress

My father's eyes twinkled and he said : 'You must be out of your mind.'

It may sound corny but the stage is my whole life. When I was a few years younger, I played big parts in operettas. Then one day I quit – *The Csárdás Princess* was my last operetta – and six months later I was playing Linda in Arthur Miller's *Death of a Salesman*. That was my first real acting part. I was successful from the start. There were no actors in my family but the whole family liked to sing. My father had a beautiful voice. He was a successful businessman. I won't say that I was his favourite child but I do think we – my father and I – hit it off very well. We always used to sing together except when he was travelling. One day when I was still a child he found me lying out in the street. I lay there and broke open an apple. I

had staged a play about Snow White and the other members of
the cast were standing around me. My father's moustache vi-
brated, his eyes twinkled, and he said: 'You must be out of your
mind.' 'Not at all,' I said, 'but I'm going to be an actress.' 'You
don't say so,' said my father with a smile. My father was simply
angelic to me and when he died I thought I'd lost everything I
had in the world. My mother was a wonderful woman but we
weren't so close. Oh, if she heard me say that now, she'd wring
her hands and say she loved me exactly the same as her other
children. Good God, when I think of the first time she saw me
on the stage. It was in Berlin. I was playing Lisa in Franz Lehar's
The Land of Smiles. After the show I went home with her. She
didn't say a word. We didn't look at each other. But in the
reflection of the shop windows I could see her shaking her head.
I was very glad that Lisa makes everybody cry in the end when
she leaves her Chinese. My mother was feeling weepy and that
put the brakes on her feelings against me. Later she was
mighty proud to show people pictures of me in all sorts of
parts and she boasted about my notices. But in the bottom of
her heart she was never completely reconciled to my going on
the stage.

You see, she'd been brought up in an atmosphere of 'With
God for King and Country'.

My good fortune was that even in my operetta days I was never
without acting ability. A lot of the women in operetta have
heavenly voices but they talk like kewpie dolls. I've always
spoken like a real actress. Even in my singing days my actor
friends thought the world of me. I remember, they used to
come to me and say: 'My goodness, Alix, it wouldn't hurt us
to take a page out of your book.' But I've never had illusions
of grandeur. I've always been too scared. I still am. But that's
something nobody believes. Nobody believes me when I tell
them I almost die of stage-fright before every performance. But
once I'm on the stage and the curtain goes up, it's gone. I don't
know if it's my mentality or my temperament that makes me

so nervous. But I fight it down all by myself. I never bother other people with my troubles. There are so many nervous actresses. They scream at the hairdresser and the customers until the whole theatre shakes. I get along with everybody. I have lots of friends, though they're all furious that I have so little private life. I can't sit in a café until four in the morning and go to rehearsal in the morning feeling like the wrath of God.

I have all kinds of friends.

One has a factory, another is a pharmacist, some are doctors. They're an entirely different kind of people, they have nothing to do with the theatre. When actors are present, I say: 'Not one word about the theatre.' No, not in my house. But the theatre people can't help it, they start talking about the theatre. That's the way they are. They always get back to the theatre. They start with the angleworm, they switch over to the elephant's trunk, and they end up talking about the elephant's theatrical way of wiggling his ears. You see, they're back at the theatre again. Well, at least we theatrical people always have something to talk about when we're together. There are so many problems. We have all sorts of things to discuss. The theatre, the plays, the plots, the parts, the other actors, Anita with her small bosom, Patricia with her weak voice, and Paul with his weak mind, who forgets his lines and keeps swallowing syllables which is what makes him so fat. That's how it is. We hardly ever read anything but our parts. I give away a lot more books than I read. I have so many parts to learn, I'm very conscientious about it and that crowds out a good many things. I only read books at night. Then I'm alone and nobody disturbs me. No telegrams, no phone calls, no director calling me up. Now I get still less chance to read, because I have a TV set. The TV gets me terribly wrought up. So much politics. It's really overwhelming. All these developments: 'Will the Chancellor go or stay? What are the Americans up to?'

And that inhuman war in Vietnam, it goes on and on and the curtain never falls. Horrible! If we did anything like that on the stage we'd be booed out of the house.

Yes, politicians can get away with anything. For a long time I didn't know what the CDU and the SPD and all those things were, but you've really got to know such things whether you like it or not, don't you agree? I realized that last night when I was watching TV, and I thought: 'No, it's not right to wear blinkers and close your eyes to everything. You've got to know what's going on in the world.' Because after Hitler I swore I'd never listen to another word about politics. Though the theatre had nothing to do with the Nazis. Oh well, maybe the management was for the Party. I still remember one time when we were supposed to go out in the snow and ice to collect money for Winter Aid, the director said: 'No, that's impossible. My people have to sing tonight.' And they were very angry with him even though he was in the Party. Well, I can put it this way: we were non-political. We didn't have to join the Party as has often been claimed. Yes, they made us parade through the streets on 1 May. I can still remember doing that, but the evening when we were back at the theatre, we said: 'What rot! Why should we go marching around through the streets?' But there were some who saw good in it. Actors too. I once explained it to an American. I said to him: 'See here,

'Actors didn't make much money before Hitler. And here's a man who encourages the theatre.

'Actors began getting higher wages. They could marry and have children and all that. No wonder they said: "Hitler's the man for us." No one thought the kind of things that happened later could happen in Germany. It wasn't until Hitler's deputy, that crazy Hess, suddenly flew off to England to overthrow the government there that people began to think: "Good God, what's going on?"' Speaking as a woman, I'll say this: At first people didn't see things in their true light. They thought it was a good idea to stop all the nonsense with the political parties, and they thought: Here's a man who's really doing something for Germany. Except that I could never listen to his speeches, he yelled so. That bothered me as an actress. It was as if I had a membrane pounding in my ear. Then we noticed that all of a sudden Mendelssohn's music couldn't be played any more because he was Jew, but unfortunately people like me didn't take that so seriously. Maybe we thought it would pass.

A few years ago I met some people in Baden-Baden. They were Jews, the members of their family had been persecuted, and the women kept saying: 'Our graves, oh, our graves!' When you hear that, there's nothing you can say. You're ashamed of the things that happened. Especially because we had really thought such things didn't exist. There was a concentration camp here, I mean, I only heard afterwards that there had been one; at the time it was always referred to as a work camp for criminals. In those days I lived quite a while in a Jewish house, and the lady – she was an orthodox Jewess – said to me: 'We are to blame. Our children don't want to be Jews any more. This is our punishment.' That was her way of looking at it. Then she went to America. And nothing happened to her. Yes, that's how it was, but now tell me, what kind of a party is this NPD that's beginning to frighten people in other countries? Are they former Nazis or people who still expect their salvation from Nazism? They must be off their rocker. But the Germans aren't the only nuts. Take a look at de Gaulle in France. Isn't he crazy too? But then I say to myself: 'Why bat your brains out over all that nonsense? Worry about your theatre.' But then I get all riled up over politics again.

We'll always be war criminals.

You can't make people forget that. Once I told an American what I thought about the bombing of Dresden. It was in southern Germany during a guest performance after the War. The American looked me in the eye and said: 'If you weren't so charming and didn't have such a beautiful voice, I'd put you in jail.' And I said: 'Please, sir.'* Why do we have to put up with everything? I had no part in the Nazis' crimes. After the War, it's true, I was accused of having said 'Heil Hitler' and of having sung for ministers and big shots. My first thought was: 'Are they crazy?' And then I told them to their face: 'Yes, of course I sang for bigshots and now I'm singing for different bigshots, and I'll sing for Eisenhower too if he comes here. And yes, I probably said "Heil Hitler" because that was the German greeting.' You can't brand everybody who wore that piece of red candy, the Party badge I mean, a criminal. There were plenty of members who never hurt a living soul. Take one of those fellows who ran around at night to see if everything was blacked out properly; he had a brown jacket on too. This idea of lumping everybody together! I can't forgive the people who do that. And what do they do in their own country? Look at the race question, all those riots. People killing each other. In my opinion that's bad too. And it really makes me sick to hear people say we're all swine. And it's not so much better today. What's wrong today? Just take a look at the paper:

They kill babies as if they were kittens.

And those awful people who do such things to children, what happens to them? They're coddled and in a few years they get out of prison and start in again. No, really, I'm against the death penalty but when I hear things like that, I'm beside myself. After a while, when I've calmed down, I remember Christ's old saying: 'It's better to let a guilty man go than to execute an innocent man.' Yes, sometimes I'm too high-strung. I'm too sensitive. I used to think you could get through life without compromises. But it can't be done. I'm seventy now and I know. Now I say to myself:

'Alix, it's time for you to stop dancing the twist and swimming too far out.'

---

* English in original.

Some people are even saying I'm eighty. If you've been on the stage a long time, they start counting the years double. When I was playing in *The Hundred-and-Sixth Birthday*, some people thought it was really my hundred and sixth birthday. Because of the way I put my heart into it. The stage really is my life.

There are some stage actors who keep saying they ought to be on the radio or on TV. To them the stage is a side issue.

All they think about is bringing home the bacon.

That's a materialistic attitude. Making money is all very well, but real actors are the ones who don't think about their private lives, who give the stage everything they've got. I'm one of those. You can't imagine the passion I put into playing Goldoni over there in the East Zone, in Weimar; it was like being young again. You see, I started my career in Thuringia, those were the days of my beauty. Sondershausen, with its wonderful Conservatory and its magnificent orchestra. Those little prince's theatres! That was culture at its height. And now again: The audience applauded almost half an hour. It was just heavenly!

But otherwise : riding through Thuringia made me sick at heart.

On the right a guard tower, on the left a guard tower. And Weimar. What a sweet little city it was! And now? An Austrian who was on tour with us said: 'Christ, Weimar looks like Sankt-Pölten during the War!' And the people were really a shock. The workers, such silence, they were all so depressed. When the little girl in the the dressing-room saw my orange – you see, I always eat fruit in the dressing-room – I was ashamed, because she actually said to me: 'We never have any oranges.' Now really, such things shouldn't be in this day and age. Of course some of the people are well off. For instance the director who comes here and puts on plays. He's the director of the Weimar Theatre. He has everything, he drives his own car. But he's so sad, he can't hide his feeling of resignation; it made me feel very badly. Oh, it's politics wherever you go ... But when I'm on the stage, it's all forgotten.

MARTHA KRUSE

49, unmarried, secretary

I think he had quite a lot of moral courage.

I'm forty, I've reached the so-called age of discretion – the age when people are supposed to get some sense. I hope that's true of me. My four brothers and sisters are also past forty. Unlike me they're all married. My father is dead. Only my old mother and myself are left there. As a young girl my mother was housekeeper in a sanatorium here. She comes from the Allgäu. My father was from Frankfurt am Main. First he was a locksmith, but he had to give it up because of an eye injury – a steel splinter went into his eye. During the War he ran a branch of an armaments factory; it was in a prison. He was a staunch old Social Democrat and was very much opposed to Hitler's régime. All the absolutism and coercion went against his grain. He never made a secret of his opinion and it got him into a lot of trouble. The Security Police took him away several times and we were terribly worried, we never knew if he was coming back. Sometimes he was gone for three days, but luckily he always came back. That was the main thing as far as we were concerned. The Nazis never succeeded in intimidating him. I think he had quite a lot of moral courage. He always helped the prisoners and made things easier for them. Mostly they were political prisoners, but there were prisoners of war too and some real criminals. My father arranged it so the members of the German prisoners' families could come now and then, and keep in touch with them. My father felt that people suffer most when they're completely isolated and cut off from the world and haven't got anybody they can talk to. He himself had quite a lot of friends and needed people he could talk to. They were mostly small artisans and government clerks. We also had friends from the university. Such a mixture was unusual in those days. It was possible because my parents were very close to nature and raised bees.

A lot of our friends were apiculturists too, so they were rather odd people.

But having this hobby in common brought them close together. It was always very gay at home. My father had a great sense of humour and in spite of his political opinions he got along fine with people who had entirely different views. For instance, we knew some teachers who were wildly enthusiastic about the National Socialist régime. Of course there were arguments but in the end they went on seeing each other because there was a human understanding between them.

Those teachers were supporters of the régime but they didn't do bad things.

Probably another reason why my father got along so well with such different kinds of people was that he was very religious. At first, I mean by upbringing, he was a Protestant. My mother had always been a Catholic and my parents were married in a Catholic church. We children were all baptized as Catholics, but my father didn't turn Catholic until later. It may sound a little funny but what brought him to Catholicism was that an aunt of mine who had been paralysed was suddenly cured in Lourdes. One fine day my aunt was able to walk again after being completely bedridden for years. That made a big impression on my father, so he turned Catholic too. One day he went to church with us children and after church he took us to the rectory and we talked with the priest. But my father forbade us children to mention it to my mother when we came home. He wanted to surprise her himself with the news because he knew she'd be very pleased. I had a strict Catholic upbringing, and once you have it drummed into you, it somehow sticks.

On the other hand I sometimes wonder whether our religion is right.

Whether it's the true religion. We're supposed to believe it is, but we don't really know. Of course the Catholic Church claims to be the only true religion, but after all the Church is run by human beings and every human being has a weak spot somewhere. So I sometimes doubt that it's the only religion. But for that same reason I believe firmly in God. We all live in hopes of a life after death, but I say to myself: those are only words that were spoken by men, even if they were inspired by God ...

All my brothers and sisters actually studied more than I did.

I went to public school, business school and business college. My eldest brother graduated from classical high school, my younger brother went to scientific high-school. They all played an instrument. I didn't, I'm sorry to say, because I was the oldest and in those days it was customary for girls just to mend and darn, which thank God isn't so true today. Anyway I was trained to help a good deal in the household, especially as my grandparents lived with us. My grandmother lived to be ninety-two. The last four years she was blind and needed a good deal of help. Maybe that's why I was so tied to the house and why I'm the only one that didn't get married. Yes, I was in the house too much, and then came the War and in 1943 I was sent to the Wehrmacht. My whole school class was drafted to work in the staff offices or as Air Force auxiliaries. But my father arranged for me not to be sent away. I only had to work in the office of an army post nearby. After the War my father got me work as secretary in the city administration, and I've been there ever since. I can't claim to be really dissatisfied, but as everyone knows the city doesn't pay as well as a private firm. I missed the boat, I didn't bestir myself soon enough to look for a private job. That too was probably the fault of my upbringing.

I'd always learned that the thing to do is to stick it out where you are and do your duty.

But what I enjoy about my work is all the people I come in contact with. I'm in the Public Order Office. People come in with all sorts of problems: housing problems, occupational problems, and so on. For years the people's main worry was finding a nice comfortable place to live. That worry has been largely eliminated but there are still emergency cases and difficult situations. Usually the families themselves are to blame because they're not willing to make any personal sacrifice for the sake of decent housing. They think they've got to have everything at once.

A lot of people find it hard to limit their personal needs.

Nowadays everybody thinks he has to have a car right away – it's what they call a status symbol – just because his neighbour has one. And all these technical innovations. Are they absolutely necessary? Of course not. Most people in Germany today are better off than they've ever been before. But a lot of them are unable to budget their money. They want more and more of everything. That gets a lot of them into financial difficulties, they can't meet their payments and then one fine day they have to move out of their apartments and end up in the homes for a-social persons. Then we have to see what we can do to get them out of there.

The people aren't attached to the democratic form of government we have now. A lot of them want tighter reins, they don't care what kind. People accept any sort of government if they think it will satisfy their wishes. Even a dictatorship. A lot of people have no desire to think for themselves.

They'd rather be led and they look for a leader to follow. Democracy actually makes them feel ill-at-ease.

Sometimes I have the feeling that they're not told enough what to do.

Under the Third Reich it was different of course. Everything was a command and that made things easy. But that was the time when the workers began demanding more and more. Just think that the Volkswagen publicity was addressed to the workers. And a lot of propaganda was made for women working. That was new. I mean, it's in the nature of things that women should be regarded as the weaker sex and that some men shouldn't treat them as equals, but I personally don't regard us women as the weaker sex. There are always times when you've got to contradict a man. And when you do, they don't take you seriously. They think:

'It doesn't mean a thing, she's only a woman'.

Yes, our people here are the same as everywhere else. Wherever you go people have their weak points. But you've got to take them as they are. I mean that every city and every region has its own mentality. What I like best here is the beautiful situation of our city. Culturally it has a good deal to offer, though it doesn't come up to the big cities. In the way of theatres and concerts, I've got to admit, there isn't so much. But I must confess that I seldom go to either, because in the evening I'm just too tired to go out. I get up between six and half past six. I've got to be in the office at seven-thirty. It takes me fifteen minutes by streetcar, but when my boss has his car he passes me and picks me up. It's taken for granted. I can't conceive of a nicer boss.

He's a work horse and naturally he expects the same of the people under him.

His motto is: 'What I do myself I expect my employees to do

and what I expect of my employees I must do myself.' My boss
is the first in the office in the morning. And I stay on with him
after hours. It often gets to be half past six or seven. That's
why I don't get to the theatre very often. I have school
friends who are still unattached, but as I told you, I have no
great friendships, only a nice little circle of friends. There's a
couple, for instance, that I see a good deal of. The husband has
a shop. I usually go on vacation with them. To Austria sometimes. But usually we stay in Germany, we go to Bad Kissingen,
Baden-Baden, the Elmau in Upper Bavaria and that kind of
place. But I've also been to Italy, that is, mostly just in the
South Tyrol.

Italy itself doesn't really appeal to me. I don't like the
people.

They're so noisy, that's what bothers me. Maybe it's a prejudice we have about the people down there. Of course there
are honest and dishonest people everywhere, but we always
used to say: 'We don't go there, oh no, you always come back
without your pocketbook.' Today that has probably changed
because the country has become more prosperous and probably
also because so many Italians have worked in Germany. I've
met a lot of Americans. When you get to know people well,
they're entirely different from what you first thought. Some
friends of mine have a one-family house. In the summer they
often rent the top floor to Americans who are travelling in
Germany. They like it here and they behave very well. At first
they weren't very nice. I mean the occupation troops after the
War. In those days the Americans were very high-handed, probably because military law was then in force, but I don't think
they were very different from our soldiers.

Our soldiers took great liberties too when they were the
victors.

I try to judge Americans and foreigners in general just as I'd like them to judge us. I wish people could have a better opinion of us than they used to. I'm afraid most foreigners still see us the way we were in the War, but then probably there hasn't been any real change in us. You can see we've already got a party like the NPD again. A lot of people have a hankering for things the way they were under the Third Reich, and that wasn't always very good. The people haven't all realized that democracy is a mode of life where you've got to respect your neighbour.

When you come right down to it, democracy is a product of the Christian faith. Don't you agree?

In a democracy we're not supposed to force people to live as we see fit. But when I think of all the things that happened here under the Nazis, I can't help saying to myself that they weren't good Christians. No, when I think back on those days, God knows I can't be proud. But have the American, English, French, etc., a right to be so proud of themselves? In my opinion they all showed their dark side during the War. Of course the others are in a better position. It paid them to win the War. While we are divided, and in the East Zone we have Communism, which has only brought dictatorship, exactly like National Socialism.

KARL BAUMGARTEN

50, married, active officer in the Bundeswehr

The comradely life has made a good impression on me.

Originally I had no intention of becoming a soldier. My father had a wholesale egg business. I was trained for business and worked in a shoe factory. Before the War I had to serve in the Army for two years and then I went back to my work. Then during the War I was drafted. After the War I became an in-

surance salesman and made good money, about the same as
my captain's pay today. But one day a friend of mine from
the Army came to see me. He had become an officer in the
Bundeswehr and he said I should apply too. That was in 1957.
Maybe it was my memories of the old idealism and my enthusiasm for the comradely life, the togetherness I had ex-
perienced during the War, especially at the front. All those
things had impressed me favourably. Maybe you could also
call it collective spirit. The War, I admit was unpleasant. I was
wounded several times, in the lungs, in the thigh, and so on.

I was in Russia, Poland, Belgium, Holland, Denmark, Norway and Finland.

In Russia I had very little contact with the population because
I was a combat soldier and didn't see much of the population.
We just kept going forward. In Belgium it was different, we
were quartered on the civilian population. At first the people
were very reserved. The man in whose house I lived was a conductor on the international sleeping cars and spoke German
fluently. He too was very reserved at first but after the first
few weeks I was really at home. The family treated me like
their son even though I was a German soldier. Some of my comrades still go to Belgium to visit their old acquaintances of those
days. Another time we were on the Polish border for four
weeks and there again we had the best kind of relations with
the population. They weren't hostile to us either. We stayed in
a village and took part in the village life. We slept in a barn
and the people stayed in their houses. We celebrated holidays
with them, we helped them with their work in the fields,
and we attended weddings and baptisms. Maybe those people
hadn't had any trouble with the Germans. That was in the summer of 1941. Actually they must have had trouble with the
Germans. Not in 1939 with the combat troops but later on
with the administration, the SS, the SD* and the Gestapo. But

---

* *Sicherheits-Dienst* – Security Police.

we saw no sign of it. At that time we didn't know much about conditions in the different countries. During the War, at the front, in the hospital and in the home garrisons I didn't hear anything about the concentration camps and those terrible things that we heard about later on.

I only remember that once when I was home on leave my father took me to see a concentration camp here in the vicinity.

It must have been a small concentration camp, a sub-camp or some such thing. My father took me there and said: 'Take a look at those people. That's what concentration camp inmates look like.' We weren't very close but I was able to get a good look at them in their striped uniforms. They were standing in columns, ready to march off. I remember clearly. My father said: 'They're criminals, but there are some politicals too.' My father hadn't been drafted and he knew more than I did about things here at home. He was an old Socialist, he joined the SPD in 1911. Naturally he was against the Nazis but in those days my natural spirit of opposition prevented me from seeing things the same way as my father. The concentration camp inmates made the same impression on me as convicts, pale and stupefied. But those people didn't look like the ones we saw later in the pictures and films. That was about the beginning of 1943. Sure, I was enthusiastic about the Nazis. That came from school if nothing else, because the schools were definitely nationalistic, they put so much stress on national feeling that it never even occurred to a young man to have different political ideas. Our education was one-sided from the start. So my education and the whole situation made me feel that everything was all right. We were practically at war and we thought people with different political ideas were enemies of the state so naturally they had to be locked up one way or another. Nobody knew at the time that those people in the camps were being killed. My father didn't say anything about it either. He only thought they were imprisoned and made to work. He didn't say a word about political murder and I'm sure he didn't know anything about it. But I remember the persecution of the Jews even before the War. Oh yes, I remember that. There was a building across the street. On the ground floor there was a restaurant that belonged to Jews. SA-men went in and threw everything out the window. Beer bottles and potatoes and furniture and egg crates. The eggs smashed and the SA-men said: 'We're not allowed to steal anything, but we can smash anything we please.' The Jews were very frightened but they stayed on in the building. Later, during the War – as my parents told me – they were loaded into trucks and driven away. My parents thought they were being taken to Poland to be resettled. They certainly had no idea they were taken to camps and gassed. Most of us were enthusiastic about Hitler, but there was also a feeling that the War was shit, and I'm convinced that a lot of my German comrades would have deserted if we'd been sent to the western front. Some of them said so. But they didn't dare to because we were up against the Russians. They were afraid they'd be worse off as prisoners than if they kept on fighting. That was in 1943, almost two years before the end of the War, and the men were just about fed up. But they carried on because they thought there was no other way. They thought that was how things had to be. In 1939 we naturally still thought it was our duty to fight for Germany, for the greatness of the Reich. We were still young enough to fall for propaganda. Today I can see that our idealism was abused.

In the Bundeswehr it's different.

The whole life is entirely different. There's no more of the old chicanery – or what you might call chicanery. In my training period in the Wehrmacht, when something went wrong, they'd march us into an alley alongside the barracks that was paved with crushed stone; the stones were still sticking out. The platoon leader would sing out: 'Break ranks!' We'd break ranks. Then: 'Sit down! Get up! On the double! Sit down.' That was just a little diversion. Naturally when we sat down, the sharp stones cut into our behinds. Well, such things don't happen any more, and if they do, the responsible parties are punished. You've heard the slogan about the citizen in uniform, coined by General Count von Baudissin who reformed the Bundeswehr. In my opinion Baudissin's idea is both right and wrong. It's right that a soldier should be regarded as a member of the population. On the other hand it's wrong because in many respects a soldier has entirely different duties. After all, he's expected to risk his life for his country. But something has changed, maybe because of Count von Baudissin: in the Wehrmacht a man had to carry out orders even if he went against his conscience; if he didn't he was risking his life unless he was a very good dodger. Today a man doesn't have to obey that kind of order. Those are our instructions. Today I can reject such orders and every soldier is so informed. I do not believe I'd be punished as long as I can justify my refusal and say: 'This order is criminal' or 'it's contrary to the rights of man.' Shooting women and children and that kind of thing. Naturally men who say such things openly tend to be passed over when it comes to advancement – it happens time and time again. And of course a soldier wants to make a career. So a lot of them say: 'I'd better keep my trap shut or I won't get ahead.'

There's still a lack of moral courage.

As long as an abuse hasn't been made public, as long as it remains an internal matter, I believe most of us prefer to keep quiet and say nothing of it. 'A citizen's first duty is to keep quiet.' That's our mentality. But it's a difficult problem. Think of it this way: A military unit is supposed to defend a river crossing. The enemy comes along and with him come refugees, our own people I mean. What should the commander of that military unit do? Whichever way he decides, things are likely to go wrong. If he commands his men to fire, and so many of his own people will be killed, women and children and so on. If the war is lost, he'll be prosecuted for giving the order to fire. How is a plain man going to make up his mind? How is he going to know what's right?

You've got to defend something.

At first there was a big 'count me out' movement, but today more men are willing to serve in the Bundeswehr; they're beginning to realize that there's some point in being a soldier, that somehow the country has to be defended. There is no longer one German fatherland. We have two German father-lands with two armies. Should they fire on each other? That's a big problem but we hardly ever go into it. If the necessity should arise, a Bundeswehr soldier would probably fire – on a soldier of the People's Army. But it's not drilled into him, nothing is done to prepare his mind for it. He's not taught to regard the soldiers of the DDR as enemies. Not at all. It's always made clear that the people of the DDR are also German. That's a contradiction of course. As soldiers of half a country, what are we actually supposed to defend? That's a ticklish question. And it will always be a problem because, when you come right down to it, our purpose in being soldiers is to defend the Federal Republic. And our oath is: 'I swear to serve the Federal Republic loyally.' In other words, it refers only to our particular state and that's what we've got to defend. It's impossible for us to develop a normal national sentiment but we've got to make the best of it. If I hadn't become a soldier, I wouldn't have to worry about these things. In case of war we'll all have to be soldiers.

Class distinctions? The classes have all been shuffled together.

I have friends of all kinds: teachers, businessmen, artisans, a cross-section of the population. No more class distinctions. The classes have all been shuffled together. There's no class pride. We don't even talk about it. Nobody pays any attention to what you were as a civilian. 'He's a soldier,' they think, 'and that's that.'

It's not exactly like that in the Bundeswehr.

A lot of the officers have titles of nobility. How much that affects the leadership of the Bundeswehr you can judge for yourself. You only have to read the paper. There are lots of aristocrats even in the regular officers' corps. They're not exactly arrogant. They behave like everybody else. But somehow they keep to themselves. They hardly associate with anyone else. They seldom invite anyone else to their quarters. They have more social cohesion.

MICHAEL GERSTENBERG
JOHANNA GERSTENBERG
42 and 36, working-class couple

His hourly pay is higher just because he's a man.

Johanna Gerstenberg: It's been a long time, twenty years, since I met my husband. I was only sixteen. It was in the streetcar. It was jammed full and he offered me his seat, so we got talking. Yes, that's how it started. I was an apprentice dressmaker. But then came the currency reform, the shop closed, so I changed over and became a metal worker. Metal work pays a lot better than dressmaking. Now I'm in testing. Heat testing of automatic devices. Eight hours a day, forty hours a week. We have Saturday off. In the testing shop we get an hourly wage and twenty per cent extra. Comes to five marks in all. I've been doing it for years. Always the same thing. A man would get more. His hourly pay is higher just because he's a man. That's why they take women for this work. That's the way it is: men are always paid better for the same work. Women are cheap labour. Only the department head is a man. The foreman, the time keeper and the adjuster are men. It's better to work under a man. He knows more about it when something doesn't work and you need his advice, because he has learned the trade. Usually he's either a machinist or a precision mechanic. An unskilled workman can't learn that kind of trade. There are five hundred of us women on the shop floor. It's no joke with so many women. Oh well, you've got to get used to it. A lot of them are foreigners, Turks, Greeks, etc. We have a hard time understanding each other, they don't speak German. Sometimes there's trouble between us and them, but more often among the foreigners themselves. Only recently some of them had a fight during working hours. Naturally they were fired on the spot.

If there were no unions the workers would be exploited more.

It's true I left the union ten years ago. I wanted some information and I didn't get it. At Christmas I was sent to the section head in a different department. I was given different work at lower hourly pay, so I was making less money. It seemed to me that there ought to be an adjustment, but the section head wouldn't do anything for me so I went to the union and inquired, but they wouldn't tell me anything definite. They said I should work it out with the section head myself. So I said: 'Then what am I in the union for? I thought the union was supposed to help me.' But they wouldn't help me so I left. I was through with them. A good many workers have walked out of the union because it was asleep.

Michael Gerstenberg: I belong to the union more for professional than for personal reasons. I'm an REFA man, that stands for *Reichsausschuss für Arbeitsstudien* (National Committee for Work Studies). We do work studies, computations, everything connected with laying out jobs. So naturally I have to deal with the shop committee, that is, the union. In such cases it's always better to belong to the union, then you're working with fellow members. You have less trouble in putting your ideas across. If there were no union, the workers would be exploited more. If there were no union the management would take advantage. There's something to be said for the unions. Without them we wouldn't have the 40-hour week.

Instalment-buying is a contagious disease.

I'm against it, but I know men who work overtime, not because
they care about doing good work but because they want to buy
more things though they could manage on less money. That's
the problem. Now and then we do it ourselves. It's a contagious
disease here in Germany. You don't know much about your
neighbour, but you see all the things he buys: you see that he's
moved into a new apartment, that the rent is more than three
hundred marks, which he can't really afford on the wages he's
making. And all the things he's bought: new furniture and car-
pets and a new car! Good God! And that's no exception. It's
what they call putting on a front. I repeat: instalment-buying
is a contagious disease, and we've caught it too. But in our case
it's not so bad, because we have no children.

Johanna Gerstenberg: If we had a child, naturally I'd stay
home. I couldn't leave it alone. I wouldn't put it in a kindergarten either. If I have a child, I want to bring it up myself and
not deposit it like a package every morning and pick it up like
a package in the evening. That doesn't appeal to me. My
friends at the factory who do that are so worn out when they
come home that they can't take care of their child properly. A
woman can only do one thing properly – be a mother or work,
not both. But the problem hasn't come up yet. Naturally I don't
exactly go to work for the fun of it. It's just that like this we
can afford to buy more things. Practically all women go out to
work.

Michael Gerstenberg: I feel the same way. We haven't been
able to make up our minds yet to say: 'Now you'll stay home.
Now we'll have children.' We sort of let things ride and now
we're practically in a panic because pretty soon it will be too
late. It's like this: There were a lot of children in my family.
I was the oldest of nine. I saw what it's like having children.
My father was a tailor. From 1928 to 1933 we were in the
United States, we went over because there was so much unemployment here at the time. My father opened a tailor shop
in Malverne, that's near Brooklyn. In 1933 when he heard that

things were picking up here, he came back. His English was perfect so he did a little interpreting now and then. I was still very little but it did me good to see something different. It's true I've forgotten most of my English, but it was good for me and my whole family to see something different from Germany.

Some Germans are so loud-mouthed.

We've spent vacations in Holland, on the French Riviera, and on Lake Garda in Italy. This year we'll probably go to Holland. We've been there before and it's the cheapest place. I've met a lot of people in Holland and seen a good deal. I think the standard of living is about the same as ours, but in France they take things easier, they have a happier life. Maybe they haven't our exaggerated standard of living, but they eat more and better. They enjoy it. They take their time about it. They live more quietly and enjoyably than we do. The southern French in the out-of-the-way villages still haven't got this hectic modern life. The French were friendlier to us than the Dutch. They've got over the War quicker. I also think that the Dutch are envious of the Germans. Especially when they see that though the Germans lost the War they can take the long trip to their country, and maybe because they don't always behave very well. Some Germans are so loud-mouthed. I've talked it over with my friends at the plant. They say the same thing, but maybe they're just as loud-mouthed. I don't know.

Yes, we can vote, but we have no influence.

Johanna Gerstenberg: We women don't discuss such things in the factory. We talk more about cooking, about work and clothes, and maybe about some article in *Die Bildzeitung*, or the latest sensation, never about politics.

  Michael Gerstenberg: With us it varies. Actually we talk about everything. A good deal about sports, but also about politics. Most of them – they're all men – are more interested in politics than they used to be. All metal workers. Yes, the

general interest in politics has increased. I think it's because
people are getting more dissatisfied. They're beginning to notice
that they're not even small cogs in the big political machine,
not even tiny screws. We're insignificant. Yes, we can go to the
polls and cast our vote, but that doesn't give us any influence.
We can vote for a party but we can't help to decide the party's
policy; they do what they please and they're always changing. I think it would be better if in the Bundestag elections we
voted directly for individuals who had been prominent in provincial or municipal politics, so we could know what they had
done. But that's not how it is. And that's why the general dis-
satisfaction has led people to take more interest in politics.
Look at our economic situation, for instance, or our foreign
relations; things are going from bad to worse. I think we ought
to come out of our isolation a little and be more independent.
In our eastern policy we want too much; we've poured out
the baby with the bath water. We thought everything was
going fine, we gloated too soon. Our government has no real
plans and antagonizes the people in the East who might be
glad to establish some contact with us.

Johanna Gerstenberg: I read sometimes, but very little. I
haven't much free time. In the summer we take a little stroll
after we get home, or we go swimming, and then television. We
haven't been to the movies in a long time. Now that we have
TV, we'd rather stay home. It's cosier. I used to go to the
theatre now and then but my husband isn't interested.

Michael Gerstenberg: But I read the newspaper. The local
paper, the *Frankfurter Allgemeine Zeitung* and *Die Welt*. I buy
them in turns.

But I believe in a higher power.

We're both Catholics but we seldom go to church. There are
reasons. Some of my relatives are very religious, there are even
a few nuns and priests, and some of my brothers and sisters are
very religious. But it isn't reflected in practice. When we're in
trouble, for instance, we can't count on the generosity of

those supposedly pious people. They're more churchgoers than real Christians. But if we had a child, we'd have it baptized. Of course. I believe in a higher power, I mean both of us do. That goes without saying. In my opinion that has nothing to do with going to church. I believe that some people who don't go to church are better than the ones who go at the drop of a hat. You can see that all over.

We don't associate with the people here in the house.

Johanna Gerstenberg: We know them, we say hello, but there's no contact between us. The apartment across the hall is rented to students. Below us there's a widow, she works in a factory too. The elderly gentleman on the floor below is in the post office. But if we needed a neighbour's help, we'd get it.

Michael Gerstenberg: We haven't many friends. Practically my only friend is a man I knew in the War. Another friend from younger days has moved away. We do all right, just the two of us. But I believe our life would be better if we had more friends.

Johanna Gerstenberg: My husband has had two long illnesses. That was hard on us with so few friends. It wasn't ideal. Oh well, life just isn't ideal.

From a political point of view I thought a good deal of Chancellor Adenauer.

Michael Gerstenberg: That was a Chancellor who knew what he wanted. I'm not a party man. I'm not in the CDU or the SPD or any other party. But I've always said: 'That's a political leader who knows his business.' In our plant, though, there was always a lot of grumbling about Adenauer. A lot of them said: 'Ah, go on with your moth-eaten old chancellor.' They were especially down on him for founding the Bundeswehr. And for being too close to America. They said he should have tried to establish better relations with the Russians in the east, because that was a better way of getting reunification. Now nobody believes in reunification any more. The division has been in force too long and nothing is happening. It's getting worse and worse. The people on both sides have got used to being apart, it's dictated from above. It all comes from propaganda. I also have the feeling that other countries think we'd be a danger if we were reunified. So they don't want reunification to get anywhere; none of them do.

These eternal concentration-camp trials.

Johanna Gerstenberg: I think they should leave us alone. That was all so long ago. It should be dead and buried after twenty years. I don't like the idea of the young people seeing all that on TV. Those concentration-camp pictures aren't nice. We didn't get to see them before, and now after all these years they've started running them all the time.

Michael Gerstenberg: I believe our young people in Germany today are well enough informed. They know what happened then but it doesn't get under their skins. They have other problems. They think of pleasure, luxury, money, and sex. That's all they see in the movies and the illustrated magazines. They all want this dream life that's put before them. It was different with us. There was the War and the hard times after it. We got no enjoyment out of our youth. Now of course we're doing very well, but at the slightest crisis people start grumbling, and some speak of mounting the barricades. But I always say: 'Your German man-in-the-street will always be a man-in-the-street. He won't mount the barricades and he won't do anything else. He puts up with everything. The Germans can only be governed with a strong hand. They are not ready for democracy yet. That's putting it mildly.

RENATE PFISTER

55, unmarried, welfare worker

I had no mind for anything but social work.

When I was ten years old, I began bringing home children I picked up on the street, who looked rather dirty and wan. Then later on a booth was set up in our school yard where mothers could go for advice. It was after the First World War. There was a shortage of everything, and rewards in the form of sugar or butter were given to mothers who had nursed their infants well. My girl friend and I were allowed to write out the coupons entitling them to those things. This brought us in contact with many needy people, and I said to myself: social work is a profession in which one can do a great deal of good. I felt it so strongly that I took up the profession of social worker in spite of all the people who tried to influence me against it. My teachers wanted me to become a pediatrician or to study law. But I stood firm. My parents were perfectly willing, though I can't really speak of parents, because mine were divorced. My father was an engineer in a large electrical firm, he travelled a good deal and was seldom at home, but he looked after us children well financially. My sister who is now a teacher and I stayed with my mother and the three of us are still living together. After graduating from high-school I worked for a year in a children's home. Then for two years I attended the Municipal School of Social Work for Women, then for a year I studied nursing and obtained a nurse's certificate. Then I received training in infant care but did not complete the course because things were so bad at the time that there was a great shortage of welfare workers and I was able to obtain a position immediately with a city department. I have now been a municipal welfare worker for thirty years. There's a singleness of purpose in all our work.

The greatest suffering and affliction come from people's disappointment in each other.

Disappointment causes much more suffering than sickness or lack of money. The purely human sufferings are the worst. Take divorce, disappointment in a false friend, unrequited love, ungrateful children, unsympathetic parents, etc. Those are the things that leave the deepest marks. All mothers, for instance, do not know when the time has come for a young person to make his way alone. You wouldn't believe how many mothers cling desperately to their children and refuse to understand that one fine day they have to lead their own lives and have a right to develop freely. This is a problem that will always exist. Other problems change with the times. When I started out as a young social worker in the early thirties, that was the time of the worst unemployment in Germany and the people's greatest cares were purely economic. After the economic situation had improved, the War came, bringing new problems and new troubles. After the War, in 1948, we had this radical economic revival. But I can't say that it has made people happier and more contented.

Man has an unfortunate capacity for making new worries for himself.

The problems don't diminish. They only change. Nowadays people come to the Public Welfare Office with problems that wouldn't have been conceivable in the past. I'll give you an example: A young government official came to me and told me that he had made friends with a girl student who had already passed her teachers' examination and was now studying sociology, but found herself in a difficult psychological situation. She suffered from states of depression and spoke of committing suicide. He had made inquiries and learned of a doctor living in another city who could help her. It was a very expensive treatment, and he asked whether we could help his girl friend on the basis of the Federal Public Assistance Law. Well, we did just that. Formerly, financial aid in such a case would not have been possible. Formerly we only helped the destitute, the people who were really in the greatest need. Today an entirely different set of people come to us for help. Today we reach into every level of society. A few months ago, for instance, the wife of a hospital physician had twins. That made five children in all. The woman's health had been impaired and she had to be sent away to rest. But what was she to do in the meantime with her five children? Her husband couldn't afford to engage special help for the purpose, so we had to contribute. In the old days that woman would have had to stay home. There would have been no possibility of helping her. And it would not even have occurred to anyone to apply for our help in such a case.

Nowadays people go to the Public Welfare Office as they would to a dentist's.

The Federal Public Assistance Law stipulates that everyone is entitled to apply to the Public Welfare Office for help. There is very wide leeway. The law offers many possibilities of assistance, because it contains many provisions for what can and should be done. You know that a law can be interpreted in different ways. Up to now the funds set aside for these activities by the Federal Government have been very considerable because the government is determined to carry on this work, come what may.

We hold out our little finger but the people take our whole hand,

and they won't let go, at least not without a great deal of grumbling, and this grumbling is something the politicians are afraid of. At the same time, of course, there are still many cases which show that we are still a far cry from a real welfare society. You have only to consider the consequences of the housing shortage caused by the War and the refugees; they have not yet been done away with, not by any means. Recently, an elderly woman came to me; in 1946, as a refugee from the East Zone, she was assigned a room with kitchen.

Because the housing shortage was much worse at that time, she was requested to share the place with another person. Now she came to me, complaining bitterly that it had suddenly become utterly intolerable; the woman with whom she shared her small apartment was always having visitors and that meant using more of her electricity. She had written down very neatly how many kilowatts it came to. You've got to remember that these old people speak very slowly and awkwardly and that it takes a good deal of patience to listen to all that. In this case it was the business of the municipal electric company to take the matter in hand and put in an extra meter. So you see how it is: When there are no real problems, people think up new ones. When you come right down to it, the two women could have solved this thing by themselves. But all the same there are plenty of problems that are almost too much for us. Yesterday we had a telephone call: It was about a woman of fifty who had been discharged from the women's hospital two weeks before with abdominal cancer and who was in such pain and screamed and whimpered and shouted so loud that the other tenants were afraid she was going to kill herself. The person who called said we must do something at once. So I called the woman's hospital and spoke to the doctor who had treated her. Then I got in touch with the home welfare service, and then the trouble really started. You know the situation. There's not a free bed in any of the hospitals. After five hours I finally found one, but it was in an old people's home, that was the best I could do. And this woman was barely fifty. There's just no room. Normally there is a vacancy in one of the homes only when someone dies. Otherwise they simply set up an emergency bed in a room that already has four or five beds in it.

People used to say that the twentieth century would be the children's century, but instead it has turned out to be the old people's century.

Thanks to medical knowledge, people live to be much older nowadays. In our homes the average age is eighty. You must try to imagine the demands that makes on the administration and nursing staff. Life can be prolonged for years by medical treatment, but so far no means has been found of preventing mental degeneration. Seventy-five per cent of our old people's homes are like small psychiatric clinics. I keep wondering: Why must this be? After all, we are living in a welfare state with a large public welfare budget. I believe that the situation was understood too late. Otherwise I can't imagine how things could have got so bad. There is always a shortage of nurses. And yet the nurses' schools train so many young people. There ought to be enough of them. We keep wondering what the reason for this shortage can be. We ourselves don't know. Of course professions connected with public welfare are not attracting as many young people as they used to.

It's a strenuous profession that calls for a great deal of devotion, and the pay is not excessive.

If today a secretary has just a little ability, she is soon in our wage group and has to work much less for it. But they are becoming rarer and rarer. For instance, I once asked a young woman how she got the idea of becoming a social worker. She said she just had no idea what to do on leaving school and before she knew it she was enrolled at the Higher School for Social Workers. In this office there are only fifteen of us in all, and if you ask me how many of us are fit for the job, I wouldn't hesitate to say: Thirteen out of the fifteen. Only two would drop out if they had a chance to go into easier and better paid work. Our group is still quite satisfactory, but it is also considerably over age. I am the oldest, but the next in line are 54, 53, 52 and 48. Then a jump down to 42, and our youngest is 27. That is my great worry. So in making new appointments I always try to choose the youngest possible candidates. Naturally that has its disadvantages too. Our young colleagues are all engaged or married when we hire them, and experience shows that they soon leave the profession. Just to think of the pace at which we work: We start at 7.30 and close officially at 5.30, but that's when our main work really begins, because many of the families can be visited only evenings and week-ends. You might call this our internal marriage problem. And we're faced with a lot of marriage problems on the outside too. For some strange reason it's chiefly men who take us for some kind of marriage advisory bureau and bring us their problems. Only men come to us for help when their marriage threatens to go on the rocks. Women are more likely to ask what they can do about getting a divorce. It's very strange. Time and time again, we find that men are much more attached to marriage. Not long ago a doctor came to see me. He was really desperate: wasn't there anything we could do? His wife wanted a divorce and he wanted to prevent it at all costs. I am sorry to say that in this case we were unsuccessful. She simply didn't want to live with him any more and had another man in mind. A source of many marriage problems is that young couples are too well-off when they start out, usually because they are both working and earning money. Then a woman has her first child, she realizes that it's really her duty to stay home with her child. But then she notices the financial loss this involves and as often as not the marriage begins to disintegrate. The husband has meanwhile developed certain hobbies that are very expensive and he doesn't want to give them up. I could put it this way:

Often it's prosperity that prevents married couples from really finding each other.

They simply lose their perspective. They have too much money. Everything is geared to externals. Then when there's a real burden to bear, they discover that inwardly they haven't really been living together and that there is no real cement to their marriage. All in all, I believe that very few married couples are immune to crises. It may come as a surprise to you, but not long ago I received the visit of a seventy-two-year-old woman who saw no hope of saving her marriage. Yes, old people have those problems too. Mostly because of dissension with married or even unmarried children living under the same roof, or with

subtenants. We have many fellow citizens who formerly, before devaluation, were able to live comfortably on their savings
or pensions, but were later obliged to sublet a good part of
their four- to six-room apartments. In time the relations
with their subtenants become strained. For instance, they have
taken in a young man or employed woman. The young woman
then marries and begins to stay home. Children are born, and
now the young couple would like to have the whole apartment
for themselves. They keep after the old people and try to persuade them to give up the apartment. They simply say: Why
don't you go to an old people's home? Then the problem is
brought to us from both sides. I often say we'd have to be like
God to handle every angle of these questions. In this country
human sympathy, especially towards older people, is in a bad
way. We have tried everything. We have given old people ready-
printed cards, so that if they are in trouble they can simply pin
the card up on the door. When the neighbour woman sees the
card she is supposed to come in and help them. It was a complete failure. It's most distressing.

Ninety per cent of the old people who live alone are lost.

If we ring the subtenant's bell because we have the feeling that
something is wrong with the old lady and ask how she is, the
only answer we get is a stereotyped 'I don't know'. Or they
simply slam the door in the welfare worker's face. In Germany
people bother very little about each other. We can't count on
neighbourly assistance. People say: That's what public welfare is
for.

People just rely on the government.

The government will attend to it. Why should I? There's an
office for it. That's how it is in the cities. Only in the country is
it still different. I know a family in a near-by village. The
woman is expecting her sixth child. She fell very ill and went to
the hospital. They are very simple people. They could have
applied to the local authorities. No, they did just what you'd

expect people to do, they distributed the children among their relatives. The grandmother who works in the laundry stopped work and ran the household for her son-in-law and the school-age children. The younger children were taken in by uncles, aunts and cousins. You won't find that kind of thing in the city any more. Don't get the idea that a young man will never carry an old lady's coal upstairs. We get such things done by going to the schools and paying the school children to help the old people, because it's not even possible through the churches to find young people who are willing to help without pay. It's a disgrace to the German nation, but I've got to admit it. God knows that in this respect our morality is really not of the best. Even so, if you approach the young people in the right way, it sometimes works. It's more thoughtlessness than conscious disrespect. If you speak very nicely to the young people and say: Do please give up your seat, there's an old gentleman standing, you must have seen him, they stand up right away and turn all red. But by themselves they don't see it. It's shocking. In other respects the young people have actually changed much less than is generally thought. Illegitimate children, for instance, have pretty much the same troubles as before. Only the mother isn't as desperate as she used to be. Formerly an illegitimate child was felt to be a terrible disgrace. This has changed radically, and purely as a result of the law. Today every unmarried mother can obtain full parental rights, though it takes time. In other words, she is the equal of a legitimate mother before the law. Even thirty years ago we had fifteen- or sixteen-year-old unmarried mothers, especially young girls working in factories. Today we occasionally find still younger ones. Girls mature much earlier. If I compare a fifteen-year-old girl of thirty years ago with a fifteen-year-old girl of today, I find an enormous difference.

The father works, the mother works, and the car is much more important than the children.

That is a very sad chapter in our affluent society. I believe a

normal citizen would find it hard to imagine how many young
people of fifteen or sixteen come to see us. What neglect!
People have simply lost all sense of shame. Three weeks ago a
young girl was picked up by the police here in town. One week-
day, instead of going to work she had simply gone out to the
Autobahn with a girl friend and hitch-hiked to Munich. Both of
them freely admitted that they had changed cars at least two
or three times and had intimate relations with the drivers.
Those used to be isolated cases. Today they have become customary. You see, that's the main reason why I take an interest
in politics. Take the whole social question; it depends entirely
on the government's policies.

Social welfare and morality were perhaps the only sphere
where the Nazis were better, though they must be absolutely
condemned in other respects.

I was in the Catholic Youth Movement, and we joined the BdM*
as a body. This, I am sorry to say, was brought about by the
attitude of our bishop. But I soon saw what was going on. I
saw what was being done to the Jews. We had a few Jewish
friends. But I'm convinced there were very many Germans who
somehow didn't really understand what was happening, because it was simply too cruel for them to conceive of. Not
everyone was able or willing to face such knowledge. The things
you had to see were too terrible. There was a family living in
the house of a friend of ours. The wife was a Jewess. At that
time I had good connexions with the public health bureau, I
knew a very nice man there. He always tipped me off when the
Gestapo was planning house searches. So we were able to warn
this Jewish lady in time and hide her. The Gestapo injected
another Jewish woman with pneumonia. This showed me how
cruelly the Jews were treated. But most people thrust such
knowledge away from them, although those things were plain
enough to see. I can still remember how we said good-bye at the

---

* *Bund deutscher Mädchen* – League of German Girls.

station to another Jewish friend when the Jews were deported.
There was a big crowd at the station. The Jews had all marched
to the station under guard. Half the city must have seen them.
But the people persuaded themselves that the Jews were just
being re-settled, that they were not going to be killed. And a lot
of people were afraid that something would happen to them if
they opened their mouths. But the German is . . . I don't know,
I've often wondered what kind of man the German really is.
On the one hand he is a hard animal and feels inwardly re-
lieved to have someone over him who tells him what to do.

I believe the Germans just have a leaning towards dictatorship.

You get that feeling time and time again. Even now they don't
really know what to do with democracy. They don't know
what to make of the personal freedom that is given them in a
democracy. We are always complaining because people in foreign countries are still so distrustful. But how can they help
being distrustful? In the opposite situation we would be too. If
you put yourself into the shoes of the people who have suffered
on account of us, you just can't expect them to let bygones be
bygones. My sister who is a teacher is often horrified in school
when she sees the way the children still glorify Hitler. Time
and again you hear people – especially people with education –
saying how furious it makes them that these trials of Nazi
criminals are still being carried on. They keep saying we've
had enough of those trials and they ought to be stopped. Instead of saying that those Nazis were pretty clever not to have
been tried and convicted sooner. On the one hand, people clam-
our for the death penalty so that everyone who murders a taxi
driver will be executed. Naturally I'm not going to defend a
man who murders a taxi driver, but in my opinion he's not as
bad as a man who slowly and ruthlessly tortured hundreds of
people to death in a concentration camp. They don't want to
see him punished but they demand the death penalty for the
man who murdered the taxi driver. I can't understand such

inconsistency in people's thinking. I suppose it's because these trials are attended by many foreign journalists and keep tearing down our reputation in the world. Lord, how happy I am to have chosen a profession in which I really help people and do no harm to anyone.

IRENE TRITZSCHKE

32, divorced, waitress

I'm just a little waitress in a restaurant.

It's a very nice place, you make good money, I can count on a thousand marks a month or I couldn't afford the luxury of this little one-room apartment. Yes, 185 marks for rent alone, though that includes heat and hot water. I refurnished the apartment only a year ago. You don't get anything for nothing. So I took out a small loan. That has to be repaid, plus two thousand marks in advance rent. Yes, I've come a long way. My parents have a restaurant in Thuringia, that's in the DDR. In other words, I started out in the restaurant business and I'm still in it. Of course my parents don't own their restaurant any more. It's a government concern and they are their own employees, sort of. Even so, they've still got fifteen waiters under them, so you can see the place isn't so small. In the summer there are lots of dances and concerts. They've got a great big dance-hall like you seldom see over here. Here there are only bars and little places.

When I left home, I was eighteen. That's the age when you think you've just got to leave home. But that wasn't the real reason. This friend of mine was a salesgirl, she'd sold some customers food without tickets. They found out and she had to clear out to West Germany. I loaned her fifty marks for the trip. But they caught her and she told them I'd given her the money.

Over there they call that 'Republic-flight-complicity'.

You know what you get for that. Ten years was about the least I could expect. So I had to clear out in a hurry. I told my parents I was going to the hairdresser and took the train to East Berlin. From there I took the E1 over to the West. I couldn't take anything with me. I was wearing a summer dress and jacket. I didn't even have a towel or a washcloth or a piece of soap. After four weeks they flew me out to Frankfurt, then I went on to Darmstadt and went to work in a little restaurant. They had a few guest-rooms too, I got eighty marks for a whole month and I had to buy my own food on my day off. I couldn't wait on table at the time because I had nothing to wear. So I worked as a chambermaid from seven a.m. to ten p.m. That was a long hard day. But I only stayed for three months. Then I went to my brother's in Düsseldorf. He's married. He's been over here for eighteen years. He found me work as a domestic helper. I made 125 marks a month but the work was too hard because the lady was completely paralysed. After six months I was fed up. I decided I'd better get out of here and go back to Darmstadt. On my way I had to wait in the station in Cologne. So what do you do to kill time? You buy a paper and look at the want ads. Well, there was a nice ad: salary 300, uniform provided. So I says to myself: What's this?

I thought I'd take a look. It was a bar.

So I went to work in a bar. I hung on for three years. But I'm mighty glad to be out of the bar business. You've got to watch your step in a bar. It's rough going. Yes, of course I met people, I had boy friends off and on. But I wanted to get out of those surroundings, out of that bar. It's terrible to be at everybody's beck and call. In a bar you're kind of free game. Most of the customers think: This is a bar, so I can do what I please. The liquor helps, and anyway most men who go to bars want to show how virile they are, or maybe they think the stuff that goes on in bars is really living. Most of them are middle-aged shopkeeper types who have decided to raise hell for once in their lives. And Cologne is famous for that kind of thing because of the fairs. The place is full of out-of-town businessmen. At home they're afraid to go anywhere, and certainly not to a bar. My oh my, suppose the wife found out! So I wanted to get out of there. I got this job through a girl friend. First I worked at a lunch counter and that was where I met my husband. You know how those things happen.

He takes you out for a cup of coffee. So you start going together, and friendship springs up.

The friendship turned into a marriage, but it only lasted four years. My husband is with an insurance company and has a very good job. He doesn't have to go from door to door ringing bells and stopping people. His line is retirement-insurance, there's a lot of demand for that nowadays. Why my marriage only lasted four years? I don't know. You meet a man, you think it's a great love, but then comes life and your great love doesn't last long. As a salesman my husband met a lot of people and naturally his deals were always closed very late at night. Sometimes he didn't come home until two in the morning. Of course I didn't swallow his story, because I'd spoken with a number of his associates, and believe it or not they were always through by nine or ten o'clock at the latest. But his coming home too late wasn't the only trouble. Other things happened and then I met another man and left. I guess it's life that drives you apart. Maybe it would have been better if we'd had children. Then maybe we'd still be married. Now I feel perfectly happy, anyway I think so.

I have my apartment and my job, I earn my own living.

Yes, I know this man. Sure, but I don't know if he's exactly the right thing for me. Of course I'm free to do as I please. I can go out when I please, I can go to bed when I please, but I don't know if I've done the right thing. I don't know if it's ideal for a woman to be alone the whole time. Of course I go home now and then to visit my parents. It's only natural. I like to go home once in a while. But live there again? No, I wouldn't go back. In the meanwhile I've developed my own 'way of life', as they say, and there'd only be complications. I've never bothered with politics. I'm not interested in politics. Sure, I go out and vote. I know which way to vote. The weakest party gets my vote. But you should never give a party your whole vote. Here in the West only the CDU was really strong in Adenauer's day.

It's not good for one party to have all the power: It had almost come to the point where you needed your prayer-book to buy a pint of milk.

That just isn't right! 'Come around on Sunday, and I'll tell you how to vote!' No, no, that reminded me of the Communists and the Nazis. At the end of the War I had just turned nine. But I'd seen and been through plenty! Believe me, a nine-year-old child often thinks more and sees more than a grown-up. A child takes things harder, and its experience goes deeper. Well, first the Americans came to Thuringia, but the Americans left and then the Russians came. My mother was alone with us four children. I'll never forget that day, we were sitting at the dinner table, suddenly the door opens, the Russians come charging in and chase us away from the table. They requisitioned our house. We weren't allowed to take anything with us. We moved in with my grandmother. We lived with her for two years and when we were allowed to move back home, don't ask me what the house looked like!

I certainly got to know the Communists!

I only know the Nazi period secondhand, from what I read about the trials later on in the newspapers. But even from that I can draw my conclusions. I don't believe that our dear good Adolf, as they say, knew all about it, the concentration camps, and so on. I mean, yes, of course he knew the Jews were sent to the gas chambers and all that, but I don't think he knew they were so cruel about it sometimes. Yes, there was a lot of cruelty, but that doesn't prove anything. There were plenty of Germans in the concentration camps too, for political reasons and so on. The guards thought to themselves: We can do as we please with these people. Do you think every little thing they did was reported? I can't imagine that all those things were known up top. You've read about it yourself, how when a commission came to investigate, the whole place was cleaned up, they were suddenly given bedclothes and all that. And the minute the commission left, it was all taken away again.

My father wasn't in the Party. He wasn't a Nazi. My father was drafted in 1939. He was in the Navy, he never rose higher than first mate, and my father never tried to push himself ahead. Now over there in East Germany he doesn't open his mouth. That's the best way. They're down on him anyway because three of his four children are in the West. Only my little sister stayed on. She studied over there and now she's a teacher. She makes good money and has a nice apartment. Will she come to the West? I don't know. I've never asked her. You know, when I go home I steer clear of political discussions, because I want to be able to go back. I don't talk about such things with my parents either. I have two brothers here in the West. One in Düsseldorf that I've told you about already and another in Bergisch-Gladbach. One is a foreman in some kind of a cutlery factory and the other's a mason. They both make good money. They have nice places to live in. The older one is building himself a second house. He's already got one, an eight-family house. The other only has an apartment in a new building, but it's very nice too. How the older one did it I don't know. He has six children but he saves money, it's a miracle. He only lives for his family, his children and his home. He's a real Christian too and has a happy family life. Well, with six children you don't need to ask.

Believe in God? That's a big question.

Naturally everybody's got to believe in something, or there's no point in life. You've got to have some little bit of content, but I don't actually believe in God, because it's always been Nature more or less that created everything, and not God at all. My first aim in life was my apartment, my second now is holding on to my money so as to have a quiet old age later on with a certain amount of security. I've also taken out a life insurance policy that I'll convert into an annuity later on, so it won't be the same with me as with thousands of old people who have an income of no more than maybe 120 or 150 marks and are glad to be taken in somewhere. Well, I wouldn't care for that. The Germans aren't exactly famous for their kindheartedness.

Oh, well, all in all the average German is a good sort, he lives for his home and family, but

if you give him an opening he'll pounce on it. He is not always exactly fair. Not necessarily. Unfortunately, that's the way the German is. If he has a tiny little bit of power, he squeezes everything he possibly can out of it. I don't think we'll ever have anything like the Nazi period again. No, it's not possible, the great powers will be on the lookout. But if they weren't, I don't know, I wouldn't guarantee anything. We would certainly make some blunder that could never be undone. We sort of need somebody to supervise us. Something like a small child. It takes a long time to grow up. It took a long time before the English had real democracy, and the Americans too. You know, there's only been one politician who had my complete sympathy, and that was our dear Kennedy. Because to my way of thinking he was the first politician who really spoke and acted the way he thought. He explained everything so it was perfectly clear to the simplest worker. We all believed in him. All my friends too. They are all Kennedy fans.

Actually I have only two girl friends here. One lives by herself, she's a waitress too, at the China Restaurant. The other lives at home. Her father owns a distillery here in town. And I'm also friends with a Danish family. The husband is marvellous. He has built up two furniture stores. I admire that Dane for doing all that in such a short time – he's only been here for five years.

It's hard here in Germany for a foreigner.

They just call them *'Fremdarbeiter'* (foreign workers). But this man has really accomplished something. The Germans are really unfriendly to foreigners and make life pretty hard for them. Sometimes very hard. Usually because they aren't getting ahead very well themselves. They're envious of anybody who has somehow managed to accomplish something. Oh yes, and then there's Doris, my girl friend, the one with the distillery. I don't really admire her. When you come right down to it, she's a poor thing because she's not independent and lives off her father and has nothing of her own. But she's very good looking and I like to be with her because she's a pleasant, open kind of person. The other one, the waitress in the China Restaurant, is an orphan. She struggles through life alone. I've always felt somehow sorry for her.

Maybe it was mostly pity that led to our friendship. Still I admire her. She has made her way and isn't dependent on anyone. That's something in itself. It's something very few people can do. Especially girls who are all alone in the world. Because they make life really hard for single women, and most of them can't manage to get ahead. People say: Oh, she's only a woman. I don't feel that way about it. I manage. But most women have difficulties because they haven't got the courage to speak their minds when there's something they want or when they have troubles. They just don't go about things the right way. Yes, I've found a second home here and I'll never leave. Take a look back there, that's where my bed is.

First thing in the morning I look out at the woods, they somehow remind me of home in Thuringia.

And I like the people here. I mean it's always hard to get accepted when you come from outside. But you've got to do your bit. You can't say: Well, now you all have to do things my way. You've got to adapt yourself, you've got to think of other people's habits. As a woman, you've also got to do that with men. You know, men are sometimes pretty bad ... You might say, free and easy. They think when they meet a woman nowadays they've got to go to bed with her right away. They're awfully fast workers. But a man can only work as fast as a woman lets him. But they can keep trying. They're more interested in their pleasure than in anything else. A woman just has to watch her step.

ARNOLD SCHULTHEISS
29, married, publisher

My grandfather had a heart attack because he was denounced to the Occupation troops.

The whole initiative rests with me, all the ideas and so on. My great-grandfather founded our publishing house in 1881. It's a small house. There are eight of us in all. When my father died, the staff consisted entirely of old hands who were perfectly capable of carrying on the day-to-day business by themselves. In that sense I wasn't really needed. What the firm did need was new ideas and the willingness to try something new. I took the plunge. I decided to take on authors with unpopular opinions that might give umbrage in official circles. So far my venture has been fully successful. I'm very happy in my work and wouldn't want to exchange with anybody. I'm my own boss, my only servitude is my limited finances, otherwise I'm free to follow my own ideas. I doubt if I'd have the same independence anywhere else. What I value most is my personal freedom. In my grandfather's day it was all entirely different. He took a very patriarchal attitude. He kept everything connected with the finances under his personal control and none of his four sons could put his nose in. My father was the oldest. He was a student of literature and his work in the publishing house was purely editorial. The second son was in the printshop and the third had a bookstore. My grandfather wanted to build up a regular little trust, but you know how it is with plans and dreams; his didn't work out. The bookstore went bankrupt and during the War the printshop was completely bombed out. Not to mention the Nazi period. For instance, we published an excellent old translation of Dante's *Divine Comedy* done by a professor from Florence; they came and said the professor wasn't an Aryan and we'd better steer clear of him, or there might be trouble for the firm. Even so my grandfather managed to keep out of the Party It was really amazing. But all the same it was the Nazi period and the charming character of some of our compatriots that killed him. After the War he had a heart attack because he had been denounced to the Allied Occupation troops as a Party member. It was a woman, a former employee whom my father had dismissed for incompetence during the thirties. She'd chosen this strange method of avenging herself. That anyone could suspect, let alone denounce him, got my grandfather so worked up it was just too much for him. He was under suspicion of perjury, because right after 1945 everyone was given the famous questionnaire to fill out, and naturally he had written that he wasn't a Party member. And now it suddenly looked as if he had been. The Occupation authorities got very angry, some soldiers came and took my grandfather away, he was given a brief hearing and then he had a heart attack. That was the end.

After that my father had a hard time of it, because he had been a Party member and was classified as a fellow-traveller.

At first it looked as if we'd have to give up the publishing house, but then my father found a well-known author with a perfectly clear slate. A very kind and generous man. He said: 'Never mind, Herr Doktor, you just run the business, I'll sign anything you say because it's all Greek to me. But I'll be officially in charge.' And so he became trustee of the publishing house until the Occupation authorities realized that they couldn't put everybody on ice just because they'd been harmless Party members. They put my father back in charge. I can't really say why my father joined the Party. Whether it was opportunism, because he wanted to save the publishing house, or whether the Nazis had a certain fascination for him, because at that time, like so many others, he hadn't seen entirely through them – I really don't know. On the other hand, my father always had a lot of Jewish friends, even during the Nazi period. I don't know whether my father knew they were persecuted by the Nazis – in any case, those friends left Germany at a relatively early date.

You can't exactly say that they emigrated, because they came back after the War. I put rather a broader definition on 'emigration'; to me there's something final about it: when a man emigrates he has no intention of coming back. How much thought my father gave to these problems I don't know, because he was very reserved, you might even say secretive. All through the War, for instance, he was a soldier, a reserve officer in the artillery. He was in Belgium, France, Poland, Russia and Czechoslovakia. After the War he once told me, and that was the most talkative he ever got, that in his opinion the front-line troops would have gone back to Germany to overthrow the régime if they'd known, for instance, what was behind the attempted assassination of 20 July 1944. Yes, that was the only thing my father ever said to me about the whole Nazi period. He was the kind of man who kept everything to himself. He never discussed business worries with my mother. Unlike him, I do it all the time.

My father never discussed business matters with my mother. I talk everything over with my wife.

I like to get the advice of someone who has nothing to do with the business. That way you sometimes get new ideas that hadn't occurred to you because you were too immersed in the problem. Our life is very different from my father's. We are not nearly so withdrawn, and we go to great pains to have a more open family life. We try, but sometimes we don't really succeed. Sometimes we feel as if we were living on an island. Yes, it's very strange. My fraternity chapter, for instance, has scattered far and wide. I was in a fraternity. It's a kind of tradition in the family.

My grandfather belonged to a fraternity, so did my great-grandfather.

I really had no great desire to join a fraternity, I thought it was rather out of date, but then I was pleasantly surprised. The spirit was entirely different from what I had thought. I had expected it to be very conservative. In the duelling fraternities there seems to be a strong leaning towards the old times, the 'fatherland principle' and that sort of thing. They say that duelling builds courage, but courage can be shown in other ways. Anyway, as I've said before, I didn't want to join a fraternity but I knew that it would please my father a good deal, especially if I joined voluntarily. By 'voluntarily' I mean without being tricked into it. You keep hearing how a fraternity that's out to enroll a certain student arranges a little gathering and then tries to convince him by every possible means, mostly beer. When the man is so drunk that he doesn't know what he's doing, he signs an application for membership and afterwards he hasn't got the spunk to say: look here, boys, that's a lousy trick, here's your application, count me out. No, they stay in the fraternity and strange to say they feel perfectly happy about it. I myself am convinced that a man can feel happy in a fraternity. I joined in 1954. The best part of it in my day was the human contacts. They aren't possible any more with the present mass influx. Of course cliques form, but they usually disintegrate after graduation. But in our fraternity the ties have lasted. We are always hearing news of one another, we exchange letters now and then. Aside from that, all I've got is the local Publisher's Association which meets regularly once a month. Of course there are big and little publishers.

The big publishers talk mostly about golf and hunting.

The small publishers are more interested in talking shop and exchanging experiences and that kind of thing. The head of a large publishing house can't have an over-all view of the business. He has his four or five managing editors and he speaks of a secretary as an underling, which isn't the case with me because when there are only eight people in a firm, such conceptions do not even arise. Yes, I'm only a small publisher but I'm quite satisfied with my life.

You don't have to have everything, that's not what happiness depends on.

It doesn't depend on having three or four millions. There's a parallel between material prosperity and worry. Worries increase with prosperity. They go hand in hand. They're synchronized. My interests are varied and I'm very fond of music. You'd think we'd go to all the concerts, but it's a funny thing: when you come home at night, you're often too comfortable or too lazy to change your clothes and go out in search of cultural pleasures. We haven't even got a television set because that would ruin our family life in the evening. We noticed that on vacation. We sat watching television almost every evening. I must admit that our rejection of television often prevents us from hearing enough about international politics. Actually I'm very much interested in it. Take an example: under the present circumstances Germany really shouldn't insist on speaking in the so-called councils of the great. I think we should be a little more modest, but modesty isn't a German speciality, anyway not in politics. We want a hundred per cent of everything, maybe a little more. We can never resign ourselves to the reality of our situation. We can never say: This is the situation and we've got to make the best of it.

The Russians were the best diplomats; they pretty well hoodwinked the naïve Americans.

I know all about the munitions the Russians received from the Americans during the Second World War. What did the Americans get from the Russians in return? When you come right down to it, nothing – absolutely nothing. It wasn't very long before the Americans realized that the Russians are their most dangerous enemy. And the Russians were very clever about preventing our reunification. Of course I hope there will be reunification some day, but hope is one thing and reality another. All the same, in my opinion Germany could have been reunited long ago if, when only the Americans had the atom bomb, they had just blackmailed the Russians politically. In the end the Russians always bow to strength. We saw that in the Cuban crisis. And I'm not afraid of what they say about Germany being too powerful after a reunification that would make us a nation of almost eighty million again. But the others are afraid of it. And in view of their past experience with us, they've got a right to be afraid. To exert the right kind of influence on our people is an educational challenge to the present-day political parties, labour unions and leading political groups. The question is whether we can really find a basis for a functioning democracy. In my opinion the democratic idea is much more deeply engrained in the English, for instance, than in us, especially as far as human relations are concerned. After all democracy isn't just something that goes on in parliament and in political parties, but also in daily life. When you come right down to it, our future political leaders come from the general average population, and if they're always fighting each other for personal advantage, if one man begrudges another the butter on his bread, how can you expect it to be any different in our parliament? If you follow the political debates in the Bundestag today, you see that most of our parliamentarians haven't the maturity to carry on a really functioning democracy such as they have in England. When you look at what they teach us in school, it's obvious that our thinking isn't democratic enough. I'm only thinking of my own school days, which are not so very far behind me.

The teachers just didn't know what to do in the hours set aside for civics.

The instruction they gave us in history was only a makeshift.

Those teachers had grown up in a Germany that was still up to its neck in authoritarian thinking, and the same is true today of a good many members of the German Bundestag and Bundesrat and also of the labour unions. When I see the uncompromising demands that the unions make on the employers, I sometimes get the impression that they're still living under the second Reich. They seem to think we still have the same kind of capitalism as in Marx's day. Many of them have not understood yet that in our present position wedged in between the two great powers, our only chance is to found a United Europe. Europe must build up a position of strength if it is to survive. Soon there will be still more power blocs, an African or an Asiatic bloc, for instance. I believe that in time the North Americans will lose their influence in South America and that another political bloc will form in South America. That might be another Communist bloc, perhaps even with a Chinese orientation. Who knows? The Americans are losing more and more of their power and prestige. Look at the war in Vietnam. I do not believe they can win that war and I think they should leave the Vietnamese to themselves. The people there have long been saying: sooner Communism than this terrible war.

CHRISTINE NIEDEREDER

28, unmarried, dancer

My father says dancing means starvation wages.

My mother wanted me to take up ballet because my aunt was a ballet dancer and so was my grandmother. My grandmother took me to the children's ballet, that got me interested, and one day I was taken to the Munich Opera for a try-out. I was seven, that's when I started learning to dance. My mother is only a housewife, she was very happy about it, but my father's a civil servant and he was dead against it. He wanted me to take up a respectable profession. He thinks a woman can make more in other lines of work and come zooming home in her own car, while we dancers have to work from morning till night. He says dancing means starvation wages. Sometimes I think he's right. It seems to me that in our profession you spend more than in a lot of others, more than you actually make. It's partly on account of the irregular working hours. Other people, you see, go to work at eight a.m. and stay until five, they have no chance to drink coffee in between or drop into a movie. But mostly it's my fault if I'm always broke. After all I gross 950 marks a month. I love my work. It gives me a lot of pleasure. First I was in the children's ballet at the opera, then the prima ballerina gave up dancing and went to Hagen as ballet mistress and sent for me. From there I went to Gelsenkirchen, and then I came here. That was eight years ago. Now I'm the first solo character ballerina, which is a good job, but I can't go any higher in this town. The only thing I could really try would be a big theatre in a big city, and I ought to be looking for something, but I'm not. That's the whole trouble. I always wait for someone to come along and say: 'I've seen you and I like you. We'll take you on at our theatre.' I don't like to write letters asking for jobs and I don't like to audition. It makes you feel like a piece of goods being auctioned off. – Dancing is my whole life. On account of dancing I only went to elementary school and now sometimes I see I don't know enough. I like to read but not enough to make up for all the things I don't know. I've just been reading *Les Jeux sont faits* by Sartre.* It's the story of a woman who has a chance to start her life all over again and makes practically all the same mistakes. Of course it gives you pause, but if I had a chance to start all over again, I think I'd do exactly the same. Only I'd like to make more money and to be luckier in love. I must confess: I've got a ten-year-old boy. He's in Munich with my parents. My love life has gone all wrong.

---

*English title: *The Die is Cast*.

I don't know why but I always get interested in the men I can't have.

The man I had my child by is married, and so is my present boy friend. He's an actor at the theatre here. It gets me down to think that I'm only a distraction for this man, especially on account of his wife, though he claims that she's not really interested in him and all she cares about is security and being known as his wife. He claims his wife isn't unhappy about our affair. She knows me by sight and it doesn't bother her. But naturally I'd rather have a man all to myself, a real partner in life. He wouldn't have to be handsome but I wouldn't like him to be really ugly or even worse if he didn't look like anything at all. Some ugly men simply look interesting. The main thing is he should love me and I'd like him to be as faithful as possible. I'd want to be faithful to him too. So far I've managed to be faithful, though I've never been married. The way I see a marriage is that a couple should really stay together and be as faithful as possible. And maybe it would be better if he weren't in the theatre.

There are so few real gentlemen.

I mean, for instance, if a lady is holding a cigarette to give her a light, to help her on with her coat and things like that. Maybe we've forgotten those things in the theatre because we work together and a man doesn't stand up to greet a fellow worker, and that kind of thing. But the truth is I've got kind of a hankering for those polite forms. Though when a man is too friendly, maybe he gets on your nerves after a while. I don't really know. I've never had dealings with a real gentleman. For instance, some men make you sick with their compliments, but a sincere compliment from a nice person is really lovely. I'm always very happy when people compliment me on my boy, and I don't think having a child frightens men away. I think it sort of appeals to them. Unless they don't say what they think. But I haven't got the feeling they mind. I think this thing with compliments all depends on whether a man is a gentleman or not. Maybe a man who is better educated can pay better compliments and is more attentive. If I ever find the right man, I'll probably discuss more things with him. That would be even more demanding than the theatre. Which would be hard on me.

If for instance he started talking to me about politics, my goodness!

I've got to admit, I'm not as much interested in politics as I ought to be. In general, I think young people, especially women, should take more interest, but I'm just not able to. I've got to admit to my shame that I don't even vote. I wouldn't even know what to vote for and if you say I should vote the same as my boy friend or my father, you've got two different opinions right there and I wouldn't know how to choose between them. So what's the use . . . If I at least had TV so I could see the daily news, I'd know more about politics. I don't read the papers either. Usually I'm dog-tired when I get home. At the most I play a couple of records to relax. What I like best is the latest hits, I don't listen to classical things. At a concert now and then, but not at home. I haven't got the patience. And probably because I haven't got time to sit down and just listen. I've got to write letters or do something else, and I can't if I'm listening to concertos. I like to go out now and then. I drink two or three whiskies and that's already nine marks. I can't really afford it. Theatre people don't treat each other. Usually I go out with my boy friend and we take turns paying. I don't go dancing. I don't know the modern dances. I only care for the waltz and the tango.

I don't think the new dances are fit to be seen.

When I go out, I fix my hair up nice and if I dance the twist and that kind of thing, I start perspiring and my hair comes undone, and then I don't feel fit to be seen. So we drink our whisky and talk about the theatre. We always discuss the play that's running or one that's about to open, and the authors. We also talk about the personal questions that come up in the plays, you know, the human problems. Which automatically reminds me of my own problems. My problems are mostly that I want to keep on supporting my boy and for that I've got to be successful in my work. You know, I often wonder how long I'll be able to keep on dancing and what will happen after that.

Some people keep on dancing until forty, but even at thirty-five the body hasn't the strength it takes.

After thirty-five dancing is really bad for the health because it's a great exertion. If I really went all out with my dancing, I'd have seven years to go at the most. But I wouldn't like to be out on the stage one day and have people saying: 'Hm, she ought to think of retiring.' There are always a lot of young people coming up to take your place and you're always afraid you won't find anything else. Of course I could try to become a ballet mistress. Sometimes I think that would be a good idea. And then again I think I couldn't stand the struggle with all those untalented dancers. Suppose I wanted something done a certain way and somebody else wouldn't do it the way I wanted, it would drive me crazy. And then there isn't much opportunity for a ballet mistress in these small theatres. What would a ballet mistress do? The programme is so limited. All they usually want is a ballet number in an operetta, a Hungarian dance or some such thing, and I wouldn't care for that. It's hard to get to be a ballet mistress in a big theatre. They all have their own people. It's hard to make the grade. You need special training, and that takes money to see you through for a few years. Good God! I'd rather think about our next ballet. I dance the part of a flower and an animal and somebody at a party. It's about a young man who's looking for his ideal or a great love or a melody, anyway, something big. And he doesn't find it anywhere, either in society or among the flowers. He keeps chasing after one thing and another but everything escapes him.

At the end he finds his melody, but by that time he's all worn out. The good, the beautiful and the melody are played by a ballerina. But whenever he reaches out for her, she's gone. You know, like the way happiness slips through your fingers.

What I like to dance best is *An American in Paris*. The choreography isn't what I'd have thought. I'm afraid the people who go to see it will be disappointed because they expect to see something in the American style like the American musicals, but of course our arrangement is classical. We've got to do it that way on the stage to keep from falling into the clichés of TV, those 'big show' ballets that always have the same hackneyed style. When we do put it on the stage, we've got to try to keep the traditional ballet style as much as possible. But whatever we dance, we have to be in perfect physical condition for every single performance.

If we're not feeling well we mustn't let anybody notice it.

Sometimes you feel weak, and then you're afraid of spraining or even breaking something. One of the girls in our ballet had a bad fall that way and hurt her knee. Suppose I hurt my feet, for instance, and have to spend six months or a year in the hospital, maybe I wouldn't be able to dance at all any more, or even if I could it would be very hard work getting back into practice. My girl friend had to give it up altogether. Fortunately she's well off. But a lot of dancers have had to go into other kinds of work to make a living and they're very unhappy. So we've got to give up a lot of things, most sports, for instance, for fear of injury. I'd love to go skiing but a dancer's contract doesn't allow it.

I'd also love to do parachute jumping.

I don't know why but that really appeals to me. I'd love to jump out into the air and have the feeling that I'm flying. Maybe this love of flying has something to do with my dancing. When my boy friend heard about it, he said I shouldn't even think about it. One day he came in with a newspaper and said: 'Look, you can jump as much as you like.' Then he showed me the newspaper and it said: 'Parachute jumping lessons eighty marks an hour.' He just wanted me to see how expensive it was. But I'd awfully like to do it. I've seen it in the movies. Just once I'd like to get the feeling it gives you. Maybe it's awful. But I'd like to know. When I fly in my dreams, it's always lovely. I dream a lot and I like to dream, I feel much better in the morning. Oh, I dream a lot of beautiful things and usually I'm the hero of my dreams. I rescue people, and I also dream that I'm the most terrific dancer. And suddenly I begin spinning, I go on and on, and people admire me.

FRITZ ALBERTUS

61, married, high city official

'Patriotic' has become a dirty word nowadays.

My brothers and I, it so happens, were brought up to be patriotic. The way we look at it, when a man has a country, it's only natural that he should serve his country in every way. We all volunteered in the First World War as a matter of course. Same in the Second. There was no question in our minds; that's what you do. Maybe it sounds a little pompous. Another thing we took for granted was that up front you yourself do what you expect your men to do. Of course some people said: 'You damn fool, why do you want to volunteer?' My answer to that was: 'Even if others don't, I know my duty.' All I can say about the First World War is that I myself, my friends, my brothers and their friends were all reputed to be brave soldiers but that they never gave a thought to bravery and heroism any more than I did. It never occurred to us. We did our duty and that was that. When a dangerous mission came up and some of your comrades were married men with children, you just said to yourself: You're not married, so that's the job for you. That's how we were brought up, we didn't have to think about it, we just took it for granted. That was the whole style of our upbringing. See what I mean? And what worries me about the younger generation who haven't been through war or anything like it, is that they absolutely reject anything connected with the ideas of country and nation and regard them as idiotic and antiquated.

I'm afraid the present generation is drifting into nihilism.

They have no ideals and even if they had any, they wouldn't be willing to make personal sacrifices for them. Maybe a little brawl, but the idea of giving their lives for them is something they've forgotten. Of course the Nazis got us to stake our lives for a wrong idea. But this younger generation that never knew the Nazis could be won over to a wrong idea too. Yes, that could happen; they have so little judgement, because so far the teaching of citizenship in the schools hasn't accomplished what was expected. Another reason is that the whole idea of authority has gone out of existence. Even in my day schoolchildren made fun of their teacher, called him nicknames and sometimes even hated him; never mind, he was still in a position of authority, and so were the parents. Nowadays a lot of people don't recognize any authority at all, but you can't have good government unless some authority is recognized. It has nothing to do with dictatorship. The Americans learn in their schools to respect the authority of their democratic government. They have an American flag in every classroom. That seems strange to us because we have gone so far from such conceptions, but it has its good side. Lax as the Americans are, they have one thing: they take it for granted that one man's freedom shouldn't interfere with the freedom of others. That's something our people here refuse to see. They all say: my freedom comes first! We're always going from one extreme to the other. Now all of a sudden we're hyper-humanitarian, so naturally we can't bring up our children properly; all we can say is: go ahead, sow your wild oats. And the result?

Everybody brings up the constitution in defence of his own petty interests.

Suppose a man wants to smoke in a non-smoking compartment and somebody objects. He says: 'No one has a right to make me stop, it's an attack on my personal freedom. I've got to smoke, it's necessary for my development.' That kind of inconsiderateness is dangerous, because when a man isn't willing to adjust to society, he isn't willing to sacrifice himself for anything either. And nobody wants to any more. Everybody just wants to live as he pleases. The lack of authority is to blame, but also the lack of respect for others. There's no more social cohesion. After the War everybody did pretty much as he pleased. After the War parents had no time for their children. To some extent that was a reaction to the strictness of the old days. And now parents are afraid to say anything. Because if they opened their mouths, they'd be called Nazis or God knows what. This eternal guilt of ours: 'Mea culpa, mea culpa, mea maxima culpa' – it's terrible how we go on and on with it, always teaching the younger generation that their parents and grandparents were the worst kind of criminals. Nobody ever says that anything was right, they just keep harping on the bad things. They treat us as if every last one of us had eaten three Jews for breakfast every day, whether we were in the Party or not. Just read what that stinking Günter Grass wrote about Kiesinger the other day. The way he attacks his whole past, just because Kiesinger was once in the Party. I know Kiesinger well. I'm not a hundred per cent for him, not at all, but it's simply intolerable that a young snotnose with his *The Tin Drum* should take that tone in writing about him.

These young people have no way of judging how it really was in those days.

You see, I joined the Party in 1933, like almost everybody else. But I was never asked to do anything wrong. In those days we took an entirely different view of everything connected with Nazism than today. After all we didn't have second sight. Nobody suspected anything criminal. But we did see how people were standing in line, how hopeless everything was. Here was a hope of improving things, and they actually did improve. We saw people suddenly taking hope, finding work, and laying the foundations of a new life. You couldn't help being fascinated. At that time I didn't realize that the Nazis were really aiming at something else. You see, I wasn't so very much interested in politics in those days. Of course there was anti-Semitism. That bothered me because of the way I'd been brought up, but the authoritarianism, the new military spirit, yes, of course, that impressed us, and in general the fact that they had finally put some order into things again. It was the same as today with the NPD. People said:

'Well, here comes a strong man at last who'll put an end to all this confusion and wishy-washiness.'

At the beginning of the War an aunt of mine was gassed. That was a big shock to me. But to show you how people felt in the main in those days, I'll tell you another story. When I went to France with my company, my soldiers were always saying: 'Lieutenant, it's awful with these people here, these French. They all do exactly what they please. What kind of a country is this? All they do is talk and complain, it's a pigpen, there's no order!' That's interesting, isn't it? That's the way we felt about it. That's the way nearly all the soldiers felt when they set foot in a free democratic country. It just seemed all wrong to them. Only a short time ago I saw something similar here in our present democratic state. A nephew of mine came over to see me. He's a pastor in Saxony, you know, in the DDR. After he'd been here about ten days he said: 'Forgive me, but I'm going back.

'It's certainly bad over there in the DDR. We're always under pressure, but somehow we're integrated, we have something to live for.

'Over here, people are just drifting. There's nothing but confusion. It gets on my nerves.' You see, what he couldn't stand was that there's no leadership here any more. I think people should stop and think about that. No sense of order, that's what worries me.

These young people today, they simply have no respect. For instance, I give a course for young men who are going into the administration. They're all high-school graduates. They started throwing spitballs at each other. But I wouldn't put up with that for very long. I put a stop to it right away. 'You're not in school any more,' I said. 'This is work, you've got to learn something here or you won't get positions.' What do you think they answered? 'Go on,' they said, 'they'll have to take us whether we know anything or not.' The day before the examination one of them came to me and said: 'We can't take the examination because you haven't given us a copy of the code. Of course we can get a copy at the office, but it's supposed to be issued.' You see, that's what they've come to: they wait for us to put the books in their hands, and if we don't, they come right out and say: 'It's your fault if we don't know anything.' They simply haven't got the personal initiative that's the basic requirement for democracy. Today there are scholarships, there's the Honnef Plan, but a short time ago some students stood up and said: 'What good does it do the German people for us to spend the best years of our life studying?' What do you think, are they sick? Of course it's not only the young people's fault if they think like that, it's partly the fault of the people who haven't taught them to think differently. But if anybody tries to teach them anything,

if anybody so much as mentions the word 'order', they start calling him a neo-Nazi, a militarist, etc.

It's so disgustingly easy. They sidestep every obligation by smearing their critics politically. Look at the Bundeswehr, for instance: first, right after the War, the new soldiers got Schlaraffia mattresses. They had maids to look after the barracks and God knows what else. But then all that went out, because the young men really wanted to be treated rough. The way they act, it's the same as when we were children when we provoked our parents until we got a box in the ear. They just want to see how far they can go. That's why I sometimes say to myself: there must be something good in these young fellows, only how am I going to find it and bring it out? What they lack are models and examples. I'm terribly sorry to say so.

But our political leaders offer neither a model nor an example,

and neither do the higher ups and the officers. Think of this: in my office there are two different kinds of soap and towels for officials and clerks in the same department. Nobody utters a word of complaint, but one fine day the union personnel adviser comes in and raises hell and takes disciplinary measures because of undemocratic behaviour, etc., etc. It's enough to make you break down and cry! Why can't they simply say: Look here, it's all the same to me, I'll use your soap. But they simply haven't got the educational background to make out by themselves. They like to be coddled and taken care of, and then they complain and yell that somebody is trying to lead them by the nose. And if they're not directed, they complain like mad all the same. It's a very strange atmosphere today. Things used to be entirely different. My father's a Saxon. My mother is from Strassburg. I was born in Giessen and grew up in Tübingen.

We've had professors in the family for generations, both on my father's and my mother's side.

Medicine, literature, law, biology, geology and so on. My brothers and cousins and I were the first to break with this tradition. One of my brothers is a medical man, used to be a general practitioner, the second was an Army officer, and I studied to be a jurist. I went to elementary school in Giessen. At first it was housed in a pawnshop. Peasant women with cheeses sat outside and the aroma came in through the windows. It was marvellous. In the second grade our class was in the Jewish poorhouse. That was about 1913. Our teacher was the cantor of the Jewish congregation. His name was Nathan Levi. When he sang and prayed with his congregation on Saturday, he left us to ourselves and a member of the class had to give the dictation. He'd come back half an hour later and say: 'Everything all right, everything all right? No nonsense please, my name is Nathan Levi and I know what I want.' He had a long beard, he was really a charming old man and very dignified. There was no anti-Semitism in Giessen. In those days I never heard of it. No, there just wasn't any. Do you know, my mother was a cousin of Max and Alfred Weber, they were all too liberal, too tolerant to think about such things. Here and there in Max Weber, it's true, you'll find a nationalistic statement. It's true, he once said: 'The unpleasant Jew' or something of the sort. But it was never meant as anti-Semitism. It was only a characterization. He could just as well have said: 'The unpleasant Berliner.' Anti-Semitism was unknown to us. We're also related to Mendelssohn-Bartholdy. That was the level of those circles of the intellectual bourgeoisie. Well, then I went to secondary school in Tübingen.

The history instruction, I've got to admit, was the way it had always been in this country. It stopped a hundred years before our time.

At that time we didn't even get as far as the War of 1870–71. We barely got to 1866. That was a lovely war, if you want to look at it that way, because the Württembergers still had a chance to shoot at the Prussians. It was a great day for the Württembergers, relatively speaking. They put up a strong fight against the Prussians, but by 1870 they were incorporated into the German Army. 1866 was their last national war. Those were entirely different times.

My goodness, when I think of it, what important people university professors were in my time!

They used to be the leaders of society. Now it's entirely different; nowadays a university professor is about as much respected as a high-school principal, anyway not much more. Except for professors of medicine. Because of their high income, they still have a privileged position in society. They can still afford the large houses or apartments which almost every professor had in those days. The big houses made for much more social life. I can't remember a Sunday when there were less than thirty, forty, or even sixty students at my father's house. The professors came into close contact with their students. Besides two students came to lunch every week, so that my father had every student in his seminar to his house at least once. In my day there were only 2,000 students in Tübingen. Today, as you know, there are 12,000. Nobody knows anyone else any more. Professors had a busy social life up to the First World War. Since then all that has changed. First came the inflation, and then there were no more servants. In those days there was much more contact between the university and the townspeople. The daughters of the families where the students lived went dancing with the students in the fraternity houses. It was taken for granted. Those were the days of the so-called 'Groschen girls'. The dancing teacher brought them along. A student had to pay his partner ten pfennigs for each dance. That went on until 1922. I saw it myself. They were artisans' daughters. Nice girls! And good dancers. They were another reason for the close ties between the students and the townspeople. Today there are still students living in furnished rooms but I hardly think they have much to do with the families. In those days the *filia hospitalis*, as they called her, fixed the students' rooms. Not just to make money, it was a point of honour. Today certain things are missing. There's no *genius loci*. It's gone. Today the students come to graduation in blue jeans. That's unspeakable! I'd throw them out. It's incredible! It's simply a question of style, of self-respect. It just isn't right. It's like going to class unshaved and unwashed.

MARTIN LINDNER

47, married, policeman

With motorization crime began to organize itself.

When I was discharged from the prison camp in 1947, a few of my Army friends joined the police. They talked it up, so I joined too. We were given seniority credit for the years we had served in the Wehrmacht. I'd never learned any trade, so they couldn't take me on as a specialist. But I knew how to type and that was needed in the police force. All the same, I had to start in again from the beginning: three months of police school and some kind of courses ever since. Why? Because the laws are always changing and we've got to keep up with them. It's hard to keep all that in your head. Now I'm a sergeant and make 1,200 marks a month. I was supposed to be retired at sixty, but now the regulations have changed and it won't be until I'm at least sixty-two. But then, it's true, we get a pension equal to seventy per cent of our last salary. As you know, we Germans aren't crazy about telling anybody how much we make. Americans don't seem to mind talking about these things, but we've got a different mentality: we feel what goes on in our home concerns only the people who live there. I don't think my wife or daughter would discuss these things on the outside. Suppose we have debts. I ask you, whose business is that? Never mind, I'll tell you. We haven't any debts. It's practically impossible to have debts if you're on the police force, because our reputations are expected to be spotless. If it becomes known that one of us is in debt, he isn't censured or anything, but his department does its best to take over the man's debts so he won't be in debt any more. Naturally they deduct a certain sum from his pay each month. I am sorry to say that some policemen are in that situation. You'll probably find these exceptional cases in any profession. One man knows how to manage his money and another doesn't, he lives high for the first ten days and for the other twenty he doesn't know what to do. But that mustn't be allowed to affect his work.

I've been on night duty now for twenty years. And for at least ten years after the War we pounded the pavement. Then came the first motorcycles with sidecars and gradually motorization became so general that today hardly anyone walks. Only a few of us still patrol on foot to keep contact with the population. Of course we all have to make a good impression and the appearance of our uniforms is checked. If my uniform isn't neat and clean when I come on duty, I can expect my boss to read me the riot act. We have an annual clothing allowance out of which we buy the items we need. Each one of us gets 285 marks a year. We can manage on that, it even takes care of the blood stains we sometimes get on our uniforms. Right after the War that happened a lot more often. Those were the black market days and sometimes things were pretty rough. Today things have calmed down, the traffic is better regulated and with motorization crime began to organize itself. Look at the bank robberies, for instance. In the old days before bank robbers had cars, their methods weren't the same as today. They couldn't make a quick enough getaway. Christ, take auto thefts and burglaries, especially the big burglaries in fur shops, jewellery shops, etc. The loot is always taken away by car. Otherwise this town is relatively quiet, it's not like the big industrial cities. Now and then we have a little trouble with the students, but it's not so bad. They break a few street lamps, run through the streets howling, and maybe making a few insulting remarks. There's no crime involved. Yes, there are often brawls in the beer halls. The people are quick-tempered and get into fights. It happens all over. Mostly in the Old City. In my radio car I stick to my own district, but over the radio I hear about everything that goes on in other districts. A lot of fights are caused by whores that make some man jealous. There are no official brothels any more but when they're standing around the street there's bound to be trouble. Now they have to do their standing in the outskirts, they used to be in the centre, but the public objected.

When a respectable woman went out in the street, a man who was looking for a woman had no way of knowing if she was a respectable housewife or a whore.

Sometimes there were funny mistakes. Some of them ended well, some of them not so well. I mean, sometimes when a so-called respectable woman was accosted by a man, she took a shine to him and let herself be led astray, so to speak. For us of course whores are only little fish. The sharks are the capital crimes. Without the active cooperation of the population we sometimes couldn't catch those brutes so quickly. But the people are okay, sometimes they give us first-class tips. The banks that get robbed most often are the branch offices in the suburbs. Last Tuesday one of them was held up. The bandit arrived all alone on a motorcycle, in broad daylight, a little before twelve noon. Twenty minutes later, we had nabbed him. The bank had an emergency hook-up, so the alarm went out quicker and we were able to concentrate our forces. The guy was a block away by the time we got there, he'd hidden somewhere. But the people in the street had seen him and turned him in. So we got him. He was a youngster.

All in all the young fellows aren't up to any more mischief than they were in my day.

I mean, things were probably a little stricter at that time because of the Hitler Youth and the Labour Service. Maybe morality was a little less lax, but all in all we had exactly the same kind of no-goods as today. After everything that happened in the Nazi period, we police officers had a pretty bad reputation. But I can say from my own experience that it has improved a good deal since then, because people finally realized that they can't get along without the police force. Of course you still find a few police-haters, but they must be characters who have somehow tangled with the police, because a reasonable law-abiding citizen never has any trouble with the police. Anyway, that's my opinion. If we catch somebody in a misdemeanour, some traffic offence, for instance, they're usually very polite.

It's very unusual for one of us to interfere with anybody unless he's done something.

and if it's politely explained to him, he's bound to understand, and if he doesn't, that's his hard luck. As a rule, the old proverb still holds good: as ye sow so shall ye reap. And we're always instructed to be polite. It's drummed into us. A policeman needs to have a lot more self control than the people he deals with and that takes years of experience. A beginner is always quick to flare up when somebody talks out of turn. But gradually it wears off and you hardly pay any attention to the things some delinquent shouts at you in his excitement. And the calmer you are the sooner the other fellow sees that he has nothing to gain by being obstreperous. I enjoy my job. I get along fine with the other men on the force. The trouble we've been through together knits us closer than if we'd been working in some factory. In some jobs it's a question of life and death. Take it from me! After all, it's not so unusual for a police officer to be killed or wounded. I just read in a department paper that 800 police officers have been killed since the War. I mean, whenever there's a fight we get it in the neck. It can't be helped. I've lost a few teeth. Sometimes we have to use our firearms. The regulations are very precise. It's only permitted in self-defence. If my own life is in danger, I'm allowed to shoot. Or in case of crimes of violence, when we're chasing criminals. When we shout at them to stop and they keep on running. All kind of unpleasant things can happen, especially because we have so many foreigners here now who don't know the regulations. At night we all carry arms, either revolvers or, on special jobs, American automatic rifles or German machine pistols.

Sometimes it's necessary, but I'll tell you something. Shooting at people doesn't interest me, I'd rather go hunting.

Hunting is my hobby. Recently I was in Austria for instance, hunting chamois. That was the first time I'd been out of Germany since the War. Otherwise I always spend my vacation around here. I take my vacation in winter which is open season for small game. We've got a big hunt club. We spend a day or two at the preserve of one of our members. I'm only a guest. A hunting preserve of your own is expensive, it would take all my pay. I came to talk about hunting because nature is kind of a part of me. When I come home from the woods, my glass of wine tastes twice as good. As a police officer, I can't afford to go to bars. You see, I live right in the middle of my precinct and I know everybody here, I'm on good terms with them, but it's perfectly possible that somebody who'd been drinking too much would make a nasty remark and we'd get into a fight. I wouldn't want that. Even a police officer is human. I'd rather stay away from the bars.

I'd think about politics even if I didn't have to.

As a police officer, it's best to be moderate in everything. The same goes for politics. All the same, I've got to think about politics, because I've got to know what I think about the government I serve in my job. My superiors expect it of me too, they want us to keep up with things and to know what's going on in the world. But even without that, I'd still think about politics. When I have time, I read two or three newspapers a day. At home I read the local paper, and at the police station we have the *Frankfurter Allgemeine Zeitung* and a few more of the big papers. And sometimes we have lectures. Only a few days ago a Protestant minister spoke to us about world politics. I was very much impressed by his openmindedness. Here at last was a clergyman who didn't keep harping on religion but spoke about the general problems of the world the way we see them. And what we didn't understand, he explained. He was a really fine man, perfectly normal.

A glance at heaven in the forest is better than a false prayer.

Of course we're all Protestants in the family and all raised as

Christians. My daughter too. She's just seventeen. We don't go to church very much, but even so I have the impression that we live like Christians. So we know the difference between right and wrong. I go by the hunter's motto: 'You think the hunter is a sinner because he seldom goes to church. A glance at heaven in the forest is better than a false prayer.' My main prayer is for peace and good health, and my only wish for our country is that the two parts should be reunited and live at peace and not try to be superior to other countries or influence or dominate them. To each man his due! People always think their own country is the only one that's any good, but then we meet foreigners and see their qualities, and we've got to admit that their way is just as good as ours.

IRENE KOLAKOWSKI
31, married, housewife

Jürgen Neven-du Mont: I'm walking across town and I see a woman standing beside her car; she's having a violent argument with a policeman. Then she drives off. A few days later, I happen to meet this lady at the house of some friends. I tell her that I witnessed her argument with the policeman. Still fuming, she tells me about it:

You see, this is how it was: I'm driving along Berlinerstrasse and I want to turn right into Hohenzollernstrasse. The traffic cop at the intersection gives the go-ahead for Hohenzollernstrasse. So I turn the corner. Just then another policeman who was standing on the corner keeping an eye on developments, as they say nowadays, comes rushing up and shouts at me: 'Pull up on the right!' So I pull up on the right. He's waiting for me, he pulls open my car door and bellows at me: 'What made you think you could turn that corner?' I say: 'Your colleague at the intersection gave me the go-ahead. What's wrong?' 'Don't hand me that,' he says. 'What do you take me for? My

colleague didn't give you anything. But I'm giving you a ticket!'
'See here,' I say, 'who told you to open my car door? You know
perfectly well you have no right to without asking me first. I
could speak to you perfectly well through the window. This is
an invasion of privacy. What's more, drop that tone of voice,
stop shouting like a feeble-minded top sergeant!' That threw
him into a complete rage, nothing came out of him but inarticu-
late sounds, he yelled and stammered and asked for my car
papers. I refused to show him my papers, anyway I said he
couldn't see them unless he told me his name first. Nothing
doing, he said. There was no number on his cap and I said if
he didn't tell me his name I wouldn't show him my papers. He
went all red in the face, the sweat ran down his ears and he
shouted at me that in that case he'd have to take me to the
police station. 'Suits me,' I said, 'if you drive with me.' But he
couldn't come with me because he was on duty on the corner.
Fuming with rage, he snarled: 'You just wait!'

'I'm going to turn you in. This is going to end very badly for
you, you can count on that.'

'On the contrary,' I said to him, 'it's going to end very badly
for you!' And then I told him that I was getting in touch with
a lawyer who specialized in traffic cases, and the last thing I
said to him was: 'My dear man, my advice to you is to take a
course in good manners at the police academy.' Oh well, then I
drove off. You were there, you saw me. That very evening our
telephone rang and it was this policeman. He said he had discussed the matter with his colleague and had to admit he
hadn't realized that his colleague at the intersection actually
had given the go-ahead for Hohenzollernstrasse. However, it
was all the same to him what steps I chose to take, I could
call in my lawyer if I felt like it. I told him I wasn't one to bear
grudges and if he apologized, that would be enough for me, the
matter would rest there. Such things are always happening
here in Germany. It's this damned German sense of authority
that sticks to people like a tick to a dog. Most people are afraid

of the police and let themselves be intimidated by any uniform.

Only recently I had another experience: I came out of a store and met an old friend of my husband's who was an officer in the First World War. He had lost a leg, which makes him a disabled veteran. It was Saturday afternoon. I don't like to drive the car on Saturday, you hardly move. So we decided to take the streetcar. It was already in sight, it was one of those big new cars, and this gentleman, his name is Reinhardt, sat down in the rear compartment and I sat down beside him. The car wasn't very full. Right away the conductor comes running. 'Go sit in the front compartment!' he shouts. At first we didn't take him seriously, but then he yells again: 'Go sit in the front!' 'You mean me?' Mr Reinhardt asked. 'I'm a disabled war veteran,' says Mr Reinhardt. 'Show me your card.' 'I haven't got it on me. I'm very sorry. But you can see for yourself that I've got an artificial leg.' 'That's all the same to me,' yells the conductor. 'You've got to go up front! And the lady too!' 'But why?' Mr Reinhardt asks. 'Because I say so,' yells the conductor. So he actually forced us to go up front. We didn't want to spend the whole day bickering with the man. Anyway, he would have told us to get out for not following his instructions. 'Well,' I said to Mr Reinhardt: 'Let's go and complain to the streetcar management.' 'Too much trouble,' said Mr Reinhardt. 'Pretty much the same thing has happened to me before. The car was full and I told the conductor I was a disabled veteran and asked him to get me a seat. He said I could go find myself one! And do you think anybody stood up for me? Not a chance! And the car was full of young students!'

It's really terrible in this country. As soon as a man has a uniform on, he thinks he can do anything he pleases.

Recently, for instance, I went to the post office. It was eleven o'clock Monday morning and the place was empty. Nobody but me. A clerk was sitting behind his window, eating a sandwich and having a cosy chat with a woman employee. He pretended not to see me, just went on eating his sandwich and talking and talking. I say: 'Would you kindly serve me? I have a registered letter.' 'Just a minute,' he says. 'A little patience, young lady.' And he goes on eating and talking. I say: 'It's what you're here for after all, it's your work and you're paid for it.' And he comes right back with: 'You're supposed to wait until I can attend you.' It was another five minutes before he took my registered letter. Of course you can't generalize. Sometimes you find a polite postal clerk.

I've got nothing against the post office, but there's got to be order.

Even people in uniform ought to be decent and polite. Nowadays you don't see much of the old Prussian civil service spirit, the idea that they're there to serve. If you say anything to a civil servant nowadays, I often get the feeling that he's offended. It's the authoritarian obsession. They're the representatives of authority and the rest of us are just people. So we've got to wait. It's always the same. Nobody tries to do anything against it. Nobody puts up a fight. I get around. I meet a lot of people. I often try to bring up the subject. But people won't listen. It's always the same lethargy and indolence where authority is concerned, they're afraid, they don't want to make trouble for themselves. Anybody with a couple of brass buttons on his coat thinks he's got a right to order people around. Actually there's no reason to be afraid of them. Nothing will happen to you if you put up a fight. It seems to be the old servility that hasn't been uprooted. The subject is inexhaustible, I'd better stop talking about it. Sometimes I could burst with rage ...

HEDWIG SCHIRMER
60, unmarried, librarian

When you're connected with popular education . . .

We're all moulded by the work we do. That was brought home to me one time during the War in an air-raid shelter. It was during a raid. To pass the time we were playing a game that was very popular at the time: if you were evacuated and were only allowed to take three books with you, what books would you take? I said I'd take one book of philosophy and one of history – I think it was Friedell's *Cultural History*, which actually you could spend a whole lifetime reading. My third book was a detective story. Naturally everybody in the air-raid shelter was indignant. They said: Why the detective story? What's the good of it? You'll read it in half an hour. But I said no, I'm not taking it for myself, I'm taking it for other people.

You see what I mean? When you're connected with popular education, you never read subjectively. I can't even listen to a concert or a lecture subjectively. I always ask myself: Would this interest so and so? Is this a subject that I should call to people's attention? Do you see what I'm trying to say? I'm trying to tell you how immersed I am in my profession. Originally I wanted to be a dancer and I took a few lessons from Mary Wigman. My father was a postal official and very conventional. He had a false sense of class and threatened to commit suicide if he ever saw me, his only child, on the stage. So I had to find another profession that would appeal to me. My father belonged to a section of the middle class that had an intense need for prestige. In those days I think there was a wide gulf between the middle class and the arts. Naturally my father didn't know anything about Mary Wigman. The art of dance, you've got to remember, was only in its beginnings, and there was something shocking about the ballet and ballet dancers. My mother, on the other hand, would have been delighted to have me become an artist. She was a gardener's daughter, but my grandfather was a very original personality and my grandmother too. There was something big about them. Their position in life might have made them more petit-bourgeois than my father's parents, but they were much more open-minded.

My grandfather decorated the table for the King.

He travelled a good deal, he had very good manners and met many people of different walks of life. When my mother was only seventeen, she felt she ought to see something of the world and went off secretly to Paris one night. She found a position as tutor in a family. My mother stayed in Paris for many years and was happy. She's always been rather partial to France, in questions of fashion and way of life. She was a genius at languages. Somehow that gift of hers aroused my antagonism and I rebelled against learning languages. This makes difficulty for me today. I'm always meeting foreigners and once I was in America for three months. On that occasion I had more trouble with the language than anyone else in the group, though I tried hard.

What I was most enthusiastic about in America was the people's tolerance.

I mean the way they respect other people's opinions and try to understand them. That was what really fascinated me. But there were other things I didn't like. Of course most of the people I met in America were colleagues and teachers. Hardly any of them had libraries in their homes. I kept asking them: Where's your library? Here, they'd say, and show me a little bookcase that might have had room for sixty books at the most. Yes, I said, but you like to read. You read quite a lot, don't you? Yes, of course, they said, but we have our public library. Then I asked:

But don't you ever want to look up something in your Shakespeare suddenly in the middle of the night?

Don't you ever feel that you want to own books? I found very little understanding for my attitude. There was no real love of books. They didn't care about bindings. When we have a favourite book, we like to see it nicely bound and printed on good paper. This doesn't mean a thing to them. Another thing that troubled me was that in an American city of three to five hundred thousand inhabitants there was no theatre and no orchestra. After I'd been there for two months, I was asked: Have you some special desire, is there something we can do to give you special pleasure? Yes, I said, I'd like to go to a concert. Of course, they said, we'll call for you at eight o'clock tonight. A car drove up and I was taken to a residential section. I thought to myself: What's going on, I haven't seen a poster anywhere or any other indication that a concert is taking place. Finally I landed in a large house and saw a number of well-dressed people gather in a large, attractive room . . .

And what was offered? Phonograph records! Imagine!

This was a city of over three hundred thousand people! Of course such things aren't very important measured against the quality of the people I met in America. All the same, in spite of the close friendships I formed with Americans, I had the feeling that there are differences in our conceptions of life and culture than cannot be bridged. Of course I've got to remember that I was fairly well on at the time, thoroughly moulded by the world in which I had lived over here. I really like it here, especially because I live in a city that is neither a small town nor a metropolis. After the War it was as if a fresh breeze had come to our town. The new contact with the western world brought a kind of cosmopolitan openness. There is a good deal of cultural and artistic activity here. True, things were difficult in my profession. It wasn't easy to build up this library. It took a good deal of fighting and strong nerves. But you can

measure our success by the number of readers. Our effort was
worthwhile. Every day as I go through the reading rooms that
thought passes through my mind. The library is used by people
of all ages.

What pleases me is that the young people read more than
I ever dared hope.

Hundreds come here every day. They pay only three marks
for the whole year. For that they can read as much as they
like and can keep books for four weeks. Of course an educational institution of this kind ought to be free of charge. In
Denmark, Sweden and England the municipal libraries are absolutely free, and of course in America too. I'm glad to say that
quite a number of German cities have followed this example.
At first we thought we'd need a lot of publicity. We thought
we'd have to canvass the schools systematically, including
trade and vocational schools, but then without any effort on
our part they began sending groups every week. The teachers
arranged these visits, but we also get a lot of people from factories. There's one firm, for example, that regularly sends us 250
apprentices. The people's interests have changed a good deal.

In general I can say that the centre of interest has shifted
from fiction to non-fiction.

Many more readers than before are interested in science,
physics, technology and medicine. Formerly eighty per cent of
the books we loaned were *belles-lettres* and only twenty per
cent non-fiction. Today the ratio is sixty to forty. The change
began shortly after 1945. Under the Third Reich certain scientific fields were inaccessible, psychology, for instance. Under
Hitler, people were not supposed to take an interest in psychology. Many books on psychology were banned. The Third Reich
wanted obedient servants of the State, who do what they are
told. People were not encouraged to think about themselves or
take a psychological view of other people. They were ex-

pected to be healthy, simple and obedient. As a reaction, works in this field were very much in demand after 1945. Today natural science, technology, sociology and contemporary history are the most popular subjects. We often wonder whether the public's interest is stimulated by the books that happen to be available or whether the supply results from the demand. It's a hard question to answer. In acquiring books librarians follow two principles: One, the democratic principle prevailing in the Anglo-Saxon countries. This means giving the reader what he wants, including popular literature such as detective stories and so on. The other principle is to supply works of literary and moral quality. I personally take the latter view. The funds available for the acquisition of books are so limited in almost all German libraries that in my opinion we shouldn't spend a penny on inferior literature.

Still, I realize that we haven't the faintest idea of how books affect our readers.

A book of high literary value can sometimes exert a worse influence than an inferior book. In the field of *belles-lettres* the greatest demand is for entertaining novels. But our young people today are encouraged in school to read problematic modern literature and to come to grips with it. They read mostly modern literature, while the older people read both. The older people are not by any means inaccessible to modern literature. They may not really approve of it but they want to familiarize themselves with it. Perhaps our public libraries in Germany wouldn't be so busy if the prices of books were lower. Even so, there are lots of cheap paperback series today. However, I have the impression that a good many people tend to buy the books that give them status.

All in all, though, the German idea of prestige hasn't got much to do with books.

For most people status attaches more to comfortable bath-

rooms, automobiles and TV sets. The love of books is a matter of upbringing. I was lucky. Because my father worked in
the post office, he was looked on as an outsider, so he read a
great deal. My friends in school also had cultivated parents who
enjoyed reading. Besides, there was a very high percentage of
Jewish girls in our class.

Most of the Jewish families had wonderful libraries.

Up to 1941 I knew next to nothing about the awful things that
went on in the Nazi period. One day in 1941 our former janitor
turned up in our library and told us about a concentration
camp where he was working as a guard. I remember it all very
clearly. He told us about some frail priests among the prisoners
who were kept running up stairs with heavy buckets of water
until they dropped. He tried to take one of the priests' buckets,
but another guard pushed him away with his rifle butt. Then
he told us other terrible things, for instance, how the prisoners
were squeezed together in iron rings until they died. It was so
awful. Before that we really had never suspected that such
things happened. At first my co-workers and I thought this
janitor, the concentration camp guard, was only trying to show
how tough he was and was pulling our leg. But the man who
was then director of the library happened to be present. He
himself was in the SA. He saw that this other man, the guard,
was beginning to tremble, and took him outside. When he came
back, I can still remember clearly, he was as white as a sheet.
He said to us:

It's true, everything he told us is true.

He hadn't been pulling our leg. The things he'd seen had made a
terrible impression on him too. You see, he had first been a
plain soldier and then suddenly he was transferred to the SS.
He was a simple soul, a good-hearted family man. Eugen Kogon
gave an excellent description of this kind of man in his book
The SS State. Our janitor was suddenly sent into the SS, he saw

all that, and he said: This won't do! He tried to stop it and naturally they said to him: You're not a man! What are you anyway? You're not a soldier, you're not a member of the national community. They systematically undermined his self-confidence. In the end he was completely confused and said: Which is the truth? Am I a coward? They all tell me I'm a coward. And here, here at home, they say entirely different things.

From 1927 to 1932 I worked in a bookstore in Celle. Then I was dismissed because the bookstore went bankrupt. I began to draw unemployment insurance. I didn't say anything at home because my father had had his first stroke at the age of thirty-five, which made it hard for him to get ahead in his profession. So we were having a hard time financially. I left home every morning without saying I was unemployed.

I wrote 487 letters applying for jobs; but I didn't get one.

Then came 1933 and then there was work. It sounds good to a young woman who likes to work when she hears them saying: Your country needs you. That cheered me up and I went along – mentally, I mean, I didn't join any organization. My father had read Hitler's *Mein Kampf* and was dead against the Nazis. He warned me. But what good was a warning? He couldn't give me work and that was what I needed. And actually I got a job right away, first in another bookstore and then in a municipal library. Things seemed to be starting up again. There was hope on all sides. And we were caught up in the current. During the first years of the Third Reich I was fully convinced that we were on the right track. But one day I happened to be standing on the Rhine Bridge in Cologne with a few of my colleagues. We heard military music and we said: What's this, have we got an army now, or are the French coming? Well, it was soldiers all right, German soldiers. And that military posture and the whole idea that they were building up a big army gave us pause. After that we listened to the foreign radio commentators and kept our eyes open; pretty soon we were getting critical. Up until then, we'd believed everything. Now our enthusiasm began to dwindle. And then one evening a lady came to see me in the library and asked me for my dues for the National Socialist Women's Organization. I said I wasn't a member. She left. But she came back and asked me again for my dues and said I *was* a member.

She said I had been automatically carried over from the National Socialist Students' Association to the Woman's Organization.

I told her I didn't want to be a member. I didn't want to belong to any organization. But the woman just said: 'Kindly do me a favour and pay your dues. My own position is rather shaky and if I report your resignation from my local group, the consequences will be disastrous for me.' I felt sorry for the woman and I paid the dues. So the snowball started rolling. I was only an assistant in the library. I still had no official position. One day the director's secretary came in and said: 'It's not at all certain that you'll get the job. Tell me, how is it you're not in the Party?' 'But I'm in the Women's Organization,' I said. 'That doesn't make any difference,' she said. 'Why aren't you in the Party? If you want a permanent job, you've got to be in the Party.' She had a friend of hers, an SA man, standing in the stacks. But I didn't know that. So I told her I couldn't join the Party because I wasn't convinced. That was stupid of me, but sincere. So she said: 'Then you don't want to join the Party?' 'No', I said. As she was leaving, she said: 'That's all I wanted to know.' Two weeks later I received a notice: 'National Socialist Party Tribunal. You are summoned to appear at 6.30 p.m. on such and such a date.' At six o'clock a young colleague of mine turned up in SS uniform. I asked him what he wanted. 'I'm going with you,' he said. He was dreadfully pale. 'I'll stand by you as much as I can.' 'Look here,' I said, 'It's not as serious as all that.' 'Oh yes it is,' he said. 'It's very serious.' So I enter the room. The district leader was sitting there, it was a regular court with a lawyer on the platform and on the side local group leaders, two typists and myself – I was on the defendants' bench.

They questioned me : Why did I lend out this book and that book? They were not exactly in the spirit of the national community.

And then came the first witness. It was my director's secretary. She had denounced me. She wanted my job. The witness against me was the SA man who had been standing in the stacks. And then I was asked if I was prepared to join the Party. I said: 'No. I'm sorry, I can't say yes when I've just said no. I haven't changed my mind.' They left me alone for a while. Then a man I knew came to see me, a friend of my father's who worked in the district leader's office. 'See here,' he said. 'They're starting new proceedings. I can still get you into the Party. Then you won't have anything to worry about.

'Don't stick your neck out again. Think of your mother who is having such a hard time.

'If you don't join now, you'll be in bad trouble. You'll be sent to a concentration camp.' I still had no idea what a concentration camp was, so I said: 'Oh, that's not so bad as long as they don't deport me.' And then I finally got sick of it and said yes. But I felt very guilty. The people of my generation, you know, didn't bother with politics in the decisive years. I wasn't the only one who dismissed his father's warning and never even thought of reading *Mein Kampf*. We didn't take enough notice of political developments. All we cared about was the arts, not public affairs. Today the young people are much more open-minded than before. A few days ago we had a meeting. It was arranged by two or three young people. There was no organization behind it. They held a discussion about the emergency laws. Our big lecture hall was packed. It holds three hundred. They all came of their own free will because they were interested in the question. There had been practically no publicity. Only a few little posters here and there. My goodness, they really talked themselves into a lather! That would hardly have been possible in my day.

EUGEN HORSELBERG
60, married, high-school teacher

I believe we haven't much to say to the young people any more.

Actually I would rather have been a doctor because I could have done more with my scientific interests, I could have applied science to living material. But it would have been too hard on my parents. A medical course costs a lot of money and I was under obligation to complete my studies as quickly as possible. My father was a small clerk working for the railroads. He had the lowest civil service rating. Sending me to the university was a big sacrifice for him. I am still amazed at his willingness to sacrifice himself for his only son, and I owe my present position in life very largely to his self-sacrifice. In my opinion the really valuable things in life are those that call for sacrifice. When I think it over, this is the way things look to me: as a doctor I'd have associated with sick people. Maybe that should make me happier. But to tell you the honest truth I'm not very happy, because association with these young healthy people is no picnic. I've got to admit that it's become very hard to deal with young people. Anybody can see that the emancipation of the young is making great strides. The over-all trend, as I see it, is toward decolonization and demythification; a man is developing into a much freer being. In my opinion this is the basic trend, it affects everybody, including the young people. But it puts us older people in a difficult position. After two world wars my generation has become very unsure of itself. I believe that we haven't much to say to the young people any more; I'm afraid they have seen through us and realize that we have our doubts about everything. Otherwise I can't account for their attitude towards us. They pretend to be terribly clever but fundamentally their supposedly bright ideas are only a feeble reflection of ours. But they use this artificial cleverness as a weapon against us.

The young people know perfectly well that our sorest point is the past, that we haven't got over it.

But the young people today are not bad. They merely sense that we don't know what to make of the mass media and the technology that are pouring in on us today, in short, of the 'modern' world. It overwhelms us and we haven't time to digest it all. In the last hundred years science has advanced so quickly that we hardly know where we stand. Of course when we were young we were sometimes in the same situation as the young people today. Youth is always critical, youth is always revolutionary. That's a part of being young; so we may as well accept the fact that the young people today are practically crazy with 'beat music'. The main difference is that these young people have more courage and also more impudence than we did. They have the courage to tell us what they think to our faces. During the First World War, when I was young, I didn't have the courage to go to my parents and say: it's a disgrace that our clergymen should preach the victory of the German people. How can they reconcile such ideas with God? How can they monopolize God for our side, even if the English and the French do the same? If I had said that, my father would have crushed me with his thunder. My parents were very strict Christians, Protestants. And I don't believe I could have discussed the subject with a clergyman. I remember the difficulties my father had on account of religion even before the Nazis, though he was only a small railroad employee. All the people he worked with were Catholics, he just had the wrong prayer book and that prevented him from getting ahead. That made me welcome the coming of the Third Reich – at first. I thought to myself: Now at last all this religious conflict will be settled. No, we didn't just march into the Third Reich without thinking.

We looked for the good in it because we had had so much bad experience.

It can't be helped. I thought it would be the end of all these religious aberrations, that there would be more justice for the working class, that working hours would be shortened, and that the workers would stop looking so miserable on their way to work with their thermos bottles and sandwiches. If all that is changed, I thought, electing Hitler was a good idea. Yes, I've got to admit, the seizure of power impressed me. During the revolution in 1918 I'd seen those mobs shooting off their guns, nothing but disorder – the way they marched was disgusting. You couldn't call it marching, at a pinch you could say they were moving forward. I suppose they thought they were shooting for some higher principle. What principle I never knew. In any case, what they were doing wasn't decent, in my opinion. The seizure of power in 1933 was decent. There's no doubt about that. The National Socialists came to power legally, that's right, legally, and when they marched, they marched properly. On the surface everything was clean and decent. Underneath? Well, I didn't look. I had no opportunity. When people talk about National Socialism today, they put too much emphasis on the end, they forget the way it began. In 1933 the question was: National Socialism or Communism, and I believe that our young people who talk so big will have to face up to that problem one of these days. Naturally not the old form of Communism or National Socialism. National Socialism is dead but Communism will continue to play an important role. We'll come to another crossroads: another either ... or? I won't say any more. The young people claim that National Socialism is still alive, that's a deliberate falsification of history. Who follows anybody today? We wouldn't even follow Christ, and God help anybody who did! He'd be beaten to a pulp. The NPD has no chance. Nothing new can be accomplished with the men who abdicated in 1945. They're out of date. Twelve hard years of National Socialist reality destroyed National Socialism. All the same, we haven't got over it and certain vestiges of National

Socialism still persist; I can only say that we would have done the job more quickly if new men had come in in 1949 instead of the old ones with their old ideas.

We simply chased the Nazis away from their desks and put back their predecessors.

I don't call that progress, I don't call it revolution, I call it regression. In this respect the situation in the DDR is entirely different. In our Federal Republic those fellows woke up one morning and suddenly had to govern. They didn't really want to. They weren't prepared. But they had to. And the result. . . . What amazes me is that there's any result at all. In the DDR it's entirely different. They wanted to govern. They wanted power. I call that a change, I call that progress! That was a revolution! Over here there was a plain ordinary restoration, from the trade unions to the religious denominations. Not a single bishop, neither Lutheran nor Catholic, has ever been dismissed. Nobody has had to look for a new job. Everywhere the same old faces. If you ask me, our situation in the West is pitiful. Yes, I believe that the whole West is inferior to the East both in ideals and in vitality.

Let's not kid ourselves, we're gradually going to the dogs.

Our political leadership is worthless. Who made the economic miracle? Not the government. It was the big managers who were careful to keep out of the government; they knew that the real opportunities for men of their ability were elsewhere, certainly not in this government. In the East it's entirely different. They want to move ahead. Over there, ideas still mean something. They've got really new men with really new ideas – and look at what we've got! We're going to fall further and further behind. The young people know we have nothing to say to them, the authority and the content are lacking. You can't get around them with old sayings. All this talk about freedom doesn't get us very far. In the War, when I saw the

Russians chasing us westward, I felt for the first time that
the days of individual freedom were over. What the Russians
did at that time was incredible. They were the only country
that had really been ruthlessly invaded, if you want to put it
that way. The Western countries were just play-acting. They
simply let themselves be manoeuvred into the war by diplomatic tricks.

In my opinion the only people with a clear conscience are
the Russians.

When you've got the enemy in your own country, every means
of driving them out is morally justifiable. In this case we were
the enemy, and it was right to use the Communist idea against
us. If I want to destroy an enemy, I can't afford a lot of talk
about freedom. People should stop saying that Communism
means the end of culture. The proletarians in ancient Rome
also thought Rome was doomed because the Germans were
coming in from the north. But today history tells us that Rome
didn't go under. No, no, I think the Russians want peace too.
In my opinion nobody west of the Elbe has very many ideas.
Just look at the power bloc the Russians set up in Europe alone,
it takes in half of Germany. And another thing: the two guar-
dian powers, the United States and the Soviet Union, can't
stand facing each other forever. One of these days they're going
to need a buffer zone between them. Whatever happens, our
main problem is our Russian policy. We've simply got to realize
what kind of man the Russian is. We've go to understand that
the Russian soul is a more enduring value than Communism.
Khrushchev demonstrated his Russian soul by taking his shoe
off in the United Nations and pounding the table with it. Russian policy is full of surprises and bluff. I can perfectly well
imagine that one day the Russian soul will give the Soviet politicians the idea of withdrawing behind the Polish border and
permitting German reunification. We might have accomplished
a good deal more if we here in the Federal Republic hadn't gone
in for politics after the War and tried to be too big for our

shoes. There are a few people in Germany who always want to put on a big act. What is the Federal Republic anyway? It's not even an appendix! But that doesn't prevent us from wanting to play first fiddle.

We ought to be more modest.

After you've lost two world wars, you really ought to draw the obvious conclusions. All this sham really hasn't made much impression on our youth. Yes, I don't think anybody, and certainly not we older men can put anything over on our young people when it comes to history. These young people are ready to mutiny. Anyone who still insists on embodying the teacher-type of my generation is going to come to grief. He won't get anywhere with the young people, he's headed for a crack-up, he'll be destroyed. Even in the scientific field it's no longer possible to make authoritative statements, and certainly not in the teaching of history and German. The old routines won't get us anywhere. We've all got to reconvert. In speaking to our students, we've got to awaken a feeling for those things which fifty years ago the patriarchal principles of those days made self-evident. The young teachers have to learn that just as much as we older ones. The only difference is that we started out with an orientation of our own, and so far they have none, they've got to look for one. We've all got to keep changing our positions like a boxer. We've got to defend our weak points from the enemy's left jabs. We've got to feel our way laboriously into the new situation if we want to be accepted with our knowledge. With the present-day youth we have to prove ourselves day after day. The young people are always nibbling at our substance and we are steadily losing substance. In a parents' and teachers' meeting I once said that the children are restless and undisciplined. A mother asked me: Is it that way with you at school too? I thought it was only at home. We parents no longer have any rights. But you in school, you still have rights to stand on. You see, that was typical of our people. Nobody wants to take his own responsibility.

Everybody wants to retreat to a legal position, so at least he has something to hold on to.

Nobody is willing to arrive at a decision by his own reason. Every human impulse is replaced by some legalistic formula. The people lack determination and courage. They're all waiting to be led by somebody. They grumble about a good many things, but at the same time they know that anyone who wants to get anywhere in Germany today had better not show any moral courage. Anyone who wants to live and think decently had better give up the idea of attaining an important position, because it can't be done without soiling your coat. I don't really think this is a sign of our German mentality, it's more a symptom of our decadence. Another symptom is the present stampede into education. It isn't right. We can't leave all the stupid peasants in agriculture and send all the bright ones to the universities. We need intelligent peasants and workers too. Under the Third Reich we were supposed to become a people of fliers; well, we flew all right, but the question is how and where to. . . . And now we're supposed to become a nation of intellectuals. The intellect is stimulated more and more and intelligence destroyed. We're ending up with a lot of egg-heads and not a single intelligent man.

ALICE NEURER
28, married, schoolteacher

As a child I played 'school' with the other children.

Even then I thought of becoming either a teacher or a pediatrician. I believe a lot of children feel that way. When you play school, you try to teach the other children what you yourself know. By the time I was eight I was very good at reading fairy tales aloud and I gave my playmates dictation. I can still remember that it fascinated me to mark mistakes with a red pencil. Those are the things that amuse a child about playing school. Of course you've got to be fair. Otherwise it's no good, the game degenerates into a quarrel. But even at that time I tried to inspire confidence in my playmates. My home of course had a good deal to do with it. I must tell you: both my parents are Protestant pastors. That is, I lost my father when I was little. He was killed in the War. I never really knew him. But my mother is a pastor too. And there are schoolteachers in my father's family. Besides, my aunt is a teacher in a boarding school. She was my great model. Before becoming a schoolteacher I took a course in institutional management. I thought maybe later I might direct a boarding school, because it gave me such pleasure to see how well my aunt, who directed a girls' boarding school, got along with the pupils – so well that the girls weren't the least bit homesick. The children felt they had someone they could go to with their troubles. So I thought it would be the ideal combination to study teaching and institutional management, so that later on I might be able to do both. Of course that would make for a very full life. Such a life is possible only if you're unmarried. So I had to give up the idea when I got married.

Formerly I just wanted to pass on what I knew. Now I try to draw out of the children what they know and place it in the broader perspective that I have as a grown-up. For instance, when the children tell about their Sunday excursions, I try to make them think more clearly and see how things hang together. For instance, if a child has observed an animal, I ask him whether he has observed certain things in other animals, so as to broaden the child's horizon. I teach in public school. I teach all subjects and I make friends with the children very quickly. I believe that is because I formerly worked in a home for ill-adapted and morally deficient children. For a time I did most of my work in the section where illegitimate children are born. Some of the mothers were only fifteen or as little as thirteen. The babies spend two years in the institution and then, if they can't be sent home, if the home environment is too bad – for instance if their mother's parents hate the child – they are sent to state institutions.

The parents of young mothers of illegitimate children often say : 'Do you expect us to bring *that* up?

'We've already got plenty to do and so little money.' Mostly they're families that have a lot of children and barely enough money to get by. But when you come right down to it, what they really lack is moral rather than financial resources. A social worker once took me to visit a neighbourhood in Düsseldorf where most of these young mothers came from. A shattering experience! The neighbourhood consisted of new houses built as part of the social housing programme. They were well built but badly furnished by the tenants. Many had pawned their furniture, but of course there was always a TV set. And the less said about the hygienic conditions the better. You can see the same in this town, in the industrial suburb where I live. They put up 'social' dwellings and in a short time they look just as bad as the tenements where the people lived before. Sad but true. Those people have no character. A perfectly normal family here in the neighbourhood is perfectly happy if they can tend their garden. On Sunday they sit in their garden, they have their flowers and a nice spot to sit in. The a-social families don't do that. It's also from mental weakness. The parents are below average intelligence and the children automatically turn out the same way. It's a vicious circle. Most of the men are unskilled workers. They can only marry a woman of their own class. Even a secretary is too demanding. I have the feeling that most of them don't even notice how miserable it is just to live from day to day instead of trying to build up a little well-being in the family. Of course those people have a hard time making a normal life for themselves because the rest of the population look down on them and reject them from the start as a-social. That's how it is: the healthy reject the sick.

The upper crust of society is represented in our school.

Most of the pupils are the children of university people. Only a few are the children of artisans and so on. And then of course there are one or two whose parents are on relief, like those people in the Old City. Yes, we have them too, but they fit in perfectly well because there are so few of them, but the parents, the people of good family, only invite children of their own class to the parties that are coming into fashion again. They say: 'These children are better suited to my child than office workers' children.' The children themselves make no distinction. In school they play together as if there were no social differences. What happens later on we don't know, because almost ninety per cent of the children in my school transfer to high school after the fourth grade. In the lower classes I have an average of thirty pupils. Twenty-five would be better. Every child over twenty-five is a burden. Beyond that number I can't give my attention to each individual child. There are so many currents that I can't quite follow them; for instance, I can't speak to every single child in the course of a class. Today there is more incentive to becoming a teacher, and I keep hearing that many more young people attend the colleges of education than before.

But unfortunately too few men.

Nowadays people say that 'a schoolteacher is a respected citizen.' But even so, men don't feel greatly attracted by the profession. Plenty of women, but nearly all the women marry and then after two or three years they leave. My principal was very sad when I got married, but I told him: 'I'll go on teaching, I enjoy it. My husband isn't opposed to it either.' Marriage doesn't hamper my activity. I'm glad to have a child now myself, so I can see what children are like before they go to school. Now I can see with my own eyes. Before I had my own, the development of a child up to the age of seven was known to me only from books. It's a fascinating profession and I have no desire to give it up. Yes, it's true that public school teachers used to occupy a lower position in the social scale. They were paid less too.

Public school teachers were always put on a somewhat lower plane than high-school teachers.

Even right after the War a high-school teacher was regarded as somebody, while a public-school teacher had to start on 150 marks, which meant that he couldn't do much in the way of improving his education. If you have more money, you can spend more on books. You can travel more. You can educate yourself. Today a public school teacher can do that too. I started out on five hundred marks a month if I remember right. But now, I think, they start on eight hundred. At present I make a thousand a month before deductions. Our salary is increased by twenty or thirty marks each year. Of course I was especially lucky because I was able to live with my mother, so I actually had my money all to myself. I was able to buy a car and take trips wherever I wanted. As long as I was unmarried, I took trips in all my vacations. I went to Greece four times with my mother. I'd read a good deal about it before. I'd love to visit Egypt.

And once I went to Israel. I knew exactly what I was doing.

I made careful preparations for the trip. First I read up on the Nazi period. There are lots of documents and books about the Jews in Germany. I read Jewish jokes too and Ephraim Kishon's satires, *Look Back, Mrs Lot* and *Noah's Ark, Tourist Class* and things like that to get a first-hand look at the Jewish humour that's supposed to be so priceless. As I later found out, it really is. My mother as a pastor had come into close contact with the problems of the Nazi period, because she was very much hampered in her church duties. She wasn't able to practise her profession as she would have liked to. For instance, baptism wasn't taken for granted. There were quarrels between parents. The mother wanted the child to be baptized, but the father said: 'No, it's not necessary any more.' And my mother had to try to find a way. Also she began at an early date to listen to foreign broadcasts so she was informed about things that other people didn't know. And she had a Jewish friend who emigrated to America, so she found out very soon that injustice was being done. And she told us children about it. I've met a lot of people who told me they were unaware of all that. It strikes me as very unlikely, the way so many people say they didn't know anything, and after I'd been to Israel it seemed still more unlikely, because there I met a lot of people who lost practically every member of their family.

That couldn't have passed unnoticed.

So it could only have been that the Jews even then were very isolated, that their plight never came to the attention of their neighbours. That's the only explanation I can imagine. But in Israel I heard the exact opposite. Most of the German Jews were thoroughly assimilated when they lived here. Most of them said to me: 'We didn't even know we were Jews any more. They had to tell us in writing.' They were Germans like ourselves. I visited the homes of Jewish families. Their bookshelves looked like those of a German professor. Beautiful editions of Goethe, Schiller and all the German classics. And the most modern German literature too. All in German, though of course all those things exist in Hebrew. And the phonograph records: all our classics. They were steeped in German music, they couldn't live without it. We young people were well received in Israel. We were a student group. We worked in a kibbutz. And later I worked in a children's home too. In 1913 the directress of this home had emigrated from Berlin, taking the whole institution with her. Israel was the biggest experience in all my life.

Naturally I came back with a terrible distaste for Germany.

I'm rather uncompromising. I said to myself: Good Lord, must I go back to the country where there are so many under-cover Nazis. I'm very sceptical when I hear people saying things like: 'Oh, the Jews, they're pushing ahead in business again. Half the

stores and businesses in our city belong to Jews.' When I hear
such things, I prick up my ears and ask: 'Well, what's your objection?' But to that they have no answer. The older generation still have this abstract conception of a 'Jew'. Not all of
course, but a good many. With the younger generation it's different. They're not anti-Semitic. But when I ask them if they'd
do anything if a new anti-Semitism should start up in Germany, with government backing, they say: 'I don't know if it's
worth fighting on the barricades for.' My own feeling is that if
such a thing happens again, I'll side with the Jews, because
racial persecution is unjust. In my opinion a lot of people are
cowards. And besides it offends their sense of honour:

'You say the Germans did that?'

'No, we don't believe it.' And then they say: 'Well, what about
the Russians, they did terrible things too, and the English in the
Boer War, and during the Nazi period they wouldn't let Jewish
ships land in Palestine and sent them away. Just remember the
business with the *Exodus*. ...' But good Lord, you can't con-
done one crime by comparing it with another. Which is exactly
what a lot of people are trying to do. It all comes from this
kind of reasoning: 'I didn't know what was going on in those
days. Of course people can blame me for that; but I refuse to
blame myself.' President Heuss put it very well: 'There is no
such thing as collective guilt, but there is such a thing as collective shame.' Unfortunately those words haven't had much
effect here in Germany. Most of the young people say – and
they're not wrong really – 'We're not responsible for the sins
of our fathers.' They try to adapt themselves to West Germany as it is. They put out feelers to foreign countries. They
read foreign literature. They try to meet foreigners as equals.
I'm pretty well informed. In our student days we had excellent
instruction in such fields as the 'methodology of current history'
and the 'sociology of the German past'. We learned about
Communism and the two German states that came into being
after the War. I am sure that civics and history are taught very

carefully in my school, because many of the teachers come from Central Germany, from the DDR. When I look into the classrooms, a number of the teachers have political maps on the wall. They try to show the children exactly the way things used to be. Of course it's hard to make a fourteen-year-old child understand what National Socialism meant and what Communism is. In elementary school it's very hard. A student of eighteen or nineteen is perfectly capable of understanding the philosophical foundations of Communism. I've noticed that the older teachers like to speak about their students. I always take that as a good sign. It shows how much interest they take in their students. They are well informed about each individual child and I think they take pleasure in it; they have good relations with them. Women teachers, I believe, have closer contact with the children. It's only natural.

Most of the men go home after classes and forget about school.

With the women it's different. We keep in touch with each other even outside of school. We get together or we phone and we talk about the children. How can I help a particular child in a certain situation? That kind of thing. We try to be good colleagues and help each other with advice. I rather doubt whether men do that. They have their families to worry about. In my case marriage is no obstacle. I discuss my work a good deal with my husband. He's studying medicine and takes a good deal of interest in the development of young people. I tell him my impressions of the children. He knows most of them by name because I talk about them so much. He's thinking of becoming a pediatrician. He hasn't started specializing yet. That comes after his examination. I can see that he's leaning towards pediatrics, but I don't want to influence him. A doctor must also be able to talk to children, like a father or a teacher. Oh yes, I met him in the student chorus. We sang the Bach B minor Mass together and the Christmas Oratorio. We used to meet afterwards and discuss everything under the sun; we discovered that we had lots of interests in common. I'd always thought a good deal about love. Actually that's why I married so late. Plenty of men were interested in me. No, I wasn't a wallflower. I'd always been looking for a man who would be a real partner, somebody with whom I could discuss everything that was important to me and who would understand me as a woman. Not all men have that quality. They don't know when you're sad or when you're hankering for some particular thing.

That's what's so surprising about my husband: he tells me what I think.

He can read my mind. It's wonderful to know that he thinks about me so much. And naturally I also try to feel out his moods and his special preoccupations and to understand his friends. I believe that love must be first of all a partnership; otherwise it's not married love. I don't know if you see what I mean. Anything else is more like a butterfly, and a woman doesn't want that, I certainly don't.

WILFRIED KORNGIEBEL, TRUDE KORNGIEBEL

63, baker; 58, housewife

ALEXANDER SEIBT

52, married, baker

My father could boast of having baked for the king and the emperor.

Wilfried Korngiebel: My father's father was a butcher and a farmer. My father learned the baker's trade. Then he became First White Dough Maker in the court bakery. White dough maker is a title that was then still in use. He was first journeyman at the court bakery because all the good things for the king's court passed through his hands. Our king was good friends with the emperor, so later on His Imperial Highness ordered his bread from the king's court bakery. Then my father set up on his own and in the course of time built a good trade. I try to carry on the bakery in accordance with his principles. My motto is that quality and craftsmanship come first. A fresh roll on the table in the morning is a good way for a working man to start his day. I have two married daughters and a son, but he doesn't work here in the bakery. He learned two trades: baker and pastry cook. But now he's still working in Trier, waiting for me to retire because – you know how it is – there are differences of opinion between us, and besides he needs to sow his wild oats for a while. Anyway I feel too young to retire. I'm sixty-three and I feel good and strong.

Mrs Korngiebel: We're not on the outs with our son and we definitely hope that he'll step into my husband's shoes when the time comes. He's sure to get married some day, to a nice woman, I hope, like I got a nice man, his father here. I was very lucky, because my father was only a switchman on the railroad. There were six of us children. I met my husband at the athletic field. I went there with a girl friend and he was playing handball. And one thing led to another. I had to wait a long time, but after we'd been friends for five years we finally got married. You know how it is, certain people talk and talk, especially our dear neighbours.

'Oh, the rich baker's son, he'll never marry Trude.'

That's the kind of thing they said. 'He's only using her.' And my mother kept saying: 'Oh, Trude, forget about him. You're only a poor girl and he's the son of a master-baker.'

Wilfried Korngiebel: But in the end the rich master baker married the poor switchman's daughter, and he didn't make a bad bargain.

Alexander Seibt: Any woman who married a baker is doing all right. I know what I'm saying because we've been bakers for three generations and the women, from my grandmother down to my wife, have never had a bad time of it. Besides, bakers are pretty shrewd. Take me, for instance. My father died of a wound he got in the First World War, after toting it around with him for years. I had to take over the business when I was very young, just nineteen. Well, then I had the same trouble as my father. The Second World War came and I was wounded and besides I caught malaria in Rommel's army, I mean the Afrika-Korps. Anyway I came home with fifty per cent disability. I couldn't work much and I had to keep one more journeyman than any other baker. But what you haven't got in your legs you've got to have in your head. So I said to myself:

'If you can't walk properly, you've got to think more. Go and do something for the people.'

No sooner said than done: I became chairman of the VDK* and besides I became town councillor, representing the *Freie Wähler* (Independent Voters). I could have gone in with the FDP or the CDU, they offered me the job, but I had misgivings. I said to myself: No, we had enough party in our Adolf's famous thousand-year Reich. But when the Independent Voters came along, I thought, that's the right crowd for me. I was appointed right away and now I've been town councillor for fifteen years. I've always had luck, top candidate, first on the list.

Wilfried Korngiebel: I'm active in public life too. I've been in the sports movement a long time. I played handball, I was a track man, and for many years I was district youth secretary for track and field events. After the total collapse in 1945 I stepped right in again to help the athletics organization back on its feet. For four years I was chairman of the '1862 Young People's Athletic Club' and in addition performed certain duties in the local gymnastics club. I was chief fight referee and organized various sports festivals. Something had to be done because sometimes the help we got from the government didn't amount to much and there were fewer and fewer idealists. The

---

* *Verband der Kriegsbeschädigten* – League of War Invalids.

times are getting more and more materialistic and the choral societies and gymnastic societies have a hard time finding new section heads to breathe new life into the organizations and preserve what our fathers handed down. There always used to be teachers who had to earn something on the side, and they were the ones who took charge of our school sections. Nowadays they're not to be had. Even so, the choral societies of our bakers' guild manage to get together sixty to seventy singers of both sexes.

We sing beautiful folk songs, but also the higher things.

Last year we put on the second act of Johann Strauss's *Die Fledermaus* at our bakers' guild meeting. And every two years we have a guild excursion. This year we're going to Strassburg to show our members the Strassburg cathedral. Last time we rented the old church in Amorbach for two hours and gave a little concert. We had the rector play the organ for us and then we sang two songs, Schubert's *Im Abendrot* and the *Jubilate*. A few guests came too. A rector was present and he thanked us and said it had been a great experience. Especially the *Jubilate* was mighty effective because of the wonderful acoustics. On the whole, singing has fallen off a good deal, especially the men's choruses. That's because people's evenings are taken up with television. And besides there's shortage of conductors. Especially the provincial societies are in very bad shape, because the societies are small and can't afford a conductor. The teacher used to do it. But now the teachers say they're too busy. The truth is that nowadays they have no need to make thirty or forty marks a month on the side. I can't find fault with them. It's a sign of the times, but it's a bad sign for our cultural life.

German *lieder* have done a great deal to keep up the reputation of Germany abroad.

Our choral societies were wonderful, but they're not what they

used to be. I can't give them as much time as I used to, because
after our former guild master had reached a certain age, that
is, five years ago, I became guild master myself. And an organization like our baker's trade takes a good deal of work, because
it's much more in the public eye than any other trade. People
measure the general standard of living by the price of bread.

When bread is too expensive people think things in general
aren't so good.

Unfortunately the price of bread has gone up steadily. Economically speaking, we bakers have a hard struggle, because
we pay very high prices for grain and flour and there's no deny-
ing that we have very high wages here in the Federal Republic
and compared to other countries very short working hours
and very long vacations. We're glad to see our fellow workers
get all these advantages and we try to keep on good terms with
our fellow workers, but somehow all that has to be paid for,
which can only be done by charging a high price for our
finished product. But an increase in the price of bread always
makes for a battle with public opinion. So we cultivate good
relations with the press because we want the press to explain
to the public why we're obliged to do what we do. We also keep
on good terms with the women's clubs and always invite them
to our meetings when something comes up for discussion. Unfortunately bread consumption has fallen off a good deal in the
last half century. At the turn of the century the per capita consumption was 440 lb. a year, now it's only 150. And the bread
consumption figures for Europe show that Germany is just
about in the last place. The reason is that our standard of living
is very high. The people eat better, they think of bread as a
side dish, though actually bread is a foodstuff blessed by God,
because it contains everything a man needs. Remember the old
proverb: 'As long as a soldier has bread, he fights.'

We also have a hard time recruiting young bakers. Everybody wants mechanical gadgets: refrigerators, TV sets, cars,
etc. And nowadays people don't feel like getting up in the

middle of the night to tend the ovens. God knows that God is the last of the young people's thoughts. All they think about is material things. Herr Seibt here is an authority on the subject. He knows, he was churchwarden of our congregation for years.

Alexander Seibt: Yes, nowadays our people are Christians only on the surface.

Look at the people that get to be deacons nowadays.

My successor, for instance, is a man who prevented people from having their children baptized under the Third Reich. But today he's a deacon, a regular weathercock, and nobody seems to mind. Sometimes I hear businessmen say: 'Good, we may as well trim our sails to the wind; some of the customers expect us to look like Christians. So let's jump on the bandwagon.' Actually their customers only pretend to be church people. It's a fraud. One is always putting on an act for the other.

Trude Korngiebel: I've got something to say about that. I'm the head of the women's chorus in our congregation. Once we sang in an old church in Nuremberg. The sacristan explained its religious and artistic significance, but nobody was much interested. Afterward the driver of our bus showed us the former Party Congress grounds. Some of the buildings are still standing there dead, all overgrown with grass. But that caught the people's interest. You see, the bus driver we had was still from the good old days. Yes, he was a character. He explained the history of the place. Good God, to think that such a wonderful thing collapsed! A crying shame!

Ah yes, if only they'd done it right ... but Adolf had too many enemies.

Too bad. They brought him down.

Alexander Seibt: When Hitler came to power, that was in 1933, I was just eighteen. I personally joined the Hitler Youth, I was even a group leader. Actually as a youngster I was enthusiastic, I refused to believe the things I had heard from the

old people. I didn't believe a word of it, for instance when somebody said to me: 'The Moustache is bound to come to grief. If
he attacks the Roman Catholics and the Jews at the same time,
it's sure to end badly. If you believe in him, you're on the wrong
track.' An old man said that to me in the year of grace 1934. He
was right but I didn't understand him then. But over the years
I came to realize that he was right. We were full of enthusiasm,
that's all. And there was something in it. Something was accomplished.

A woman could go out on the street alone even when it
was blacked out during the War.

Nothing happened to her. Unfortunately that's not true any
more. In those days offenders were punished good and proper.
They weren't sent to rest homes like today. What kind of
punishments do people get today? ... Maybe we haven't got
the right idea, but in those days there was order. The laws
were hard but they were fair. When you think of the days when
a worker could visit Spain or Norway with 'Strength Through
Joy'. No other country in Europe or America ever had that.
The socialistic idea *was* good for the working man. Maybe Adolf
Hitler's main idea was all right, but it's like in the proverb:
'When a beggar rides, he spurs his horse harder than a noble-
man.' And anyway Hitler lacked something. Things were just
too much for him, and you can't drive history. We've just had
the anniversary of the air-raid on Dresden. That was a terrible
thing, and now they're arguing to see whether England gave the
order or America. Each one puts it off on the other. Anyway it
was a sin what they did. There's another old proverb: 'Woe to
the defeated!' I think it sounds better in Latin: 'The vanquished
must bow to the victor.'

   Wilfried Korngiebel: Once we had the Zurich Athletic
Club here; we ate dinner with them at the Hotel Adler. The
wife of the Swiss club president was sitting next to me. 'Look,'
she said, 'what do you think of Russia and the Communists over
there?' And I answered: 'To tell you the honest truth, we're

glad they're there, because if they weren't we couldn't enter-
tain you so well today, we'd still have bread tickets and meat
tickets, and England, France and America would still be sitting
on us hard. If there were no threat from the East, we'd never
have got this far. The Americans fed us well, but they milked
us well too. That's the situation now.'

GLOSSARY OF ABBREVIATIONS

2 A O. *Offiziersangelegenheit* and *Ordensverleihung:* Officers' affairs and the conferring of decorations; a wartime administrative department

ASTA. *Allgemeiner Studentenausschuss:* General Students' Committee

BdM. *Bund deutscher Mädchen:* League of German Girls

BHE. *Bund der Heimatvertriebenen und Entrechteten:* League of those who have been driven from their homes and disenfranchised

CDU. *Christlich-demokratische Union:* Christian Democratic Union

DDR. *Deutsche Demokratische Republik:* East Germany

DRP. *Deutsche Reichspartei:* German Reich Party

EK II. *Eisenkreuz zweiter Klasse:* Iron Cross, Second Class

EWG. *Europäische Wirtschaftsgemeinschaft:* The European Common Market

FDP. *Freie Demokratische Partei:* Free Democratic Party

HIAG. *Hilfsorganisation auf Gegenseitigkeit:* Mutual Aid Organization

KPD. *Kommunistische Partei Deutschlands:* German Communist Party

KVK II. *Kriegsverdienstkreuz zweiter Klasse:* War Merit Cross, Second Class

NPD. *Nationaldemokratische Partei Deutschlands:* National Democratic Party

NSDAP. *Nazionalsozialistische Deutsche Arbeiterpartei:* National Socialist German Workers' Party; the official designation of the Nazi party

REFA. *Reichsausschuss für Arbeitsstudien:* National Committee for Work Studies

SD. *Sicherheitsdienst:* Security Service

SPD. *Sozialdemokratische Partei Deutschlands:* German Social Democratic Party

VDK. *Verband der Kriegsbeschädigten:* League of War Invalids